# The Economics of Social Problems

D0026846

# The Economics of Social Problems

## THIRD EDITION

**Julian Le Grand**

**Carol Propper**

and

**Ray Robinson**

MACMILLAN

First edition 1976
Reprinted four times
Second edition 1984
Reprinted four times
Third edition 1992

Published 1976 by
MACMILLAN PRESS LTD
Houndmills, Basingstoke, Hampshire RG21 6XS
and London
Companies and representatives
throughout the world

ISBN 0–333–55257–1 hardcover
ISBN 0–333–55258–X paperback

A catalogue record for this book is available
from the British Library.

11   10   9   8   7   6
03   02   01   00   99   98

Printed in Hong Kong

# Contents

# Acknowledgements

Again we are greatly in debt to the many colleagues and students who have commented on earlier editions of the book and on the manuscript of this one. In particular, we would like to mention Gillian Court, Damaris Le Grand, Phillipa Marks, Robin Means, Tony O'Sullivan, Randall Smith and Christine Whitehead for helpful comments on specific chapters. A succession of editors at Macmillan have patiently endured a succession of missed deadlines without any flagging in their encouragement or commitment; the most recent (and the most patient) is Stephen Rutt. Finally, we are deeply grateful to Lorraine Cantle, who had not only to do much of the typing, but also to manage three authors and several word processors, separated geographically and often technologically. All this she did with her customary speed, efficiency and, above all, good humour.

*Julian Le Grand*
*Carol Propper*
*Ray Robinson*

# Introduction

This book is the third edition of *The Economics of Social Problems*, the first edition of which appeared in 1976 and the second in 1984. The two original authors, Julian Le Grand and Ray Robinson, have been joined by Carol Propper to produce a radical revision and updating of the book. We have also taken the opportunity to incorporate numerous changes and extensions suggested by colleagues, students and reviewers who have used and commented upon the earlier editions.

However, the basic approach to the analysis of social problems remains the same. Indeed, this approach – the systematic analysis of alternative methods of economic organisation within the social policy area – is of even more relevance now than when the book first appeared. Since then, privatisation proposals in health care, housing, education, and so on – discussed originally as possibilities suggested by academic inquiry – have assumed a central position on the policy agenda. As such, both the approach of the book and the topic areas to which it is applied are of considerable contemporary concern. The basic aim of the book is to introduce students to certain key economic concepts and methods of analysis through the study of a range of contemporary social problems. It is our deliberate intention to move away from the more abstract theoretical approach that is a feature of many introductory economics textbooks and instead try to provide a book that emphasises 'learning-by-doing'. This is done through the simultaneous development of the relevant theory and its application to particular social issues. The success of the earlier editions of the book has shown this approach to be both popular and effective.

All the relevant concepts and theories are explained in the text, and so no prior training in economics is required. Accordingly, the book may be used as part of an introductory economics course. If it is used in this way, the student will acquire many of the basic skills of economic analysis usually obtained in a less appealing manner from more conventional introductory textbooks. Alternatively, it may be

used as a supplementary text to provide students with an appreciation of the relevance of economic analysis to a range of intrinsically
interesting social problems not normally dealt with in introductory
textbooks. In addition, our experience has shown that the book is of
value not only to students who will go on to specialise in economics
but also to students in other disciplines, such as social policy,
sociology and politics. Indeed, the book should be of interest to
anyone new to economics who would like to discover the contribution that the discipline can make towards understanding some of the
pressing social problems that confront us today.

Although, for these reasons, the book has been designed primarily
for use at the introductory level, we have found that it is of interest to
those with a more extensive background in economics and/or the
problem areas studied. We believe that the approach we have
adopted for the study of each topic is a useful way of clarifying the
issues involved and has some claim to originality. This approach is
discussed more fully below.

## The Problem Areas

We have called the issues discussed in this book 'social' problems, so
as to distinguish them from the more conventional 'economic'
problems (such as inflation, unemployment and economic growth)
that are usually dealt with in introductory principles books. This is
not a distinction we would seriously defend – all problems faced by a
society, including economic ones, are presumably social problems by
definition – but we feel that it has support from popular usage.

The problem areas chosen for investigation are health, education,
housing, social care, the environment, transport and the distribution
and redistribution of income and wealth. Those familiar with earlier
editions will realise that some of these have been changed so as to
reflect current concerns. The chapter on social or community care –
the care of elderly, mentally ill or physically disabled people – is
completely new. The chapter on pollution has been completely
rewritten to produce a new chapter on the environment. The
discussion of urban congestion has been incorporated into a wider
chapter on transport. All the remaining 'problem' chapters have
been extensively rewritten to reflect current issues, and to respond to
developments in the economic analysis of those issues.

What has not changed from earlier editions is the adoption of a common structure and analytic approach to all the areas studied. Since this is a crucial feature of the book, it needs to be explained in more detail.

## Structure and Approach

In the process of teaching the material on which this book is based, we have learned a great deal about the difficulties that the study of social issues involves when used at the introductory level. In particular, we have found that students usually lack any framework that would enable them to introduce some order into their inquiries about particular problems. Teachers whose earlier education has provided them with such a framework sometimes forget the sense of confusion that the student feels when confronted with highly complex issues. For this reason we believe it to be imperative that a consistent approach for examining problems should be used throughout. This is a key feature of this book and its main claim to originality. We have not produced a set of separate essays on individual topics or a discursive examination of 'some economic aspects' of each of the problem areas. Instead we have adopted an integrated and systematic framework for studying each problem in a consistent way.

Thus the reader will find that each chapter contains three basic sections. First, we ask what are society's objectives in the area concerned. In most cases we decide that these objectives can be conveniently summarised under two main headings: the achievement of *efficiency* and of *equity*. Efficiency considerations refer to the provision of the quantities of housing, hospitals, schools, residential homes and so on that yield the greatest level of aggregate (net) benefit to the community. Equity issues are concerned with the justice or fairness of the way that these goods and services are divided between different members of society. However, while we concentrate upon efficiency and equity, there will be other objectives that society will also wish to pursue. The promotion of consumer choice and the fostering of a sense of community or altruism, for instance, are two others that figure in some of the areas in this book. Consequently, attention is drawn to them when it is considered relevant to do so. Having so specified society's objectives we can say that a social problem exists whenever the existing system fails to meet the objectives set for it. The next question to ask is: 'What kind of economic system could best meet these objectives?' Since the private market system is the dominant means of providing the goods and services that we use in our everyday lives, it is the obvious place to begin an examination of alternative systems. In some of the areas we examine, the market is the main means actually used (housing, for example); in others, the market has been either replaced or stringently regulated (education and health care, for example). Hence the second main section of each chapter considers the arguments for and against the use of the market system as a means of allocating and distributing the good or service in question. Then, in the light of certain shortcomings of the market, in the third section we examine the desirability or otherwise of government intervention. Although we consider numerous forms of public policy, ranging from minor adjustments in the market's operation to its complete replacement, we show that they all fall into one or more of three general categories: direct public provision, tax or subsidy policies, and regulation. But each of them is shown to be subject to the same tests of efficiency and equity that were relevant to the private market.

Those familiar with earlier editions of the book will find that we have included a much more explicit consideration of 'government failures' in the areas concerned. This reflects changes in economic thought. In recent years, there have been major developments in the economic analysis of government policy, showing how governments, as well as markets, may fail to achieve social objectives such as efficiency and equity. Although the theory of government failure is not yet as well developed as that of market failure, we have tried to give an exposition of the relevant arguments. Moreover, throughout the book, we have emphasised that the task of the social or economic analyst is not to contrast one perfect system (market or non-market) with another, but to compare two or more imperfect ones to discover which is the 'least-worst'.

The first and last chapters do not have this structure since they are not concerned with specific problem areas; but they are none the less an integral part of the whole approach. Before students begin to study a particular problem, we feel it is important that they have at their disposal some general discussion of social objectives and their relationship to the operations of the market system. Chapter 1 is an attempt to provide this. Students will find it useful to look at this chapter before they consult the one dealing with the area in which they are interested. The last chapter, Chapter 10, is an attempt to pull together the links between all the previous chapters. In the context of a general discussion about the merits and demerits of the market and of government policies, it draws attention to the common elements in the discussions of each problem area and to their wider implications. Again, it differs from the last chapter in earlier editions in that it now incorporates a far more developed theory of government failure: one that, so far as we are aware, has no direct equivalent in other economics texts.

We believe that this format has two advantages. First it has the unity of approach that, as we emphasised above, is essential for the student to obtain a good understanding of the generality of economic analysis and indeed of the specific problems themselves. Second, it does, in fact, enable us to cover most of what economic analysis has contributed to these subjects. Much of the debate between economists has been about market versus non-market systems of allocation. But the contributions to this debate are dispersed among countless books and journals. By bringing together the disparate strands of this debate into an integrated study at the introductory level, in the context of social issues of wide concern, we hope to make accessible to the maximum number of readers a systematic critique of market and non-market economic systems.

## Note to the Teacher

Each of the chapters is largely self-contained and hence can be read quite separately from one another. This feature – which is deliberate – has involved some repetition in the later chapters of theoretical material that appears in the early ones; however, our experience suggests that when students are 'learning-by-doing', repetition is no bad thing. Within each chapter, sections and sub-sections have been carefully indicated so that, if necessary, they too could be read independently. Moreover, each chapter contains suggestions for further reading and a set of questions for discussion. Some of the questions relate directly to material presented in the relevant chapter, whereas others are designed to extend discussion beyond the limits of the chapter.

If a full course is to be taught from the book, the following advice as to the order of topics might be helpful. We have found that it is useful to begin the course with a brief examination of society's objectives and the operations of the market, as in Chapter 1, then to continue with health and education – the discussions of which have strong analytic similarities and which also arouse passionate debate (and hence student interest). Housing and social care continue the 'welfare' theme. The environment and transport chapters raise rather different issues from the earlier ones and can usefully be taught together. The distribution of income and wealth, as one of the fundamental issues underlying the discussions of most of the other topics, is a good subject with which to culminate the course. The final session can review the first week's discussion of the market and government as alternative mechanisms of resource allocation in the light of the subsequent course work, along the lines of Chapter 10.

# Social Objectives and the Allocation of Resources

# 1

This chapter describes the analytical framework that is used in each of the subsequent chapters for the study of particular social problems. Those readers who have studied economics previously will recognise certain parts of the analysis (such as the theory of demand and supply), but are unlikely to have seen it incorporated within the general framework presented here. This is because we have endeavoured to explain at an introductory level the relationship between social objectives and methods of resource allocation, notably the market system. Explaining this relationship involves dealing with a number of theoretically complex issues and it is for this reason that most economics textbooks delay dealing with it until the intermediate or advanced level. However, the study of social problems is greatly assisted if some appreciation of the subject is acquired at the outset. Moreover we feel that it is possible to retain an acceptable degree of theoretical precision and at the same time convey key elements of the subject to a more general readership.

Accordingly, this chapter proceeds as follows. After a brief consideration of the concepts of scarcity and choice, we begin by specifying social objectives in relation to economic activity. We suggest that one such objective will be to select the quantity of output for each good and service that results in the highest attainable level of economic welfare. We term this the efficient level of output. Another important objective is to distribute the goods and services produced between the members of society in a way that is considered to be fair or just. This we term the equity objective. Finally, we suggest that other objectives within the social policy area are likely to include the desire to promote consumer choice, preserve individual freedoms and the encouragement of what is variously termed community, citizenship or altruism. Having considered these objectives we go on to explain the way in which a private enterprise or market system of economic organisation will organise economic activity, and to consider the extent to which it can be expected to realise these objectives. We conclude the chapter by describing the forms that government policy may take in its efforts (which may or may not be successful) to realise social objectives more fully.

## Scarcity and Choice

Economics is concerned with the way in which we use scarce resources to produce the goods and services which satisfy our material wants. Because it is through the consumption of various goods and services (commodities) that people satisfy their wants, we can say that these commodities yield economic benefits. Moreover, the amount of benefit enjoyed may be expected to increase as the quantity of goods and services made available for consumption increases. Thus additional housing, improvements in the quality of education or health care, and increases in the stock of housing will all yield positive benefits. But unfortunately the resources of land, labour and capital which are used to produce these commodities are not available in unlimited supply, and so we cannot hope to produce a sufficient quantity to satisfy all our wants. The scarcity of resources in relation to the demands made on them leads inevitably to the need to make a series of choices about the quantities of different commodities that are to be produced.

Production of a particular commodity will therefore have costs in the form of the other goods that could have been produced with the resources it uses up. For example, labour time or machinery that is devoted to car production is obviously not available for providing hospital facilities or schools. Because it is possible to look at the costs of production in terms of the alternative goods and services that could have been produced, economists have devised the term *opportunity cost*. So the opportunity cost of producing cars is the forgone opportunity of providing other commodities such as hospital facilities.

In many situations the market price that is paid for the use of a resource reflects its opportunity cost. Thus we may expect the price a hospital has to pay for the services of plumbers or carpenters to be the same as they would receive when employed in the construction of new housing. Therefore the price paid by the hospital measures the value of plumbers' or carpenters' services, not only to the hospital, but also in their alternative use in the housebuilding industry. But market prices do not always measure opportunity costs. In situations where society's resources are not being utilised fully, the decision to employ an additional resource in, say, the provision of hospital services will not necessarily imply a reduction in the availability of resources for alternative uses. So if there is unemployment of labour, or if machines are standing idle, the decision to put them to work may incur a zero opportunity cost (for otherwise they would be producing nothing) even though the market price for their services will almost certainly be positive. In any discussion of the costs of resources used in production, the concept of opportunity cost should always be borne in mind.

# Efficiency

When deciding on the quantity of a particular commodity that should be produced, we will need to consider the way that both benefits and costs vary at different levels of output. In general, benefits are desirable and costs are to be avoided, so it would seem logical to try to select that output at which the excess of benefits over costs, the *net benefit*, is largest. When society has selected this level of output and has allocated its resources accordingly, we say that there is an *efficient* allocation of resources or, alternatively, an efficient level of output. In the next two sections we shall investigate a little more closely the level of output that will satisfy this condition by considering the way that benefits and costs arise through the consumption and production of an everyday foodstuff – butter. Butter has been chosen because it is a fairly simple commodity familiar to most people, although this is only for purposes of illustration – those cholesterol-conscious people who have forsaken butter will find that the arguments presented here are equally applicable to margarine! Indeed, as we shall show in the remainder of this book, the arguments can be extended to practically all commodities.

## Benefits to Consumers

If we look at a typical person we will probably find that the total benefit (*tb*) she derives from eating butter will vary according to how much is eaten. In general we would expect *tb* to increase as more is consumed. However let us look a little more closely at the way in which benefits increase; specifically, let us consider the benefits which are derived from each separate gram that is consumed. Most probably, this will depend on the quantity of butter that has been consumed already. If the person has had no butter at all, considerable satisfaction is likely to be obtained from spreading it on bread or toast. As the amount that is available already increases, the options facing the consumer will tend to satisfy less mouth-watering needs: spreading it a little more thickly or using it for purposes (such as cooking) for which inferior substitutes were used previously. By and large, we would expect to find that the benefit derived from each gram becomes less as more immediate needs are satisfied. Hence each additional gram will yield less benefit than the previous one. If we define the last unit of butter consumed at any level of consumption as the *marginal unit*, we can say that the benefit derived from the marginal unit – that is, the *marginal benefit* (*mb*) – declines as the quantity of butter consumed increases. Note that to say that mb declines does not mean that the consumer does not derive positive benefit from the marginal unit; it simply means that the benefit is less than was derived from the previous unit.

Now we can extend this analysis beyond the individual consumer to society as a whole. If we define society's benefits as the sum of the benefits received by each consumer of butter, we can add up each person's *tb* to obtain the *total social benefit* (*tsb*). Similarly we can add up the *mb*s derived by each person to obtain *marginal social benefit* (*msb*) – that is, the increase in *tsb* recorded as we increase society's consumption by a marginal unit. (Note that this process of adding up does require us to be able actually to add the amounts of benefit received by different consumers. Usually this is facilitated by expressing benefits, which are obviously subjective, in terms of a single objective unit of measurement, that is £s. However, this procedure can present problems if not everyone values a £ equally).

When we are considering society's consumption of butter, we are more likely to ask what is the *msb* of increasing consumption of a thousand tonnes than by a single gram; but although the scale of analysis is different from that of the single consumer discussed above, the general principles of the example are unaffected. In particular, just as we would expect *mb* to decline as butter consumption increases, so we expect *msb* to decline. Society will also derive successively less benefit from each marginal unit as the total level of butter consumption increases. This information is depicted in Figure 1.1.

In Figure 1.1(a), *tsb* is measured in £s on the vertical axis and the quantity of butter consumed per week – in thousands of tonnes – is recorded on the horizontal axis. The *tsb* curve shows that as butter consumption increases *tsb* also increases, but that the increases in benefit become less at successively higher levels of consumption. For example, compare the increase in benefit between 40 000 and 60 000 tonnes with that between 120 000 and 140 000 tonnes. These increases in *tsb* are of course the *msb* at each level of consumption; the pattern of *msb*s implied by the *tsb* curve has been extracted and presented separately in Figure 1.1(b). This time the vertical axis measures *msb* while the horizontal axis continues to measure the quantity of butter consumed. The *msb* curve slopes downwards from left to right, showing that the *msb* declines as the level of butter consumption increases.

## Costs of Production

Let us now look at the costs incurred in the production of butter – that is, the value of the resources of land, labour, and capital that are used up. The actual chain of production of even a reasonably commonplace foodstuff such as butter will be quite complex – extending from the dairy farmer, and the equipment and labour that is used, through the manufacturing process, to the packaging and marketing in retail shops. It is not our intention to get involved in a detailed examination of all these costs, but instead to draw some broad conclusions about the way we can expect costs to vary as output increases.

If we take the typical firm engaged in the process of butter production, we would expect to find that its costs of production increase as its level of output expands, for it will need to employ a greater quantity of resources. Hence total costs (*tc*) will increase with

**FIGURE 1.1**
**Benefits and costs of Butter Consumption**

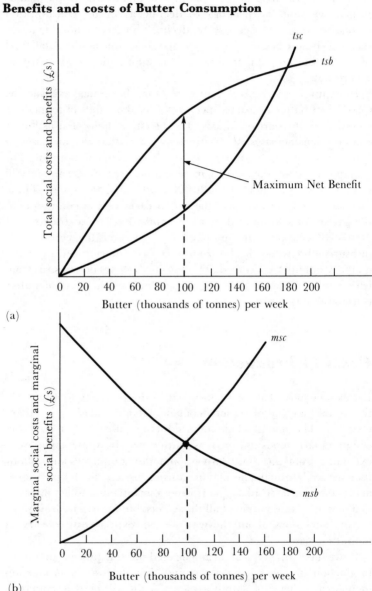

(a)

(b)

output. But how will the costs of producing each additional unit of output – the marginal cost (*mc*) – vary as output increases? Numerous studies by economists have shown that when we take a reasonably short period of time (in our example it is one week), although the *mc* of production may at first decline as output increases, there is a level of production beyond which it becomes increasingly difficult to expand output without incurring heavier costs per unit produced. This phenomenon is commonly known as diminishing returns. It is caused by such factors as the need to pay higher wages to induce people to work overtime or to attract new labour to the firm quickly, and to purchase new machines or to bring older, less efficient equipment into service as production increases. Therefore, over an important range of possible outputs, we can expect to find the firm experiencing a rising *mc*.

Now in the same way that we added up individual consumer's benefits to obtain social benefits, so we can add up the individual firms' *tc*s to obtain the industry's *tc*. Moreover, if we assume that all the costs of butter production are borne by the industry, its costs will represent total social cost (*tsc*). Similarly the individual *mc*s can be added up to obtain the marginal social cost (*msc*) at each level of output. The *tsc* curve of Figure 1.1(a) shows the way that *tsc* is expected to increase with butter output and the *msc* curve of Figure 1.1(b) shows the corresponding behaviour of *msc*.

## The Efficient Level of Output

Given this description of the way in which social benefits and social costs vary as butter consumption and production increase, we are now in a position to identify the level of output at which the excess of *tsb* over *tsc* is greatest – that is, where net social benefit is at a maximum. This will be the efficient level of output. This position is most easily identified by again considering Figure 1.1(a). The level of output at which the *tsb* curve is at the greatest distance above the *tsc* curve is 100 000 tonnes per week. At any other level of output the excess of *tsb* over *tsc* will be less. A glance at the corresponding *msb* and *msc* curves in Figure 1.1(b) will show that this point of maximum net benefit will occur where *msb* = *msc*. A moment's thought should confirm why this must be so: as long as the *msb* of a unit of output is greater than its *msc*, society will gain by more being produced, for each unit will add more to benefits than to costs. Conversely, if *msc* is greater than *msb*, society will gain if butter consumption is curtailed, for in this situation the last unit produced is adding more to costs than to benefits. Only where *msb* is equal to *msc* will it be impossible to increase net social benefits by changing the level of output. Hence an equivalent way of defining the efficient level of output is to say that it occurs when *marginal social benefit* equals *marginal social cost*.

As we said earlier, this analysis of the efficient level of butter output is not only relevant to the production of butter but to all goods and services. Hence we can define the socially efficient output of cars, health care, education, housing or any other commodity in exactly the same way. Overall efficiency is achieved when every commodity is being produced at its efficient amount. In such a situation it will be impossible to increase net social benefit by reallocating resources from one area of production to another. For the reallocation of a resource will lead to a reduction in output in the market from which it is taken (and hence a departure from its efficient level) and an increase in the market in which it goes (and, once again, a departure from the efficient level).

Thus to say that we have an efficient allocation of resources is a powerful statement, for it means that net social benefit cannot be increased by a reallocation of resources and/or a rearrangement of production. This would indeed seem to be an important aim that any economic system should set itself. However this will not be the only social objective. It must be stressed that an efficient system does not necessarily imply a fair or equitable one. At first sight this may seem to be a strange thing to say, for we have defined an efficient system as one that produces the maximum net benefit for society. This might be taken to imply that it will be equitable, because a society in which there are gross inequalities of income – where Rolls Royces exist alongside widespread poverty – is hardly likely to produce the maximum benefit for all its members. But such a conclusion would misunderstand the meaning of maximum net benefit. It only refers to the overall level of net benefit for a given distribution of income; it does not concern itself with the way benefits are distributed between the individual members of society. The notion of equity is not dealt with by the efficiency criterion in the way the latter is generally used by economists. Let us examine more closely why this is so.

# Equity

The distinction between efficiency and equity can probably be explained best by means of an example. Suppose there are just two members of society – Adam and Eve – who produce and consume their own butter (with, of course, a little help from their four-legged friends). Now assume there are a variety of ways in which Adam and Eve can organise their time and work, but that the amount of butter produced per week for which their total benefit is greatest is ten kilograms (kg). Therefore, following our earlier discussions, we can say that the system of work that produced ten kg per week is an efficient system. Now there are a number of ways in which they could divide these ten kg between themselves for consumption. For example, they could have five kg each, or Eve could have six kg and Adam four kg, or Adam ten kg and Eve none. They are all possible combinations, and all could occur at an efficient level of output, but we would probably not consider them all to be fair. Questions concerning the distribution of butter between Adam and Eve are matters of equity and need to be considered as distinct from the question of efficiency.

The distinction is stressed in Figure 1.2. On the vertical axis we measure the quantity of butter consumed by Adam and on the horizontal axis the amount consumed by Eve. The straight line $UU'$ is called the consumption possibility frontier, for it traces out the maximum combinations of consumption (and hence benefit) open to Adam and Eve. For instance, at point $A$ they both receive five kg, while at point $B$ Eve receives eight kg and Adam receives only two kg. Now clearly any combination, such as $C$ (where both receive four kg and there are two kg left over), is an inefficient combination because it would be possible to move to a point on the frontier where both Adam and Eve are better off. The same will be true for any other combination inside the frontier: it will always be possible to make at least one person better off without affecting the other, or to make them both better off. Only when a combination on the frontier is selected will we have an efficient solution.

But the fact that the solution is efficient does not mean that it will be equitable. There will be many combinations lying on the frontier, but a number of them will involve quite uneven distributions. The judgement about the equity of these various combinations will depend on one's ethical views about the way that butter, or benefits, should be distributed between Adam and Eve. It is because questions of equity involve personal value judgements about the way in which benefits should be distributed among members of society that many economists claim them to be outside the realm of their professional competence. Economists, it is argued, are no better equipped to supply answers to these questions than are any other citizens. Accordingly they have confined their attention to the allegedly value-free efficiency condition, claiming that questions involving equity or the distribution of benefits are matters for the political process.

**FIGURE 1.2**
**Efficiency and Equity**

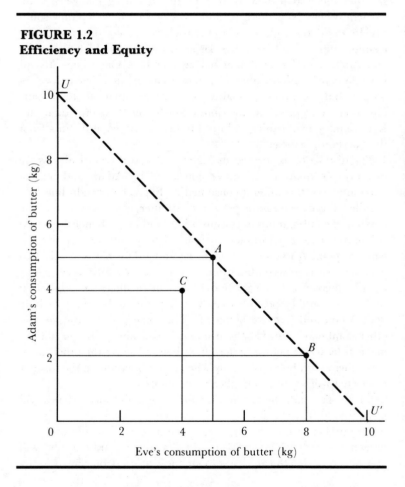

However, one should always be wary about claims of value-free (and hence superior?) social science. Some people who recommend the pursuit of efficiency imply that this is a value-free, technical matter without apparently realising, or revealing, that their prior acceptance of a given income distribution (often the existing one) itself involves a value judgement. In fact, the only difference between the objectives of efficiency and equity – in terms of their dependence upon value judgements – is that there is greater consensus among economists about what constitutes efficiency (as described in the previous section) than there is about what constitutes equity: but this is a difference of degree, not of kind.

Consequently the view taken in this book is that the economists' methods of analysis may be used to evaluate alternative methods of economic organisation in terms of their success in achieving both efficiency and equity; and, indeed, other objectives such as the promotion of consumer choice or the fostering of a spirit of community. Furthermore, while we shall always be careful to distinguish between the inevitably value-laden process of *specifying* an objective (be it efficiency, equity or whatever) and the largely value-free methods of *achieving* a given objective, it is relevant to note that economic reasoning may also actually serve to clarify the definition of objectives.

To illustrate this last point, consider the two interpretations of equity often associated with the social policy areas investigated in this book. One of these is the concept of full equality: everyone should have equal treatment for equal health care needs, everyone should receive equal education subject to their ability and so on. The other interpretation is in terms of minimum standards: no person should fall below a socially specified minimum level of income or consumption. Thus every family should live in a decent house with all the basic amenities even though some families would still have better quality housing than others; each person in need of health care should receive at least a minimum level of such care, and so on.

Now both of these objectives can be illustrated in terms of our earlier discussion about Adam and Eve. This is done in Figure 1.3. In the diagram the line $OE$, running from the origin at an angle of 45°, shows how different total amounts of butter could be distributed equally between Adam and Eve, and thus indicates distributions that would satisfy the full equality criterion. With 10kg of butter available, it would obviously indicate that 5kg each was the most

**FIGURE 1.3**
**Full Equality and Minimum Standard Deffinitions of Equity**

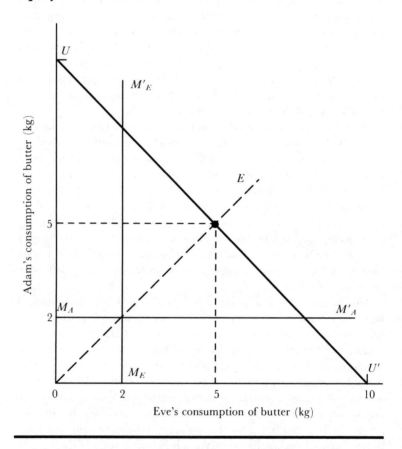

preferred combination on both equity and efficiency grounds. On the other hand, suppose that in this two-person society agreement has been reached specifying a minimum level of consumption of 2kg of butter below which no-one should fall. This minimum standard objective is depicted by the two lines $M_A M'_A$ and $M_E M'_E$. They indicate that only combinations of consumption enclosed by the two lines to the north-east of their point of intersection will satisfy the minimum consumption constraint. And with a consumption possibility frontier $UU'$ defined for 10kg of butter, they indicate a range of distributions on the frontier that will be considered equitable and efficient.

There is one final point concerning the relationship between equity and efficiency that needs to be stressed. In the example we have assumed that the distribution of butter between Adam and Eve was independent of the total amount of butter available: that is, the redistribution of the butter did not affect the amount of it that was produced. However, this may not be the case. Suppose that Eve actually did most of the work involved in producing the butter. If she knew that some or all of the butter she produced was subsequently to be redistributed to Adam, she might not feel inclined to work so hard and, if she followed her inclinations, the total amount of butter produced would fall. The net social benefit from butter production would also therefore fall; hence efficiency would be less. So the attainment of equity would have reduced efficiency. More generally, in the real world, where the amount people produce may depend on the rewards they receive, there may be a *trade-off* between equity and efficiency; the single-minded pursuit of one may result in the other not being achieved and vice versa.

# Other Objectives

Because this book is concerned with the economic analysis of social problems most of our attention is devoted to the two social objectives most commonly considered by economists: efficiency and equity. However, there are obviously other ends which the members of a society may wish to pursue. For instance, the importance of *consumer choice* is often emphasised in industrialised societies. Another important value is that of *freedom* or liberty: political freedom, freedom of movement, and freedom under the law are all aspects of freedom that relate to some of the issues discussed in this book.

Another objective to which a society may subscribe, and which is of particular importance in the social problems area, is that of *community*, or the linked ideas of 'citizenship' and what in many

European countries is referred to as 'social solidarity'. Much of our behaviour is governed by the pursuit of self-interest or the interests of our immediate family and friends. However, within most people there is a strong belief that to act in the interest of the community, without any expectation of personal gain, is an honourable activity. Self-sacrifice by war heroes or lifeboatmen, donations of blood to hospitals or cash to charities all enjoy a prestige deriving from our recognition of the need at times to temper self-interest by displaying consideration for others before ourselves It has been argued that society should endeavour to develop a system of economic organisation in which opportunities for altruistic behaviour of this kind are expanded: a society in which the spirit of 'community' complemented the individual pursuit of self-interest.

Again it is important to recognise that it may not be possible to achieve all these aims simultaneously. A society where individual liberty is paramount is unlikely to be especially communal; one that emphasises consumer choice may not be equitable. In any social decision concerning the 'best possible' allocation of resources, there is likely to be a trade-off between objectives: no aim will be followed so far that the attainment of other aims is seriously damaged.


# The Market System

As we stressed earlier, wherever scarcity exists society is confronted with problems of choice. A variety of ways have been devised, at different times and in different places, to provide particular societies with a set of 'mechanisms' by which these choices can be made. For instance, in certain primitive societies chiefs or councils of elders typically made decisions about what foods should be grown, gathered, and hunted. They also decided how their members were to go about these tasks and who was to receive the food and other goods produced by the community. At a slightly more complex level, feudal societies also operated on a similar system of central direction.

Until recently, two dominant methods of performing these tasks of allocation could be identified among large-scale societies. On the one hand there were the so-called 'command' or planned economies of Eastern Europe, the Soviet Union and China, where primary emphasis was placed upon the administrative planning of production by government appointed decision-makers. Within these societies the main means of production were in public ownership and decisions about what and how goods are produced, and to whom they should be allocated, were made via a government bureaucracy. The particular economic systems of individual countries varied quite considerably, especially in relation to the amount of decentralisation of power they displayed, but they all – to a greater or lesser extent – shared a common reliance upon government decision-making as a means of co-ordinating everyone's activities. However, with the partial exception of China (at the time of writing), all these countries are in the process of dismantling their command economies. Instead they are adopting the mechanism for resource allocation that dominates the economies of North America, Western Europe, Australasia and Japan, and newly industrialised countries such as Taiwan, Singapore, and Hong Kong: the market or free enterprise system. This is a form of economic organisation in which the majority of allocation decisions are made through the ostensibly unco-ordinated actions of large numbers of individuals and private firms. The co-ordination of activities within these countries comes about because each factor of production (land, labour and capital) and each commodity has a price to which diverse groups respond in a way that reconciles their separate actions.

Because of its current dominance as a means of economic organisation throughout the world, a major focus of attention in this book will be on the way in which the market system operates (or could be expected to operate), especially in areas where social problems arise. As a preliminary to those discussions, most of the remainder of this chapter is devoted to an explanation of some of the essential elements of the market system. Let us continue to use the butter example for illustrative purposes. As in the case of all commodities we shall distinguish between those people who buy and eat the butter, the consumers, and those who provide the butter for sale, the producers. In general, consumers comprise private households while the producers are usually organised groups known as firms. Of course, a particular individual will be both a consumer and producer at different times; the categories refer to the actions taking place while performing a particular role rather than to distinct categories of individuals. By looking at each group in turn we can see how their respective, apparently unco-ordinated, actions are reconciled by the market system.

## Consumer Demand

Each individual has a set or tastes of preferences that will determine, among other things, how much butter she would like to consume. However, a general preference for acquiring a commodity only becomes a demand for the commodity when the consumer is willing and able to pay for it. Hence the price of butter and the amount of income the individual possesses, as well as her tastes, will also determine how much she demands. Also the prices of other commodities, such as margarine, may affect the quantity of butter she demands.

Let us for the moment confine our attention to the way the demand for butter varies as its price varies, with all the other factors remaining unchanged. There is a certain amount of intuitive appeal in the proposition that a consumer's demand will increase as the price falls: that, as butter becomes cheaper, a person is induced to buy more of it. If we then add up all the individual demands that would be forthcoming at each price we should be able to see how much butter would be demanded within the economy at each price. This information will be embodied in a market demand curve of the type presented in Figure 1.4(a). In this diagram the vertical axis measures the price of butter per 250g packet and the horizontal axis measures the quantity demanded in thousands of tonnes. The demand curve slopes downwards from left to right, showing that the quantity demanded will increase as the price falls. Thus 100 000 tonnes will be demanded at a price of 70p per 250g, while 150 000 tonnes will be demanded at the price of 50p per 250g. Later we will describe how this relationship between demand and the price of butter is affected when the other factors that determine demand – such as income – change, but before then let us look at the conditions under which we would expect butter to be provided for sale.

## Producer Supply

We said earlier that production takes place within firms. These firms may have a variety of objectives that will determine the terms on which goods are offered for sale. Many economists have looked at the objectives that firms pursue both from theoretical and empirical points of view. Some claim that firms aim to maximise profits; others

**FIGURE 1.4**
**The Demand and Supply of Butter**

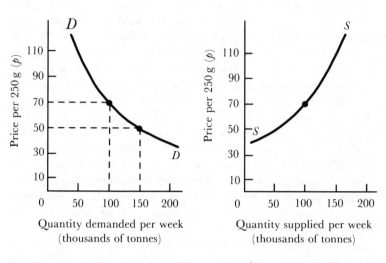

(a) The Demand for Butter

(b) The Supply of Butter

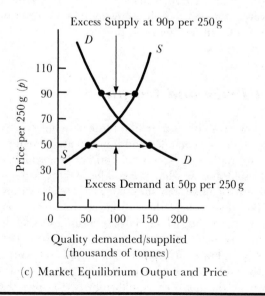

(c) Market Equilibrium Output and Price

maintain that they try to maximise sales; still others believe that firms do not pursue maximising targets at all but are more interested in a quiet life free from the pressures of extreme competition. These are complex theories and beyond the scope of this book. We shall simply assume that firms are interested in making some profits, and since the profit made on each packet of butter is the difference between the price at which it is sold and the cost of producing it, the quantities of butter that firms offer for sale will depend on the price per gram they receive and the costs of producing different quantities.

As the price rises – other things remaining equal – the firm initially makes a greater profit on each item it sells and therefore it is likely to be induced to expand production. However, it may be, as we argued earlier, that as production expands it becomes more costly to produce more if output goes beyond the level of production for which the firm planned. So production costs increase because of the need to pay overtime wages and to use older, less efficient equipment to supplement that used in normal times. Hence firms may need higher prices to induce them to supply more.

By adding up the quantities that each firm is willing to supply at different prices, we can see the quantity that the industry will supply at various prices. This information, commonly presented in the form of an industry supply curve, is depicted in Figure 1.4(b). The curve slopes upwards from left to right, showing that a greater quantity of butter will be offered for sale as its price rises.

## Market Price and Output

We have now established a relationship between the quantity of butter that would be demanded and supplied at different price levels. By combining these two figures we can see how much is actually bought and sold and at what price. This is done in Figure 1.4(c), where both the demand and supply curves are shown on the same diagram. The point where the two curves intersect represents the price and quantity at which both consumers' and producers' requirements are met. In this case, consumers are willing to buy 100 000 tonnes of butter at 70p per 250g packet and firms are willing to supply that quantity at that price. This price–output combination, known as the point of equilibrium, is the one that will be established in the market and it will persist until some outside influence disturbs the situation.

We can see why the equilibrium point is the one towards which market price and quantity will move by considering what would happen if the market price were above the equilibrium, say at 90p per 250g. At this price firms are willing to supply 125 000 tonnes of butter but consumers are willing to buy only 75 000 tonnes. If this price persists firms will over-produce and stocks will begin to pile up. The only way to rectify the situation is to lower the price. This has two effects: it increases the demand for butter and at the same time reduces the supply coming on to the market. In this way the discrepancy between demand and supply is reduced until it is eliminated at the equilibrium price.

The same process will also ensure that price cannot remain *below* the equilibrium level. If, for example, the price were 50p per 250g consumers would demand 150 000 tonnes per week while firms were only willing to supply 50 000 tonnes. In this situation butter would be snapped up as soon as it was offered for sale and shelves and stockrooms would soon be bare. The more astute firms would soon notice that a lot of demand was remaining unsatisfied at this price and that they could, in the next week, sell all they had to offer at a higher price and thereby make larger profits. Prices would therefore begin to rise. Once again this would have two effects: it would reduce the demand for butter and induce producers to supply more. The tendency for prices to continue to rise would only end when the equilibrium price was reached, for then demand and supply would be equated.

Such are the rudiments of the way the market system operates: the ostensibly unco-ordinated actions, and possibly conflicting interests, of consumers and producers are reconciled by the way they both respond to common price 'signals', and in this way market output is determined. For simplicity we have confined our discussion of the way the market system operates to the case of butter, but obviously the application is far more general. In each commodity market, whether it is butter or bread, health care or housing, decisions regarding the level of output can be decided by the interaction of demand and supply. Furthermore this process is not only confined to markets for commodities. It also applies to the markets for 'factors of production' such as labour, capital and land. If one looks at the number (that is, the quantity) of construction workers or lawyers who are employed, and the wage or salary (that is, the price) they receive, one can see that demand and supply factors often play a key role.

The discussion thus far of the way in which consumers and producers react to price levels different from the equilibrium price has shown how their respective actions tend to move market price and output to the equilibrium level. These same reactions can also be expected to establish a new equilibrium price–output combination if a change in market circumstances renders the existing one inappropriate. Indeed, one of the most important attributes claimed for the market system as an allocator of both commodities and resources is its ability to respond quickly and smoothly to change. In the next section we look at the way in which it does this.

## The Market System and Change

For the sake of continuity we shall ask for the reader's tolerance and continue with our butter example. When the demand and supply curves of Figure 1.4 were constructed it was stated that they showed the way in which the demand and supply of butter were likely to vary as its price varied, when all the other factors that might be expected to affect demand (and supply) remain unchanged. We shall now relax this assumption and see what happens when one or more of these factors changes. We will consider one example of a change in the determinants of demand and one of a change on the supply side of the market.

First, let us look at demand. Suppose that for some reason the incomes of a large section of the population increase. We would expect that some of this additional income would be used to buy more butter: that is, some consumers who were not able to afford to buy much before will be able to use butter instead of cheaper substitutes and others will be able to become more lavish in their use of it. In terms of our diagrams society's increased affluence can be conveyed by constructing a new demand curve to the right of the original one. (This is referred to as a shift in the demand curve). Thus in Figure 1.5(a) the curve $D'\,D'$ shows that a greater quantity of butter will be demanded at each price – at the new higher level of income – than at the previous level. At the original equilibrium price of 70p per 250g packet there is a new, higher level of demand – 150 000 tonnes. However, since there has been no change in the

# FIGURE 1.5
## Change and Market Equilibrium

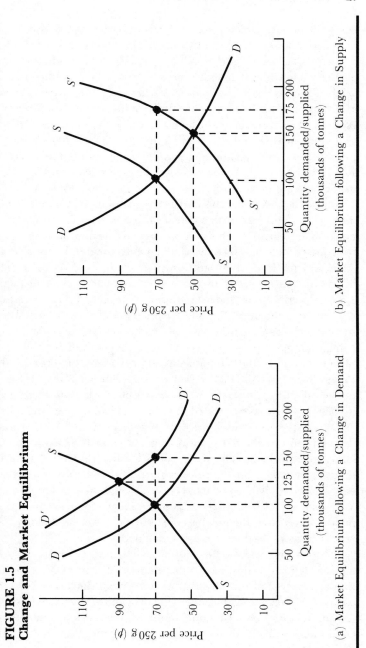

(a) Market Equilibrium following a Change in Demand

(b) Market Equilibrium following a Change in Supply

conditions under which producers supply butter, the quantity they are offering for sale is shown by the original supply curve (*SS*). So at a price of 70p per 250g, they still offer 100 000 tonnes. Thus we have a situation in which demand exceeds supply at the prevailing market price. Then, as we know from our earlier discussion, we can expect some upward movement in the price until a new equilibrium is established. This is shown in Figure 1.5(a) by the point of intersection between *D'D'* and *SS* – that is, an output of 125 000 tonnes at a price of 90p per 250g. The 20p rise in price has induced producers to supply more and 'choked off' some of the excess demand that existed at the old equilibrium price.

Now let us look at the effects of a change in supply. Consider a new discovery in butter-making technology that enables firms to produce butter more cheaply. This may be expected to lead firms to lower their prices and still make the same, or even greater, levels of profit. Thus, at each level of output, firms will charge a lower price. This information is conveyed by the new supply curve (*S'S'*) in Figure 1.5(b). (Verify your understanding by checking to see that each quantity is being offered at a lower price than before. Where would the curve lie if a change in supply conditions led to higher prices being charged?). Now producers are willing to sell the old equilibrium output of 100 000 tonnes at 30p per 250g or to offer 175 000 tonnes for sale at the old market price of 70p per 250g. However, neither of these alternatives is compatible with consumers' willingness to buy, as indicated by the unchanged demand curve (*DD*). At the new lower price of 30p there would be too much demand, and at the old price of 70p not enough demand, for the larger amount being offered for sale. Clearly an intermediate price needs to be found. Such a price is given at the point of intersection between the unchanged demand curve *DD* and the new supply curve *S'S'* – that is, 150 000 tonnes at 50p per 250g. The new equilibrium price is lower than the previous one, but the lower production costs permit firms to produce a larger equilibrium output.

These examples show the way in which changes in the determinants of demand and supply – other than price – can be incorporated into an analysis of the way the market system functions. We have only considered two such changes but, obviously, many are possible. (Again, test your understanding of the way that changes in external factors may be accommodated by considering the effect on the initial price–output equilibrium of the following events: (a) an increase in the price of margarine, (b) an increase in the price of cattle food-stuffs, and (c) a health education campaign pointing out the link between coronary heart disease and the consumption of fatty food stuffs. After considering the effect of each of these events separately, suppose they happen simultaneously!).

As we mentioned earlier, the way in which the market system reacts to change is often claimed to be one of its main attributes. There is no need for a complex administrative system to make decisions about changes in the composition of output. This is achieved by the supposedly unco-ordinated, individual actions of a vast number of consumers and producers, each acting in response to price 'signals'. If butter production becomes more costly, price will reflect this and demand and output will probably fall while the production of some other good increases. The system is automatic or, in the words of Adam Smith – the father of modern economics – there is 'an invisible hand' at work.

# The Market System and Social Objectives

We have now discussed both the concept of an efficient level of output and the level of output that will be established in a market system in terms of our butter example. However, the link between the two approaches is far more fundamental than this choice of an arbitrary example might suggest. The reader will no doubt have noticed that the marginal social benefit and the marginal social cost curves have the same general appearance as the demand and supply curves. This is no coincidence. In fact an essential part of the theory underlying the market system is that in certain circumstances the demand curve is an alternative presentation of the marginal social benefit curve and the supply curve is an alternative form of the marginal social cost curve. Under those circumstances, the equilibrium output obtained through the market system will be the efficient level of output. Let us look a little more closely to see why this is so.

For any rational individual who wants to maximise the net benefit obtained from consumption, it must be the case that the maximum price that she is willing to pay for a commodity is determined by the marginal benefit ($mb$) derived from it. An individual will not be willing to pay a price greater than the *mb* received because this would lead to higher costs being incurred than benefits obtained. Similarly a rational consumer will always be willing to pay the market price if it is less than the *mb* obtained, for net benefit will be increased through each extra unit of the commodity consumed. In such a situation a person will continue consuming additional quantities of the commodity until the *mb* derived falls to the level of the price. At this point there is no further possibility for increasing net benefit. Thus the price a consumer is willing to pay for different quantities of a commodity, or the demand curve, is defined by the *mb* curve. Now when we discussed the marginal social benefit (*msb*) curve we said that this was obtained by adding the individual *mb* curves of each consumer. Similarly the market demand curve is obtained by adding all the individual demand curves. So if each individual *mb* curve is identical to the individual's demand curve, the *msb* curve must be identical to the market demand curve. From society's point of view the price that consumers collectively are willing to pay, or their demand, is determined by the sum of their individual marginal benefits, or the marginal social benefit.

As long as there are many firms in competition with one another, the link between the marginal cost and supply curves can be established in a similar fashion. For each firm, the price at which it will sell a particular quantity of a commodity will equal the costs of production it incurs on the last unit of output as production increases, or the marginal cost (*mc*). If it were to sell a commodity at a price less than the cost of producing the last unit it sells, the firm would lose money on that last unit. If it were to sell the commodity at a price more than the cost of producing the last unit, other firms could undercut it by reducing their prices to the level of marginal cost. Therefore under competitive conditions the marginal cost and supply curves must be the same thing. Further, if the marginal social cost (*msc*) is the sum of the individual firms' *mc*s at each level of output the result is that the *msc* curve and the market supply curve also are identical.

Thus the interaction of demand and supply can be expected to lead to an efficient level of output. Now this is obviously a very important prediction. We are saying that an unfettered competitive market system in which both consumers and producers are intent on maximising their individual net benefits will lead to the maximisation of society's net benefit. Or as Adam Smith put it:

**It is not from the benevolence of the butcher, the brewer, or the baker that we expect our dinner but from their regard to their own interest. We address ourselves not to their humanity but to their self-love, and never talk to them of our own necessities but of their advantages.**

It is the claim that a market system will produce an efficient allocation of resources which provides the major theoretical basis for preferring it to other methods of economic organisation. But because this claim is often obscured in emotion-laden debates between ideologues of the political left and right, it is important to establish exactly what it asserts.

First, it is necessary to recognise that the prediction that a market system will achieve efficiency rests upon certain assumptions about the way in which the market operates. These have not been spelt out in this chapter because an examination of them, and the possibility that they will not be met in specific problem areas, constitutes a major element of the remainder of this book. However, to anticipate our conclusions, the reader will find that we identify a series of important market imperfections which can be expected to prevent it achieving efficiency in the areas discussed. Second, we must emphasise again that despite its dominance in the economics literature, efficiency is likely to be only one of society's objectives. From among the others we have selected the aim of equity for special attention. And as we have seen, an efficient system is compatible with a number of different distributions of benefits between the members of society, many of which may be highly inequitable.

We have also mentioned other objectives such as consumer choice, freedom and community. Advocates of the market have argued that it is only through a market system that consumer choice and more general freedoms can be preserved. Under a competitive market system no one individual can direct or coerce another in economic matters, for individuals can always take their business elsewhere. So competitive markets offer choice. But they also decentralise economic power. Since the latter is often linked to political power, it is argued that their existence is an essential element in avoiding the centralisation of political power and hence the erosion of political and other freedoms. On the other hand, the existence of markets may be antithetical to the aim of community. For many of the social reformers who were influential in the establishment of the 'welfare state' the market system, with its dependence upon the pursuit of self-interest, was inconsistent with the objectives of community, citizenship and altruism which they wished to promote. This belief is still held strongly by some present day supporters of the welfare state who maintain that government finance and provision of services such as health care and education is more likely to produce a sense of community and commom citizenship than is private finance and provision.

So the ability of markets to achieve different kinds of social objectives in the allocation of scarce resources raises fundamental and controversial issues. In the rest of this book, we discuss these issues with respect to specific social problem areas in the chapter devoted to that area. Finally, we return to the general question of market success and failure in the last chapter.

# Government Policies

The perceived failure of the market system to realise satisfactorily the objectives which our society has set itself has led to various types of government intervention. The precise form of government policy in the areas of health care, education, housing and so on, will be the subject of extensive discussion in the individual chapters of this book. However, because it is easy to become immersed in the detail of individual policies at the cost of losing sight of the general principles they are meant to embody, it may help the reader if we specify at the outset the general categories within which government policies fall. First there is government *regulation* of the market system. This involves specifying, via law, what activities may, or may not, have to be undertaken. Examples of regulation include pollution control standards (for example, smokeless zones), rent control restrictions, compulsory schooling until 16 years of age and public health legislation. Second, a government may use *tax or subsidy* policies to deter those activities it wishes to restrict (by taxing them) or to encourage those activities it wishes to expand (by subsidising them). Examples of the use of tax/subsidy policies are student grants, tax concessions to house owners, home insulation grants, and congestion and pollution taxes. Third, the government may seek to achieve the desired allocation of resources through direct *provision* which actually replaces the market system. The National Health Service, the provision of council houses and public transport provide examples of this policy.

Now through the use of regulation, tax/subsidy policies or direct provision the government tries to achieve the social objectives it has set more fully than the market system by itself can achieve them. But it should be stressed that it does not always realise this aim. In subsequent chapters, we shall be discussing, not only the potential failings of the market system, but also the failings of government policies designed to rectify market failure in the specific areas concerned. Again in the last chapter we return to the general question of government success and failure, paralleling so far as possible the similar discussion of the market.

## Summary

Most societies pursue a number of objectives in the allocation and distribution of resources. From these we have selected *efficiency* and *equity* for particular attention, although we have also discussed *choice*, *freedom* and *community*. We have defined the efficient level of output as the one which yields maximum net social benefit; that is, where the *marginal social cost* of production equals its *marginal social benefit*. We have shown that, under certain conditions, the interaction of demand and supply within the market system will achieve an efficient level of output. It may also promote freedom, according to some definitions of that term. However, there is less reason to be confident that it will achieve an equitable distribution of resources or promote altruism and a sense of community.

Given the likelihood that a market system will be able only partially to meet the objectives set for it, we have described methods of government intervention that may be used in an attempt to meet these aims more fully, viz, *regulation, taxes* and *subsidies*, and direct *provision*. The ability of these various forms of intervention to meet social objectives, together with that of the market, is examined more thoroughly within the context of specific social problems in the remainder of the book.

## Further Reading

There are a large number of introductory textbooks that develop the ideas contained in this chapter at greater length and depth.

Individual students and teachers will no doubt have their favourites and so we have just provided some suggestions for the reader who is totally unfamiliar with these texts. Probably the most widely used introductory textbook in Britain at present is Begg, Dornbusch and Fisher (1987). Another useful textbook, with something of a social problems flavour is Culyer (1985). Barr (1987) and Culyer (1980) provide useful discussions of the application of economic analysis to the areas to be discussed in this book; however, they both require a basic knowledge of economics. Definitions of *efficiency* are given in most economics introductory texts including those mentioned above. Conceptions of *equity* are discussed in detail in Le Grand (1991), some parts of which are accessible to non-specialists. Altruism and *community* are discussed in Titmuss (1970) and Collard (1978), although the latter may be hard going for non-specialists. General arguments in favour of markets, including their contribution to efficiency and liberty, can be found in Seldon (1990). The use of markets to achieve 'socialist' ends is discussed extensively by Miller (1989) and the contributors to Le Grand and Estrin (1989); in the latter see, particularly, the chapters by Miller, Plant and Estrin and Winter. The last of these provides a useful critique of command economies.

# Questions for Discussion

1. If, as some people argue, 'there is no such thing as society', does it make sense to talk of 'social' objectives such as efficiency or equity?
2. The concepts of social benefit and social cost involve the summation of individual benefits and costs. What problems does this procedure pose?
3. 'The specification of an efficient allocation of resources, unlike the definition of an equitable distribution, does not involve personal value judgements'. Do you agree?
4. The market system is based upon consumer demand; how does this differ from consumer need?
5. Will the achievement of an equitable distribution of resources inevitably involve inefficiency and a restriction of personal freedom?

6. Explain how you would expect government regulation in the form of price controls to affect the operation of the market system.
7. Do you think that reliance upon the market system precludes the promotion of community spirit or altruism?
8. In what ways would you expect the development of large firms to affect the model of the market system presented in this chapter?
9. Consider the concept of freedom and the extent to which it is promoted by alternative economic systems.

# Health 2

Good health is one of the most important factors contributing to individual welfare. It is an essential prerequisite for enjoyment of almost every other aspect of life. A high income or a good education yield little satisfaction to the chronically sick. And, at the extreme, ill health that leads to death will make all other sources of satisfaction irrelevant.

It is not surprising, therefore, that throughout the world considerable resources have been devoted to the maintenance and preservation of health. In Britain, health care expenditures account for over six per cent of the Gross National Product; in the United States they account for over eleven per cent. In most Western European countries the proportion lies somewhere between these two figures. Despite the amount of resources involved, however, the area has only become of interest to economists relatively recently. Perhaps because it involves dealing with highly emotional and sensitive issues, economists have not traditionally viewed it as suitable for the application of economic analysis. Even now there is a strong feeling among many non-economists that health is a matter of 'social' and not 'economic' concern, and therefore that the tools economists use for studying problems of resource allocation in other areas are simply not appropriate for the field of health and health care.

It is one of the aims of this chapter to show that this feeling is mistaken. The fundamental problems of resource allocation apply to health just as they do in any other area of life. What proportion of the nation's resources should be devoted to the maintenance of its citizens' health? What is the best method of achieving a given level of health care from limited resources? Should health care be privately or publicly provided? All these are economic problems in the sense that they are problems of resource allocation, and they are all therefore problems for which the economist's tools can contribute to finding the answers.

Many factors contribute to individuals' states of health. These include diet, work situation, housing, public health measures (such as sewage disposal and rubbish collection) and the availability and quality of health care. Resource allocation problems arise in each of these areas, and to treat them all adequately would be beyond the scope of this chapter. Accordingly we shall concentrate on the last of them: health care. First we look at the objectives society might have with respect to the provision of health care. Then we examine the possibility of using the market system to allocate such care: its advantages and disadvantages as a means of achieving the objectives. In the light of certain market shortcomings, we discuss the various ways in which the state can intervene and the associated advantages and disadvantages of intervention. Finally, we examine recent reforms in the UK health care market.

# Objectives

We saw in Chapter 1 that two important aims that have to be considered in any question of resource allocation are the attainment of efficiency and the promotion of social justice or equity. Let us see how these can be interpreted in the context of health care.

# *Efficiency*

It is sometimes stated that an efficient health care system is one that provides the highest possible standard of care, regardless of cost. As an American doctor has put it:

> **It is incumbent on the physician . . . to practice not 'cost effective' medicine but that which is as safe as possible for that patient under the particular circumstances. Optimization of survival and not optimization of cost effectiveness is the only ethical imperative . . . A physician who changes his or her way of practising medicine because of cost rather than purely medical considerations has indeed embarked on the 'slippery slope' of**

compromised ethics and waffled priorities. (Loewry, 1980, p. 697).

This point of view has a strong influence on the way that medical practitioners actually behave; understandably so, since it is of obvious ethical appeal. Unfortunately as a policy guide it is a non-starter, for costs cannot be ignored in making policy choices. The building of hospitals, the training of doctors and nurses, the manufacture of drugs and technical equipment, all consume scarce resources. That is, they use up land, labour and capital; resources that could have been put to other users, such as building schools, training teachers or making cars. The 'best possible' standard of health care could only be achieved by devoting all of the economy's resources to it; hardly a wise course of action, since no other commodities (including those vital to health, such as food) could be produced.

Even within health care itself the idea that physicians should always provide the best possible treatment regardless of cost makes little sense. Doctors who give their patients 'Rolls-Royce' treatment are likely to be taking resources from other patients. Keeping patients alive as long as possible cannot be a target for the allocation of resources, even within the health sector, for the survival prospects of one patient can only be increased at the expense of the survival prospects of others.

What is needed is a definition of efficiency that takes account of the costs of, as well as the benefits from, health care. An obvious starting point is the definition suggested in Chapter 1. There an efficient level of production of a commodity was defined as one where the difference between benefits and costs is greatest: that is, where the marginal social benefit ($msb$) from a production of the commodity equals its marginal social cost ($msc$). A simple example will show how this might be applied in the field of health care.

Suppose we are trying to decide what is the efficient number of hospital beds to provide in a particular town. Imagine that we can measure the benefits and costs of providing hospital beds in terms of money (how this might be done is discussed below). Looking at these benefits and costs, we find that to provide 1000 hospital beds would yield a social benefit of £20 million and would cost only £10 million. To provide a second 1000 beds would benefit the town rather less than the first: say, by £12 million. It would cost slightly more: say, also £12 million. To provide a third 1000 beds would cost yet more – £16 million – and create benefits of only £8 million. Thus the benefit from providing each extra 1000 beds, the *msb*, declines while the cost, the *msc*, increases. This is as would be expected. Once the major needs of an area have been satisfied the benefits from providing more and more hospital beds are likely to diminish, while with each new hospital built the resources available for building yet another one become increasingly scarce and, therefore, more expensive.

These figures, together with their equivalent for fourth and fifth thousand beds, are summarised in Table 2.1. From this table we can deduce what would be the efficient number of hospital beds to provide. The gain (the *msb*) from providing the first thousand beds is £10 million greater than the cost (the *msc*). So those beds are worth providing. The *msb* from the second thousand equals the *msc*; hence they are also (just) worth providing. However, the costs of the third, fourth, and fifth thousand beds are greater than the benefits, and so it would not be efficient to build them. Therefore the efficient number of beds is two thousand, the point at which the marginal social cost of providing more beds begins to exceed the marginal social benefits.

**TABLE 2.1**
**Social Costs and Benefits of Hospital Beds**

| Number of hospital beds (000) | Marginal social benefit (£ million) | Marginal social cost (£ million) |
|:---:|:---:|:---:|
| 1 | 20 | 10 |
| 2 | 12 | 12 |
| 3 | 8 | 16 |
| 4 | 6 | 22 |
| 5 | 5 | 30 |

We can make the same point by use of a diagram. In Figure 2.1 the curve running downward from left to right shows how the *msb* declines as the number of beds provided increases, while the curve running upward shows how the *msc* increases. The point at which the two curves intersect is the efficient number of hospital beds.

## FIGURE 2.1
## Social Costs and Benefits of Hospital Beds

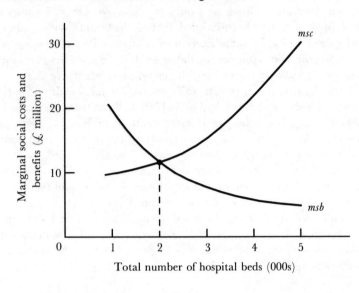

This is an example of how the concept of efficiency outlined in Chapter 1 could be applied in the field of health care. It is, in fact, perfectly general; in principle, it would be applied to any problem of allocating resources in the area (such as that of determining the efficient number of doctors to train, or of kidney machines to provide). But to use the concept in practice is not so easy. Difficulties arise in measuring the quantities involved, particularly the benefits.

The benefits from a course of medical treatment are the value of the improvements in health that result from the treatment. Any attempt to measure these benefits therefore requires information concerning the value people place on improvements in their health. But this is not easy to obtain. Ill health usually involves a loss of earnings or earnings-potential, and one method of measuring the benefits from a particular health improvement is to calculate the associated reduction in lost earnings. However, this takes no account of the value of any reduction in pain and suffering; moreover, it assumes that individuals with no earnings or earnings potential place no value on their health. An alternative is to try to find out how much people would be prepared to pay to reduce the risk of their health deteriorating; another is to calculate this sum by looking at the extra amount people are paid to work in industries where their health may be affected. Yet another is to ask individuals to value different health states. Research on this is currently under way in several European countries and in North America. Whilst not uncontentious, it is intended that the results can be used to establish the benefits of particular types of medical intervention.

The fact that measuring the benefits from health care is difficult should not obscure the essential truth that it is impossible to make any reasonable decision concerning resource allocation in the health field without taking some view (however crude) of the benefits involved. The hospital administrator who decides to allocate money to heart transplants rather than to kidney machines is making an implicit judgement about the relative benefits to be derived from each. The decision to use labour and capital to build a clinic rather than, say, a school or a mile of motorway implies that the benefits from extra clinic are greater than those from an extra school or more motorway. The difficulties in measuring benefits do not invalidate the definition of an efficient level of health care as one that maximises the difference between benefits and costs, for that definition is simply a formal way of stating a social objective already implicit in most decisions concerning resource allocation. That being the case, it is worth attempting to measure benefits, however crudely, for the alternative is simply to rely on what may often be ill-informed and arbitrary assessments.

## *Equity*

There is agreement amongst most people that the health care system should be fair or equitable. However there is much less agreement about the appropriate definition of fairness or equity. In Chapter 1 we discussed two ways of defining the equitable allocation of a commodity: one in terms of a minimum standard – everyone should have at least a minimum quantity of the commodity concerned – the other in terms of full equality – everyone should consume the commodity equally. Both of these have figured in discussions concerning the equitable allocation of health care. Some believe that there should be a *minimum standard* of treatment for those in need.

Others prefer the broader objective of full equality, usually phrased in the health care context as *equal treatment for equal need*.

A third interpretation of equity found in discussions concerning the organisation of health care is that it should promote *equality of access*. What is meant by this is rarely specified, but one interpretation is to define it in terms of the costs or sacrifices that people have had to make to get medical care. These include any fees or charges that may be levied, any money lost through having to take time off work, and the costs of travelling to the medical facility concerned. If these differ between people – for instance, if some individuals have had further to travel than others – then there would seem to be inequality of access. Hence this interpretation of equality of access implies equality of personal or private cost.

# The Market System and Health Care

In the United Kingdom the market system is used to allocate a wide range of basic necessities including clothing and food: it is not employed (by and large) in the allocation of health care. It is apparently believed in Britain that food and clothing will be distributed roughly in accordance with social objectives under the market system, but that health care will not be. The purpose of this section is to examine the basis for that belief. Is medical care in some way fundamentally different from food, clothing or any other commodity which is distributed through the market? Are there special characteristics distinguishing medical care from these other goods? Why should society's objectives be better achieved by non-market provision?

First, let us see what the features of a perfectly competitive private market in health care might be. Hospitals would charge their patients a price varying according to the type and length of the treatment. Doctors would operate similarly, charging for consultations and treatment. People in need of medical care could go to the doctor or to the hospital of their choice, provided only that they could pay the appropriate charge or were covered by an insurance policy that would pay the fees. The principal argument for this system is that it would be efficient. Since people would be free to choose, doctors and hospitals who provided inferior treatment at high prices would lose customers to those who provided better and/or cheaper services. For instance, a doctor who acquired a reputation for making wrong diagnoses, holding half-hearted consultations, and overcrowding the waiting room would lose patients to one known for her medical successes and ease of access. A hospital that did not use cost-saving technology would have to charge higher prices than its more efficient competitors and would eventually be driven out of business. Thus medical practitioners of all kinds would have a strong incentive to improve their standards of service and/or reduce their costs.

Furthermore, there would be freedom of choice; people could choose the doctor, hospital and treatment that suited them best. Doctors and hospital staff, knowing that their livings depended on it, would be attentive to their patients' desires and preferences. The result would be a system of health care that catered for individual's wants at the least possible cost – an efficient system.

These arguments are essentially the same as those used in Chapter 1 to demonstrate that the market can allocate butter efficiently. They imply that the *msb* curve in Figure 2.1 coincides with the market demand curve for hospital beds, and the *msc* curve with the market supply curve. Hence the point of intersection of the supply and demand curves – the quantity of hospital beds that would actually be supplied under a market system – will be the efficient quantity. Therefore, the argument goes, if the allocation of health care is determined by the market, the outcome would be efficient.

But will the outcome of market allocation of health care be efficient? Many argue that it will not. It is claimed that health care possesses certain characteristics that render market allocation inefficient. In particular, inefficiency in markets in health care arises because of *uncertainty of demand, imperfect consumer information* and *externalities*. Moreover, it is argued, efficiency is not society's only objective: there are others, such as *equity*, whose requirements are generally violated in the market. Let us look at those arguments in more detail.

## Uncertainty of Demand

One of the features of health care is that the demand for it is likely to occur unexpectedly. Generally people cannot predict when they are likely to want health treatment, and it is difficult for them to plan their expenditure and savings so as to ensure that they could always meet any unexpected medical expenses. This perhaps would matter little if the sums involved were small, but many forms of health care – such as those requiring long stays in a hospital – involve the payment of sums that can be very large indeed.

Within the market system there is a mechanism for coping with the problem of uncertainty: insurance. In theory – and indeed in practice in some countries such as the United States – the majority of families could have some kind of insurance plan to help them cope with expenditures for medical care. However, there are two difficulties with private insurance for health care that may reduce its efficiency. These are termed *moral hazard* and *adverse selection*. *Moral hazard* is the phenomenon that once a person is insured against an eventuality her actions may make it more likely to occur. It arises in the health care field because if a person is fully covered by insurance the incentives to both patient and doctor to economise on treatment are virtually eliminated. The insured may visit a doctor for frivolous ailments; the doctor, secure in the knowledge that the patient does not have to pay, may recommend highly expensive treatment. Both factors may raise utilisation and costs well beyond the efficient level. *Adverse selection* arises when insurance companies find it difficult to distinguish between good and bad risk individuals. The bad risk individuals are more likely, at a given price, to demand insurance than the good risks. With no way of telling a good risk from a bad risk, insurance companies will set their premiums to reflect the average risk of all the insured. As a consequence, some of the good risks may then not buy insurance, because the price will be above what they would be willing to pay. As a result, the ratio of bad risks to good risks amongst the insured will rise, claims will increase and the cost of insurance, the premiums, will go up. More good risks will not buy insurance. The end result will be fewer persons with insurance cover.

The existence of moral hazard and adverse selection will mean the insurance market will be more limited than if the insurance companies had full information about the actions of buyers. As a result certain people will not be able to buy insurance and will not have cover against the costs of medical care.

## *Imperfect Information*

Health care is also considered to be different from other commodities because there is an imbalance between the knowledge of the supplier of the treatment (the doctor) and that of the consumer (the patient). For many commodities, consumers have a fair idea of what constitutes quality. Even if they do not, provided that the commodity in question is one that is bought repeatedly, they can acquire knowledge of quality from their use of the good and employ this information to decide whether to purchase it again. For instance, if the shoes bought from a particular shop wore out quickly, consumers would acquire this information through several purchases of shoes – and presumably would shift their custom elsewhere.

But the situation for health care is very different. Before the treatment starts consumers usually have little idea of the extent of their illness, of the suitability of various possible treatments and of the likely effectiveness of treatment. Therefore they have to rely upon their doctor for this information. Furthermore, much medical care is not repeated, so that even if a consumer finds out that a treatment was not suitable, it will in many cases be too late to change to another. In other words, neither before nor after the treatment can consumers easily acquire information that will enable them to make an informed choice. Instead, the supplier of medical care – the physician – is also the supplier of information. The supplier of care thus acts as the consumer's *agent*, informing her both about her illness and its treatment.

This being so, the claim that an unregulated market in health care provides an incentive to doctors and hospitals to provide good service through competition becomes of doubtful validity. If consumers do not know (and cannot find out about) the difference between good treatment and bad treatment, then they are unlikely to shop around for better service. Instead, they will seek to build a long term relationship with a supplier – to establish a relationship of trust. Given this, consumers will not 'shop around' whenever they get ill, but will seek care from the supplier with whom they have built up a long-term relationship.

## Monopoly

The existence of this information imbalance confers considerable *monopoly* power on the suppliers of medical services. The fact that patients find it difficult to 'shop around' makes it less likely that doctors and hospitals will compete with one another. Instead, each can operate as a monopoly, raising prices without fearing a substantial loss of customers. It is also argued that the information imbalance between suppliers and demanders of care can lead to *supplier induced demand.* According to this argument, because patients rely on doctors to provide them with information, doctors can persuade patients to have more medical care than they would have done had the patients been fully informed. It is obviously very difficult to establish whether this occurs in practice, as it is not possible to know what amount of care patients would demand if they were fully informed! It is also likely that doctors' ethical codes act to limit such demand inducement. Nevertheless, in a system in which doctors are paid for each service they supply, the incentives are to provide more rather than less treatment.

## *Externalities*

A feature of health care that may create problems for market allocation is that it has 'external' benefits or *externalities* associated with it. The consumption (or production) of a commodity is said to create an externality when a third party who is not involved in the decision to consume (or produce) it is none the less affected by it, but receives no compensation or payment. If the effect is adverse, it is described as an *external cost*; if it is beneficial, as an *external benefit*.

Certain types of health care, particularly those concerned with communicable diseases, can create external benefits. For instance, if some people decide to be vaccinated against whooping cough, then not only do they reduce their probability of getting the disease, but they also reduce the probability of others getting it. The vaccination has thus benefited the people vaccinated (an *internal* or private benefit); and it has benefited others (an *external* benefit). Similarly, a hospital treatment that cures someone of a particular communicable disease confers external benefits, since it reduces the probability that others will contract the disease.

Since society includes both those who undertake any externality-generating activity and those affected by the externality, the total social benefits (or costs) of an activity is the sum of the private (or internal) benefits (or costs) and the external benefits (or costs). Thus:

private benefits (or costs) + external benefits (or costs) = social benefits (or costs)

This can be illustrated by our example of hospital beds. Suppose that treatment in hospitals confers external benefits: that is, it benefits not only people who become patients, but also the rest of the population (through, say, the reduction in the spread of communicable diseases). Let us assume that the size of the external benefit created by an extra thousand hospital beds – the marginal external benefit – decreases as more beds are provided, ranging from £22 million for the first thousand to £14 million for the fifth. Suppose, also, that each hospital still confers the same benefits on patients as before; but we now have to call these the marginal private benefits. Then we must draw up a revised cost and benefit statement, as shown in Table 2.2. From this table we can see that the socially efficient quantity of hospital beds has changed. It is now four thousand, where the *msb* – the sum of the marginal private benefits and the marginal external benefits – equals the *msc*. For each thousand of the first four, the msb is at least as great as the *msc*; whereas for the fifth thousand, the extra cost is greater than the extra benefit.

But under the market system only two thousand beds would be provided. While it would be socially profitable to provide the third and fourth thousand beds, it would not be privately profitable. Why not? We saw in Chapter 1 that the market demand for butter equalled the sum of the marginal benefits that individuals derived from butter. However, in this case, when external benefits are present, the market demand only equals the sum of the marginal *private* benefits, because under a market system a hospital only receives payment from its patients. It has no way of making non-patients (those who receive the external benefits) pay. Hence the maximum revenue that could be extracted for the third and fourth thousand beds would be only the amount that the patients using them are prepared to pay (that is £8 million and £6 million respectively). Since in both cases this would be considerably less than the costs of providing the beds, no profits could be made by any firm providing them; hence they would not be provided.

Again, this can be illustrated by a diagram. In Figure 2.2 the marginal social benefit (*msb*) and the marginal private benefit (*mpb*) curves are plotted along with the marginal social cost (*msc*) curve. The point of intersection of the *msb* and *msc* curves shows the socially efficient quantity of hospitals; the point of intersection of the *mpb* curve (which, for the reasons explained above, is the same as the market demand curve) with the *msc* curve shows the quantity that

**FIGURE 2.2**
**Social and Private Costs and Benefits of Hospital Beds**

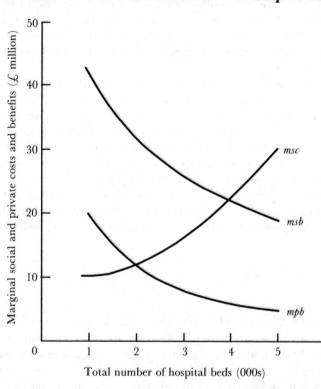

will be provided under a market system. Thus, when there are external benefits, the market demand curve and the marginal social benefit curve are no longer identical. The result is that the quantity provided under a market system will not necessarily be at a socially efficient level. So the existence of externalities can prevent the market from operating efficiently. The degree of inefficiency will depend on the size of the externality (that is, on the divergence between the *msb* curve and the *mpb*, or market demand, curve in Figure 2.2).

Now it has been argued that in fact the external benefits from the type of health care provided in developed countries are relatively small. Hence the degree of inefficiency from this source will also be small. The basis for this argument is first, that communicable diseases are now fairly rare and second, their treatment is the only form of health care that confers external benefits. Both claims have been challenged. Some communicable diseases are still prevalent (such as venereal diseases and now AIDS). Furthermore, communicable diseases may not be the only form of health care to create external benefits.

Many people feel concern when others fall ill, even if they themselves are not directly threatened. They feel that the sick should always receive the medical care they need. Thus the consumption of health care by the sick affects the utility or the well-being of the not-sick. If this is the case, then treating the sick results in positive externalities. The existence of these *caring externalities* has been used to be justify subsidisation of health care. In practice, it is very difficult to establish either the extent of these externalities or to put a value upon them. It is therefore difficult to know how much intervention is justified on the grounds of externalities.

## *Equity*

Will a market allocation of health care be fair or equitable? It seems unlikely. Earlier we saw there were three equity concepts commonly used in the health care context: a minimum standard of treatment for all in need, equal treatment for equal need and equality of access or cost. In a private market poor people may not be able to purchase the treatment they need or to afford health insurance. There is no market mechanism to ensure that everyone will be able to obtain at least a minimum. Nor is there a mechanism to bring about equal treatment for equal need. Those with higher incomes are likely to purchase better treatment; those who are healthier will face lower insurance premiums and so will buy more insurance and be entitled to more treatment if they fall ill. Finally, while the forces of competition might ensure that most people faced the same financial cost or price for each unit of health care, that price would represent a greater sacrifice for the poor than for the better off (because it would represent a larger proportion of their income). Therefore it could be argued that inequality of cost or sacrifice, and therefore inequality of access, would persist under market allocation.

# *The Role of Giving*

A further argument that has been put forward against the use of a market system in health care is that the introduction of commercial considerations would destroy the relationship between patient and doctor – or more generally – the relationship between the supplier of the service and its recipient. Titmuss (1970), the principal exponent of this view, claimed that to give (and to receive) a service where no financial remuneration is directly involved is a more satisfying form of human relationship than one involving direct payment for services rendered, and because of this is ethically superior.

The basis for the argument is this. To introduce a system linking payment to the quantity and quality of treatment provided is to relate treatment to the supplier's self-interest. This, it is argued, would make the system more efficient. But the Titmuss view states that even if there is an increase in efficiency, the social welfare might none the less be reduced by the use of the price mechanism. This is because its use diminishes the role of altruism and increases the role of self-interest. In a society such as our own where, ostensibly at least, altruism is valued more highly than self-interest, to decrease the opportunities for the exercise of the former while increasing those for the latter might be a retrograde step.

There is also an argument that in some cases giving may be more efficient. If the good is given for free, suppliers have no incentive not to reveal the truth about the quality of the good they are giving. Thus, in the case of blood, donors will have no incentive to hide infections such as hepatitis or HIV. If they were paid for this blood, they would have an incentive not to reveal such information and the quality of the product given would fall (as indeed it has done in the US market for blood).

# Government Policies

In the previous section we saw that there are a number of reasons why a market system may fail to achieve an efficient and equitable allocation of health care resources. Faced with these limitations it should come as no surprise to learn that in just about every country governments intervene in the health care market. But the form of this intervention varies a good deal. In Chapter 1 we classified government policies into three main categories: regulation, direct provision and taxes/subsidies. Examples of all three types of intervention can be found in health care.

# *Regulation*

Most regulatory policy is designed to ensure that the quality of health care meets acceptable standards. Doctors have to complete a lengthy period of education and obtain recognised qualifications before they can practice medicine; nurses have to follow specified courses of training and receive registration; post-registration courses are required for specialised nursing such as midwifery; drugs have to satisfy safety standards before they can be marketed, and so on.

Often the government lacks the specialised information necessary to carry out these functions effectively and so the responsibility for regulation is delegated to professional bodies within the health service itself – so called *self-regulation*. Thus, for example, in the UK the British Medical Association, the Royal College of Surgeons, the Royal College of General Practitioners and the Royal College of Nursing engage in different forms of regulation for their members.

In some countries regulation of quality goes beyond the general specification of education and training standards. The United States, Canada and Australia, for example, all have hospital accreditation boards. These boards monitor standards on a regular basis and if a hospital fails to meet the criteria laid down, it will have recognition withdrawn and may fail to qualify for government funding. Again, in the United States, state and federal government regulations control the level of private hospital investment that can be undertaken in an area through the administration of Certificates of Need. These mechanisms are clearly more necessary in a system where the bulk of providers are employed privately and therefore less able to be controlled directly by the government.

The lack of direct government control over doctors' and hospitals' fees has also led to the emergence of price regulation in countries where patients are charged fees. In the US, for example, the federally funded medical programme – which meets many of the costs of health care incurred by people over 65 years of age – specifies, in advance, the price it will pay per hospital in-patient case according to the diagnostic group to which the patient is assigned.

# *Provision*

In the UK (and in several other European countries) most health care is provided by the state. In the UK the government owns most of the country's hospitals through the National Health Service (NHS). Within these hospitals services are provided by salaried doctors and nurses employed by the Department of Health. Similarly, community health services are provided by NHS midwives, district nurses and health visitors all of whom are public sector employees. Primary care is delivered by general practitioners who are formally self-employed but, in practice, work under close NHS contracts and have the costs of most of their activities met by the public sector. In addition to these services, the government assumes responsibility for public health and health promotion activities, such as campaigns about AIDS, drug abuse and heart disease.

# *Taxes and Subsidies*

In most advanced industrial countries governments play a major role in the funding of health care. In 1987 in OECD countries government expenditure, on average, accounted for just over three quarters of all health care expenditure. Even in the USA public spending accounted for over forty per cent of health care spending.

In Britain, the NHS combines direct public provision with extensive subsidisation of the costs of medical care. Hospitals and general practitioners are funded by the government and services are, for the most part, offered free at the point of use. So because they do not incur user-charges, patients are subsidised. For some services – opticians, dentistry and drug prescriptions – the level of subsidisation has been progressively reduced over the last ten years, but nonetheless, over eighty five per cent of total health care spending is still financed from taxation.

In other health care systems, subsidies may be targeted at specific groups – such as elderly people, unemployed persons and others on low incomes – to decrease the price of health care supplied by private, fee-charging suppliers to these individuals. Some countries also subsidise the purchase of private health insurance by making premiums tax deductible (this operates in a similar way as tax relief on mortgage payments in the UK). Such a measure was adopted in the UK in 1990 for private health insurance for persons over 60 years of age.

# Government Policies and Objectives: an Assessment

Each of these forms of government intervention can be viewed as a response to the problems associated with allocation by the market. Thus regulation is an attempt to deal with the problem of monopoly, subsidisation with externalities and equity concerns, direct provision with the power of providers. But although market failures exist, government intervention does not necessarily improve the situation. The system of incentives created by intervention may also lead to inefficiencies and inequities. To examine these government failures we look at the effects of intervention in the UK health care market.

# *Regulation*

Consumers do not have the level of medical information necessary to judge the professional competence of doctors or hospital services and acquiring such information would be extremely costly. As a result the government acts as the custodian of the consumers' interests and assumes the responsibility for ensuring that standards meet an acceptable level. In this market regulation is often delegated by the government to regulatory bodies established by the providers – *self-regulation*. This is in part inevitable as providers are better qualified to assess other providers' performance. However, it may mean that regulatory agencies operate more to serve the interests of those they are supposed to be regulating than to protect those of the consumer. For instance, it is argued that the medical professions' power over length of training has been used more to restrict the supply of doctors (and hence raise their incomes) than to protect the public against poor quality treatment. Regulation may also set up incentives which reduce efficiency. If prices are regulated to limit monopoly power, prices in health care markets will not act as efficient signals to purchasers and providers. If when regulating for quality, volume of work performed is used as a proxy for quality, the effect of regulation may be to reduce the number of hospitals in which certain operations can be performed. This may reinforce tendencies to *spatial monopoly*, which arises when there is only one hospital in a large geographical area.

## Provision

The imbalance in information between demanders and suppliers may result in higher prices for medical care, overprovision and an emphasis on 'high-tech' medicine. Direct provision may counteract these tendencies. If the government provides health care for a large enough proportion of the population, it becomes the dominant or sole buyer of doctors' services and other inputs. It becomes a *monopsonist*. It can then use this power to counteract the monopoly power of suppliers, both to reduce the price charged and, in some cases, to alter the nature and the geographical distribution of the health care produced. In the UK, direct provision, through the operation of cash ceilings, appears to have limited the spread of high cost, high technology medicine. Use of the RAWP formula – designed to reduce inequalities across regions – to distribute resources appears to have reduced geographical inequalities. However, direct provision may introduce other inefficiencies.

When the government provides a good, competition is often either prohibited or limited by the size of the public sector. Thus in the UK, although a small private health care sector exists, it is dwarfed in any size based comparison with the NHS. This means the state provider is a *monopoly*. It is argued that the lack of competition from other suppliers allows inefficiency to develop in production; because no competing suppliers exist services will not be produced at their lowest cost. It could be argued that the extent of production inefficiency may be reduced by limiting the funds available to the producer, for example, by imposing cash limits as in the NHS during the 1980s. However, as the state monopolist has no incentives to monitor costs (since it has no competitors) it may be difficult to identify those services which are inefficient. The imposition of cash limits will not necessarily guarantee that efficient services remain and the inefficient ones are squeezed out. The pattern of services that develops will probably depend more on the power of individual doctors and bureaucrats than on relative costs and benefits.

# Subsidies

As subsidies may have considerable distortionary effects, we look first at their impact on efficiency.

## Subsidies and efficiency

Subsidisation may be one method of dealing with externalities. As noted above, where there are external benefits from health care the amount of health care consumed in a private market will be less than the socially efficient level. Reducing the price for a service by a subsidy will increase the demand for the service. For instance, suppose a charge is made for treatment for a contagious disease. If an individual has the disease and weighs up the costs and benefits of being treated and decides not to be treated, other people are put at an increased risk of getting the disease. Hence they are made worse off. However, if the price of treatment is reduced, the individual may find that the benefits now outweigh the costs; they will take treatment and other people will be better off. Subsidisation may therefore move society closer to the efficient level of health-care provision.

Subsidisation reduces the price of a good or service to the buyer or user and this may be an efficient way of dealing with the problem of externalities. However, if the price is reduced too far, subsidisation may result in either *overconsumption* or to *excess demand*. We illustrate this by means of Figure 2.3. In this diagram the marginal social cost of producing the health care is given by the line marked *msc* (as the line is flat it is assumed the good is produced at constant marginal social cost). The subsidised price, marked by the line *mpc*, is below this cost. The subsidy per unit sold is the distance between the *msc* and *mpc* curves. The marginal social benefit (that is, internal plus external benefits) is as given by the line marked *msb*. It is assumed, as above, that the marginal benefit of each new unit consumed is lower than that of the previous one. If the consumer acts to maximise total benefit, she will consume where private marginal cost equals private marginal benefit. This is at $Q'$ units in Figure 2.3. However, because of the subsidy, the true cost per unit produced is higher than the perceived private cost. The socially efficient level of consumption is at $Q^*$. Thus there will be over-consumption of the good.

The larger the subsidy for any given *msb* schedule, the higher the over-consumption. In the case of a good provided free – for example, health care in the NHS – the consumer will try to expand her consumption to the point where the benefit from the last unit of the service consumed is zero (as at this point $mpb = mpc = 0$). In this case the price mechanism no longer serves as a *rationing* device. Unless the government expands supply up to this point (which would be both inefficient and in the case of health care probably extremely costly), there is a situation of *excess demand*. More health care is demanded than can be supplied.

In this case, the government must use some other rationing device to determine who gets what. In the NHS two forms of rationing

**FIGURE 2.3**
**The Effect of Subsidisation on the Quantity of Care Demanded**

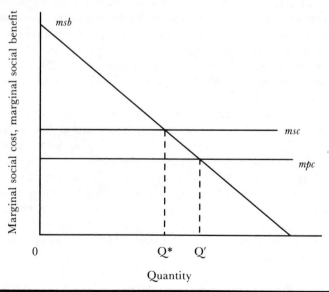

device are used. The first is the queue (the wait to see a doctor in a surgery or in the outpatient department of a hospital), the second is the waiting list.

Being in a queue takes up time for the demander of care. Waiting in a queue is least costly to those who have lots of free time and most costly to those with little free time. Unless the amount of free time demanders have is in inverse proportion to their willingness to pay, there is no guarantee that those who get the health care first are those who are willing to pay most. Thus the good is not received by those who value it most highly, so the allocation is not efficient. There are people who would be willing to pay more but cannot get the good. The outcome may also not be desirable on equitable grounds. People who are in manual jobs or low paid jobs frequently cannot take time off work to attend the doctor. They may also receive sick pay for less time than people in higher paid jobs. Thus these people who face the highest cost are amongst the poorer segments of the population.

Individuals are referred to a waiting list by their doctor. The problem with delegating the decisions about who gets what to health care professionals is that in making those decisions, the latter may pursue their own interests as well as those of the patient. It is argued, for example, that doctors may treat 'interesting' cases more rapidly than less interesting ones. In this case, people requiring 'uninteresting' treatment are more likely to be on the list than those whose cases are 'interesting'. It is not necessarily these people who want or need treatment most. Another problem is that those people with the right contacts or who know how to 'play the system' may be able to get to the head of the queue first. Again, such allocation is unlikely to be either efficient or just.

In the UK the government both subsidises and produces health care. As health care services are not sold, the incomes of producers do not depend on meeting consumers' wishes. The outcome that emerges, and its efficiency, depends on the way in which producers are reimbursed. This is illustrated by the system of payment to general practitioners (GPs) used in the NHS. Under this system GPs are basically paid according to the number of people registered with them, rather than according to the amount of treatment they give. Hence they have an incentive to maximise the numbers of people on their register, but to minimise the amount of time spent with each person. In other words, they have an incentive to 'under-doctor'. In contrast, if doctors were paid according to the amount of treatment they provided and patients paid nothing at point of demand, they would have an incentive to 'over-doctor'. Both systems of reimbursement are thus likely to be inefficient, but, under the first system, there will be underconsumption, and, in the second, overconsumption, of health care.

A further difficulty arises when the government forsakes the use of prices as an allocation mechanism. It becomes extremely difficult for it to assess the overall efficient level of provision, for it has few signals to guide it. It has to rely either on the outcome of the political process or on allocative decisions of professionals and bureaucrats. In the UK the amount spent on the NHS is determined as part of the public expenditure planning process. This is a highly political as well as economic exercise in which the spending patterns of each department are determined for the following year. Ultimately, government policy should reflect the wishes of Parliament and hence the electorate. In a perfect world, voters' preferences on health spending would be translated into expenditure allocations. In practice, though, such a close link between individuals' preferences and spending as a single programme is impossible to achieve. Governments have to balance a range of policy options. In particular, there is the desire – usually showed by the majority of the electorate – to reduce taxation, as well as to provide health and other services.

This introduces a clear tension: a tension that has been resolved in the UK in recent years by keeping a tight rein on public expenditure. As a result there is evidence that spending on the NHS has been too low. This judgement is suggested both by the increasing demands being placed on the system by growing numbers of elderly people and the costs of new medical technology and new demands, and by the low proportion of the national product devoted to health care in the UK compared with other countries at similar levels of GNP. In short, government funding seems to have failed to produce the level of health care provision that most commentators consider to be desirable. Of course, in the absence of precise knowledge of the benefits of the UK level of provision, it is impossible to say with certainty that total expenditure is below the efficient level.

## Subsidies and equity

Subsidies may be used to lower prices of medical care or increase the rewards from provision of care to achieve equity goals. To improve access by the poor, they may be used to lower the price of care. To promote geographical equity, governments may pay for the medical education of, or pay higher wages to, doctors to work in areas which have too few doctors – for example, remote or rural areas.

Whether such subsidies are an effective way of promoting equity will depend on the type of subsidy and on the definition of equity. Some subsidy schemes, such as Medicaid in the United States, involve a means test; that is, they are confined to people with income ('means') below a certain level. Others, such as the NHS, are universal; that is, all those who need treatment receive it free or at a heavily subsidised price. Both universal and means-tested subsidies can be justified on the grounds that they promote equity defined in terms of minimum standards, for they both reduce the price of medical care to the poor and therefore encourage their consumption. However, it is often argued that universal subsidies will be the more successful of the two in this respect. For means tests are often regarded by those eligible as stigmatising and socially humiliating; moreover, the procedures involved in decisions over eligibility are often complex and time-consuming. Hence the take-up of the service will not be as large as it would be if there were no means test.

On the other hand, means tests are possibly superior to universal subsidies in meeting the other interpretations of equity – equal treatment for equal need and equality of access or cost. For means tests imply a lower financial cost of health care to the poor; they therefore make the actual sacrifice involved more in line with than incurred by the rich (thus creating greater equality of access) and perhaps also thereby increase the poor's use of the service relative to that of the rich (thus promoting greater equality of treatment).

## *Quasi-Markets*

We have seen that both market provision and government intervention may have efficiency and equity failures. Recognition of this has led to a search for solutions which draw on the benefits of both market and government allocation mechanisms of health care. The aim of reform has been to introduce *incentive* structures that will counteract some of the failures of either market provision or government intervention.

The idea of the reforms introduced in 1989 for the British NHS is to create an *internal* or *quasi-market*. Under these reforms, the provider and purchaser functions of the hospital service are to be separated and a market will be created on the supply side. Providers, both public and private, are to compete for the budgets of publicly financed purchasers, known as budget holders.

The reforms proposed the creation of two types of budget holders. The first type are general practitioners (GPs) working in practices of over 9000 patients. Under the system in operation prior to the reforms, GPs provided primary care, but referred patients for secondary care to the hospital sector. The costs of such care were met by the district health authority. Under the reforms budget holding GPs are to get cash limited budgets for certain types of secondary care for their patients. These services are to be purchased from competing public and private providers. The second type of budget holder are District Health Authorities. These purchasers will hold the majority of funds now available in the hospital sector and can buy care from the most efficient provider, be they public or private, within or outside the district where the patients live. Budget holders are to seek out providers, compare prices and quality and place contracts with the most efficient providers. Thus competition will be introduced on the supply side of the market. The intention is to reap the efficiency gains of the introduction of competition – lower costs and greater responsiveness to patients – without sacrificing the equity goals met through tax provided finance.

It is too early to assess the outcome of these reforms. However, there are a number of potential problems. First, for a competitive market to operate in the short term there needs to be excess capacity in provision or providers must be able to expand capacity quickly. Whether providers can respond quickly is an open question. Certainly, reduction in capacity may be difficult – electoral pressures may make closure of hospitals difficult and the information advantage of physicians may make it difficult to reduce excess staffing levels or change production technology rapidly. Second, the absence of data on the quality of outcomes may make the system cost driven. The availability of quantifiable financial criteria may lead to the neglect of quality. Thus rather than achieve efficiency in production, where maximum benefit is derived for a given level of expenditure, the system will tend towards cost minimisation. Finally, by ignoring the level of finance provided to the health care sector, the reforms have not tackled the issue of whether the overall UK budget for health care is too small.

Attempts to alter the incentives facing providers of care have taken place during the 1980s in other health care systems. For instance, in the USA, the level of state subsidy for the aged and the poor has steadily risen through the 1970s and 1980s. Private expenditure has also risen rapidly. To limit this growth in expenditure, new (to the US) methods of delivery of care have been introduced. Prior to the 1980s, most health care was provided on a *fee-for-service* basis, in which suppliers were reimbursed for each item of care supplied. Generally, finance for this care was provided by insurers who were not the suppliers of health care, known as *third party insurers*. During the 1980s different forms of insurance and of supply have emerged. One example is the *Health Maintenance Organisation* (the HMO) in which a group of doctors provide care for their patients at a fixed price, paid in advance by an employer or by the patient. Essentially, the insurer and provider roles are merged, so reducing the moral hazard problem. This form of organisation is not dissimilar to that for GPs in the UK, except that in the UK the government, rather than the patient or private insurer, pays the annual fee.

There are several other examples of convergence in health care systems within developed countries. Lack of space precludes a discussion of these reforms here, but the interested reader may consult the Further Reading at the end of the chapter. Similar developments are also occurring in other areas of social policy and some of these are discussed in other chapters of this book.

# Summary

There are two principal objectives with respect to health care: *efficiency* and *equity*. An efficient level of health care is one where the *marginal social cost* of further care equals the *marginal social benefit*. Equity can be defined in a number of ways in the context of health care: the most common definitions are a *minimum standard* of treatment, *equal treatment for equal need* and *equality of access* or cost. Health care has certain characteristics which in general mean that it will not be allocated efficiently by a market system. These include *uncertainty of demand*, *imperfect consumer information* leading to *monopoly*, and *externalities*. Nor is the market likely to achieve equity under any of its interpretations.

The state may intervene through *provision*, *regulation* and *taxes/subsidies*. Under the National Health Service all three are used. Each can be seen as a response to the various failures of the market. Thus state provision is a means of dealing with the problem of monopoly; regulation, with the problem of imperfect consumer information; subsidies, with uncertainty of demand and externalities. However, each has problems of its own. Thus provision can create inefficiency due the absence of competition; regulation often services the interests of the regulated; and unrestricted subsidies can lead to over-use and an inequitable distribution of public expenditure.

In response to these failures, recent changes adopted in several health care systems seek to change the incentives facing suppliers of care. In the UK, an *internal* or *'quasi'*-market in health care was introduced in 1990.

# Further Reading

The classic article, for those with some economics background, on health care and insurance failure is Arrow (1963). Textbooks surveying health economics and containing discussions of the economics of the UK health care system are Cullis and West (1979), McGuire *et al.* (1988) and Barr (1987). The UK system pre-1990 reforms is described in any of these. Cullis and West (1979, Chapters 6 and 7) discuss production and cost functions; McGuire *et al.* (1988, Chapters 2 and 3) discuss health and health care as an economic commodity. A discussion of the role of equity in health care is provided in McGuire *et al.* (1988), Le Grand (1982, 1991). The use of cost-benefit analysis in health care is examined in Williams (1974) and a specific case examined in Williams (1985). Discussion of outcome measures is contained in Williams (1987).

An early review of international differences and similarities provided in McLaughlan and Maynard (1982); a later one in OECD (1990). A detailed description and analysis of developments in health care policies during the last two decades in the UK can be found in Le Grand, Winter and Woolley (1990). An account of recent developments in the medical care market in the USA is given in Stiglitz (1988). Critiques of the NHS can be found in Seldon

**64**  *The Economics of Social Problems*

(1981); the case for reform and a discussion of internal markets in Enthoven (1985). An outline of the 1990 quasi-market reforms and a preliminary evaluation of their impact is given in Culyer, Maynard and Posnett (1990); see also Le Grand (1990). Evidence on equity in the NHS is provided in Le Grand (1982) and in O'Donnell and Propper (1991).

# Questions for Discussion

1.  How would you define health?
2.  Should a doctor's aim be 'optimisation of survival' or 'cost-effective medicine'?
3.  What is an equitable distribution of health care?
4.  'To place a money value on human life is both immoral and impossible'. Discuss.
5.  Discuss the various ways in which the benefits from health care can be measured.
6.  'In the market medical care will tend to be under-supplied relative to the efficient level'. 'Profit-maximising doctors have an incentive to over-supply treatment'. Reconcile.
7.  Are there any reasons on the ground of efficiency for replacing the National Health Service by a system of private health insurance?
8.  'Food is as essential to health as visits to the doctor, yet under the NHS the latter is provided free while the former is not'. Is this an argument against the National Health Service, for a National Food Service or neither?
9.  Should blood donors be paid? Should users of donated blood be charged?
10. Why may reducing the price of care to zero not achieve equal access costs for all?

# Education 3

A hundred years ago the leading English economist, Alfred Marshall, wrote:

> **There are few practical problems in which the economist has a more direct interest than those relating to the principles on which the expense of education of children should be divided between the State and the parents. (Marshall, 1890, p.180).**

Of course, since Marshall's time the education system has expanded beyond recognition. Moreover, government finance and provision dominate. Today there are nearly ten million children and students in a public system which extends from nursery education for the under-fives, through primary and secondary schooling, to colleges of further education, polytechnics and universities. By 1990 total public expenditure on education and science amounted to £25 thousand million or, put another way, to approximately five per cent of the Gross Domestic Product.

But the massive expansion of the education system has not meant that questions concerning the appropriate sources of finance have gone away. Quite the reverse. For example, in presenting its proposals for the reform of student finance and the introduction of top-up loans, the government recently announced that one of its objectives was:

> **'to share the cost of student maintenence more equitably between students themselves, their parents and the taxpayer' (Department of Education and Science, 1988).**

Clearly, Marshall's remarks still have topical relevance.

In this chapter we shall investigate alternative ways of financing and providing education. In order to do this, we shall start by defining the objectives of the education system. These are often expressed in a variety of ways. For example, education may be viewed as a means of training the future workforce. For many people, however, it is also concerned with the provision of more general social skills. For others, it is a major means of equalising opportunities in subsequent adult life. Having considered these various objectives, we shall go on to consider how far a market system can be expected to realise them. As few societies have left education exclusively to the market, it should come as no surprise to anyone to learn that we conclude that there are strong reasons for some form of government intervention. But what form should this take? Is the dominance of government provision and finance satisfactory? We deal with this issue in the final part of the chapter where we examine some of the major changes introduced through the 1988 Education Reform Act and other proposals for radical reform.

# Objectives

Just as in the case of health care, we can discuss the objectives of the education system in terms of two main categories – namely, those concerned with efficiency and those concerned with equity.

## *Efficiency*

Stated in general terms, the efficiency objective is to try to specify the amount of education (that is, the size of the education system) that will maximise aggregate net social benefit. To translate this into a working definition we need to be able to identify both the costs and the benefits of providing education. Now while the costs are relatively easy to specify – being the costs of teachers' salaries, books and materials, school and college buildings and so on – the benefits are less tangible. Basically, however, it is possible to distinguish two categories of education benefit that any system will be expected to produce. We may term these production benefits and social benefits.

Production benefits accrue because one of the main functions of any education system is training the future workforce. Through education individuals acquire knowledge and develop skills that will increase their productivity when they enter employment. Thus expenditure on education is an investment that yields benefits in the form of additional production in the future. Of course, the link between education and production benefits is more pronounced in some forms of education than in others. Clearly it is stronger on skill-based, further education courses than in general primary education; or on an engineering or accountancy degree course compared with those in English literature or art history. But practically all forms of education will lead to the acquisition of some skills that will prove useful in the workplace. For example, consider the benefits which derive from basic literacy and numeracy learned as part of general primary school education. When basic communication through reading and writing becomes possible, there is scope for the use of more efficient techniques in a whole range of economic activities. Similarly, basic numeracy makes access to an increasing range of computer-based production techniques possible. Furthermore, an increase in the number of people with the elementary qualifications which are a necessary prerequisite for more advanced training will lead eventually to a larger number of highly trained workers. Economists refer to this as the 'option value' of elementary education; that is, it provides the option of further education or training.

In most cases it is not possible to identify the social benefits of an education system with the same degree of precision as the production benefits. They tend to assume far more diffuse and less tangible forms. But this should not be allowed to diminish the importance attached to them. For example, most forms of education perform an important socialisation function; that is, they seek to provide pupils or students with a set of values and range of skills that will enable them to function effectively in the wider society outside the school or college. These may be expected to extend from consideration of major ethical and moral questions to more routine advice on out-of-school leisure activities, job application procedures and so on. Of course the precise form of socialisation can be expected to vary between different parts of the education system. Thus while certain values are likely to be shared by all institutions within a given society (for example, a belief in the superiority of reasoned argument over emotional prejudice), others will vary between institutions, depending upon the social context in which they expect their students to find themselves. For some, the attributes of punctuality, reliability and discipline will be important whereas others may be encouraged to question and criticise rather than conform.

In addition to this socialisation function, many people would argue that the transmission of knowledge through education is a good thing in itself, irrespective of whether or not it serves any ulterior objective. Thus an appreciation of literature, the arts, the discoveries of science and technology and so on are seen as desirable ends in themselves.

## Equity

In Britain certain basic human rights guaranteeing equality of treatment have long been recognised. The right to vote and to receive justice before a common law are two examples. More recently it has been argued by many people that *equality of opportunity* in education should be a basic right. That is, there is a certain amount which, as a society, we believe everyone should receive. This view is based on the recognition that education is not just another consumer service but a process that has a fundamental effect on the recipients' – and their children's – lives. For many people it is not only a major determinant of their lifetime incomes (and hence their access to market goods and services), but also the quality of their lives. Tastes cultivated through education enable individuals to enrich their lives in numerous ways.

Given the importance attached to education for these reasons, it is hardly surprising that society should require that it is distributed equitably. But what is an equitable distribution? Just as in the case of health care, it is not usually taken to mean that everyone should receive exactly the same amount of education, because their needs and capabilities may vary. Not everyone wants or is able to benefit from a three year university course. Rather it is usually taken to mean that there should be universal *equality of access*. That is, no student who is willing and able to benefit from a particular course should face a higher cost of doing so because of irrelevant or discriminatory criteria, such as income, race, sex or religion. However, sometimes it is felt that although this objective is desirable it is not possible to achieve with the limited resources that are available for education. Accordingly, the less stringent definition of equity presented in Chapter 1 is often adopted; this states that everyone should have a certain minimum quantity of education. Some students may obtain more education than others but no one should be denied the minimum amount considered socially necessary.

# The Market System and Education

The general advantages claimed for a market system were discussed in Chapter 1. In the case of education, supporters of the market claim that the quantity provided, its form, and (with some reservations) the people who receive it will be determined best by a free market. Two main reasons are usually cited in support of this claim. First, the need for consumer freedom of choice is emphasised. In a market system consumers are able to express their preferences when they make decisions about the type and quantity of education they purchase, and through the expression of these choices the socially efficient quantity of each type of education will be indicated. The second and related point ensures that the required education is, in fact, made available. Educational institutions will be in competition for students (as this will be the source of their income) and will need to respond by offering those types of education that are in demand. Moreover, as students will be deterred by unnecessarily high fees, providers will need to ensure that they employ cost-effective methods in running their schools and colleges. In this way, supporters of a market system argue an efficient system responsive to consumer needs will be established.

But can we be confident that the market will operate in this way? Critics of this view argue that there are specific failings that will prevent the market in education from operating efficiently. These are capital market imperfections, imperfect information, externalities and monopoly in the supply of education. Moreover critics also question the ability of a market-based system to achieve an equitable distribution of education. Let us look at each of these points and try to assess their validity.

## Capital Market Imperfections

We have already seen that most education embodies a vocational element and can be expected to increase students' future productivity. Thus they (or their families) know that through education they can acquire knowledge and learn skills that will widen their future employment choices and, in most societies, increase their future earnings. Therefore when considering whether to undertake further or higher education beyond the age of 16, individuals are effectively faced with an investment decision; should they incur costs in the present in the expectation of receiving additional income in the future?

We may illustrate the situation confronting a typical person in the following fashion. Consider a student who has obtained the necessary entrance qualifications for a three-year degree course in economics and wants to decide whether to accept the offer of a university place or whether to enter a firm directly on a school-leavers' trainee management scheme. Confronted with this choice, the student will want to know the relative costs and benefits of each option.

As far as the costs are concerned, she will want to consider the additional costs that would be incurred through following the university course. These are likely to include the costs of study materials, such as books, possible additional costs incurred through living away from home (if the student would remain at home otherwise), and tuition fees if these are not paid for by the government. But the major item of cost will be the salary forgone through undertaking education instead of going directly to work. (Note this is an opportunity cost of the type discussed in Chapter 1). For most students, however, these costs will be reduced by the amount of any maintenance grant they receive while at university. After considering the costs, the student will want to know about the likely benefits of a three-year degree course. These will generally accrue in the form of higher expected earnings over her working lifetime.

A plausible time profile of the flow of costs and benefits is shown in Figure 3.1. In the figure the potential graduate's annual costs and benefits are compared with those she would expect as a non-graduate. The shaded areas $A + B$ represent the costs to the student of a three-year degree course. Area $A$ is the additional cost of attending university compared with working as a management

**FIGURE 3.1**
**Investment in Education**

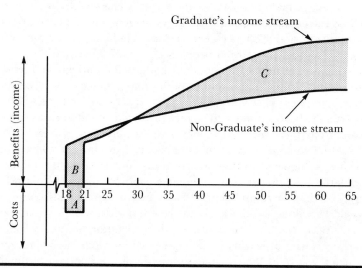

trainee. This will cover the costs of books, additional living expenses, fees, and so on. Area B is the opportunity cost of forgone income; that is, the non-graduate's net income minus the student's grant between the ages of 18 and 21 years, and thereafter, the lower income received initially by the graduate compared with the non-graduate who is already established in the workforce. Area C represents the benefit of a degree course. It indicates that from her late 20s until retirement the graduate can expect a higher annual income than her non-graduate counterpart. By comparing the amount represented by Area C with A + B the student can estimate the likely rate of return on an investment of A + B in education. This is referred to by economists as an investment in 'human capital'.

Now this discussion is not meant to imply that every student consciously makes these calculations before choosing an education course. Rather it is intended to demonstrate the economic implications of education choices, some of which are almost certainly taken into account by prospective students. In fact, the government, when putting forward its proposals for the introduction of top-up loans for students, published figures which, it claimed, showed the rates of return obtainable by graduates. Between 1981 and 1985, when comparing a male graduate in the social sciences with an A' level school leaver, the government's figures suggested a rate of return of between 26 and 32.5 per cent. Taking graduates in all subjects together yielded a return of between 22 and 27.5 per cent.

What are the implications of these findings for a private market in education? Simply that if returns of this magnitude can be obtained from investment in education we would expect students to be willing and able to borrow money to finance their studies and to repay these loans from their subsequent increased earnings. In general there should be no need for government financial assistance to students in further or higher education as lenders would recognise the returns available from investment in human capital. However, this pre-supposes that the capital market (banks or other lending institutions) would be willing to offer loans on these terms. In practice financial institutions tend to be cautious about lending to low-income borrowers with little collateral. (Try persuading your bank manager to lend you £30 000 on the sole basis of your future earnings potential!) At the same time many students – especially those from low-income households – will be unused to entering into this type of credit arrangement and are likely to be reluctant to commit themselves to long-term debt. For these reasons we cannot be confident that the private market would finance the efficient amount of investment in education.

## Imperfect Information

It is a basic assumption in economics that consumers know their own interests better than anyone else. However, in most cases consumers of education are not mature adults. Consequently most people would be a little wary about ascribing to them all the usual attributes of sound judgement and rationality that consumers are usually assumed to possess. Generally, however, this problem is overcome because decisions regarding education are made by, or in close consultation with, parents. But in some cases the need for an adult to act on behalf of a child does present problems of its own, for adults may not always act in their childrens' best interests. This may be particularly important in the case of education, which has been described as a process that sometimes protects children from their families. Failure to act in their childrens' best interests may result from neglect on the parents' part, but it is more likely to arise because parents cannot always be expected to possess all the information necessary to make wise decisions.

Education is a complex process with many facets that are not readily apparent to those viewing it from the outside. The benefits of education – especially higher education – are not always clear to those parents who have not experienced it. Moreover, collecting information on courses, teachers, facilities, out-of-school activities and so forth – which are necessary in order to make wise choices – can be very time-consuming, even if we assume that all parents are able to assimilate and evaluate the information they collect. Against this view, it is sometimes argued that the complexity of choice is just a matter of degree and that choosing a personal computer or video cassette recorder is an equally complex task which is, nevertheless, left to the consumer's discretion. Further, it is pointed out that when educational institutions are competing for students there is an incentive for them to disseminate information more effectively. It is also argued that only by giving parents the responsibility for making choices can they be expected to have sufficient interest to develop the expertise necessary to make wise decisions.

How convincing is each of these arguments? Certainly computers are complex pieces of equipment of great variety about which the average buyer has only limited knowledge. But are the consequences of the decision as to which make or model to buy quite as important as those concerning education? If we accept that education goes a long way towards determining subsequent job opportunities and the quality of a person's life, we may well feel that the scope for individual mistakes of judgment should be minimised beyond those considered permissible in the case of purchasing a computer. But if this view is adopted, it is important to recognise that it involves an element of paternalism; a restriction is being placed on consumer choice on the grounds that consumers may not always act in their own best interests.

Because they dislike such restrictions upon freedom of choice, most economists prefer strategies that simply provide consumers with the information necessary to make wise choices. But this approach requires effective methods for the dissemination of information. Can we rely upon these being produced within a market system?

Advertising is obviously a means of making information available that is widely used in market systems. But discussions of advertising practices usually distinguish between informative and persuasive advertising. While most people might support the production of prospectuses in which information is provided on teaching staff, courses offered, out-of-school activities and so on, college advertisements which emphasised the quality of skiing facilities or the merits of the local beer might give some cause for concern.

There is also some debate about the desirability of increasing information on schools through the publication of examination results, which reveals another problem. According to critics of publication, examination results can be misleading because they rarely take account of the starting ability levels or social backgrounds of different school populations. They may also act as a mechanism for attracting more able, middle class children to apparently successful schools while consigning lower achievers to 'sink' schools. This may well jeopardise the overall equity aim of the education system.

Finally, we might accept the claim that individuals can be expected to collect information and act responsibly only if they are given the opportunity to do so, without necessarily accepting that the best way of encouraging responsibility is by making people paying consumers. There are other ways of encouraging parents to participate more fully and responsibly in their childrens' education. Parent-teacher associations are just one example of non-market systems of mutual involvement in the education process.

## *Externalities*

As we saw in the case of health care, wherever external costs or benefits exist, a private market cannot be relied upon to produce an efficient allocation of resources. This is because the existence of externalities will cause private and social costs and benefits to diverge. Neither producers nor consumers will normally take these externalities into account. However, from society's point of view, they will have an effect on the level of welfare enjoyed by each member and so they need to be considered. In the case of education there are a range of external benefits which do not accrue directly to the student, but are passed on to others in the community. We may divide these into two main categories: employment benefits and benefits to society in general.

Employment benefits arise because modern production techniques require high levels of co-operation between workers. People who have been educated, as well as increasing their own productivity, will be able to increase the productivity of their fellow workers through their contact with them. Educated workers may achieve this by the use of more efficient methods of supervision and management, thus permitting their less educated colleagues to use their own time more productively. Similarly, education may increase a person's flexibility and adaptability. Hence an educated person is likely to be more able to respond to changes that arise through rapid technological progress. Flexibility is likely to prevent breakdowns or 'bottlenecks' in the production process. Against this view, some economists argue, that although these benefits result from education, they are not externalities. According to this argument, these benefits will be reflected in the earnings of the people who have received the education. Thus the benefit will accrue to them as a private benefit and not to others. It is difficult to resolve this disagreement because measuring the different components of earnings presents substantial problems. Clearly, separating those which are attributable to the education of others from those attributable to the worker's own efforts, her own education, and other factors affecting her productivity is no easy matter. None the less, given the interdependence of modern production techniques it is difficult to believe that everyone is paid strictly in accordance with his or her own contribution to productivity and is not affected by others working for the same firm or organisation.

The second category of external benefits comprises those which accrue to society in general. These arise because certain aspects of education can only be realised fully if other people share them. Our scope for communication will be severely restricted if we can write but you cannot read! So if communication is in our mutual interests, we benefit from the literacy you acquire through education. On a more general level, we have already spoken of the socialisation function of education, and this obviously provides a benefit to society at large. By contributing towards a common standard of citizenship, education will tend to produce a degree of social cohesion that is in most people's interests. Of course, education does not always produce this effect. It also leads to the questioning of accepted practices, some-

times resulting in social unrest and even the unseating of governments. Those politicians who clamp down on universities in times of
trouble clearly believe they impose external costs rather than benefits.

Even more so than in the case of employment externalities, the
measurement of social externalities poses enormous problems. In
consequence, economists' attempts at quantification have tended to
concentrate on some of the more tangible items. Unfortunately, these
have not always been the most important ones. For instance, the
benefits of socialisation have been approximated in terms of 'crime-
avoidance costs' – that is, the police and other law-enforcement costs
that are avoided because people are more law-abiding. Again,
literacy benefits have been measured in terms of the cost savings
that arise through people being able to fill in their own income tax
returns. These obviously represent highly imperfect measures of
external benefits, and probably under-estimate the true scale of
their full range.

## Monopoly

In a market system competition between firms can be expected to
lead to each firm adopting the most efficient method of production.
To do otherwise would lead to higher than necessary costs and a
need to charge higher prices. This would lead to a reduction in
demand for its products. However, if a firm enjoys a monopoly
position it is protected from the competition of rival firms and is able
to charge higher prices without a substantial loss of trade. Now
monopolies can arise for a variety of reasons but they all introduce
the danger of prices being set higher than would obtain in a
competitive market.

Within the education system, monopolies can be expected to arise
because certain geographical areas are not sufficiently densely
populated to support more than one school. Thus without some
children making very long journeys to more distant schools, or
becoming boarders, one school may have an effective monopoly of
education in its area. Such a monopoly is known as a spatial
monopoly because it is space – or distance – that is protecting the
monopolist from its potential competitors. Wherever a spatial
monopoly exists there is reason to fear that a market system will
not produce an efficient allocation of resources.

# *Equity*

The principal objective concerning equity is that there should be equality of access to education. Now if education is sold on the market, access will depend, to a large extent, on income. In a world where there are unequal incomes, access to education will also tend to be unequal. Even if the less stringent definition of equity is adopted – namely, that everyone should receive a minimum quantity of education – it is virtually certain that a large number of families would not be able to afford the minimum of ten years of schooling that our society feels is necessary, if they are required to pay for it from their own resources. In higher education, even if the direct costs are borne by the government, opportunity costs in terms of forgone earnings, are likely to impact more heavily on students from low income backgrounds than on those whose parents are better off. In short, wherever access to education is determined largely by incomes that are distributed unequally, or where large numbers of families have insufficient incomes to afford the full expenses of education, we are likely to get a socially inequitable distribution.

In view of all the above factors, we may conclude that there is a case for government intervention in education on both equity and efficiency grounds. But this does not establish the form that this intervention should take. Debates on this subject have covered much ground. In the remainder of this chapter we shall consider the way in which the government has chosen to deal with the problem in Britain. This will involve looking at the traditional form of government intervention and the important changes that have been introduced in recent years. We shall also look at some proposals for further reforms that have attracted the attention of a number of economists.

# Government Policies

The traditional form of education in Britain, as it has developed over the last thirty years, has resulted in over ninety per cent of children attending state schools. In these schools, education is provided free to the user and financed from central government and local government funds. In further and higher education, the vast majority of students receive education free of charge in government-financed colleges and universities. In addition, most students also receive non-repayable maintenance grants from the government which contribute towards their living expenses while studying. Hence education policy relies heavily on both government provision and subsidy.

As we have seen, there are a number of efficiency reasons why the government has chosen to intervene in the education sector. In particular, its policies have been designed to ensure that there has not been under-provision of education. It has also, of course, attached considerable emphasis to the equity aim; namely, the establishment of equality of access. By controlling the provision of education, and making it available free of charge, the government has sought to ensure that no one is denied access because of income limitations.

In recent years, however, there has been an increasing body of criticism which has questioned whether existing methods of direct provision and subsidisation represent the most effective way to achieve these aims. In particular, claims have been directed at the alleged lack of responsiveness of the monopoly, government system to the demands of students, parents and, especially, employers. This dissatisfaction has resulted in a number of reforms designed to increase consumer choice and providers' responsiveness to users' preferences. All of these reforms involve the introduction of internal or 'quasi'-markets into education; they have a basic similarity to the quasi-market reforms in health care discussed in Chapter 2. The 1988 Education Reform Act introduced a system of open enrolment. Under this system, parents are permitted to enrol their children at any school of their choice. Schools, in their turn, receive funding based upon the numbers of pupils enrolled. These provisions are designed to increase the amount of choice facing parents and to encourage schools to respond to parent's preferences by making funding dependent on schools' success in attracting pupils. Competition between schools, in their quest to attract pupils, is also expected to increase their efficiency.

Increased efficiency is also a major aim of the opting-out provisions and devolved budgeting introduced as part of the same legislation. Opting out will allow schools to opt out of Local Authority finance and control and instead receive grants directly from central government. Similarly, greater freedom will be offered to all schools as a result of the transfer of budgetary responsibilities from Local Authorities to the schools' boards of governors. This will enable school head teachers – in consultation with their governors – to exercise greater control over the ways in which their budgets are spent.

The Department of Education has also introduced a new funding system for polytechnics and universities. They are now required to bid for funds for teaching purposes from their respective funding councils. In deciding between rival bids, the funding bodies are expected to pay attention to the costs per student at different institutions and thereby provide an incentive for the cost effective provision of education.

Amidst all of these changes, however, there is one major paradox. At the same time as it is offering greater autonomy to providers to respond to consumer preferences, the government has chosen to impose a major new instrument of regulation: namely, the national curriculum. This is designed to ensure that certain subjects form a predetermined part of the syllabus in all schools. It has been justified on the grounds of raising standards. Whether or not it achieves this aim, it clearly represents an example of increased state control in education policy.

Taken together, the above reforms represent a significant shift towards the incorporation of key elements of a market system in education. However, there are critics who argue that they do not go far enough. According to these people replacing the existing system of financing schools directly with one operated through an education voucher scheme would lead to even greater choice and efficiency.

## Subsidies: Education Vouchers

A voucher scheme is designed to combine the advantages of a market system with the guarantee of ensuring that everyone is able to obtain at least the minimum quantity of education considered socially necessary. It does this by allocating education vouchers to families with which they can 'buy' education services for their children at schools of their choosing. Each voucher would entitle a student to a given quantity of education services and would be presented to a school as payment for the services it provides. The schools – which could be state run or owned privately – would then redeem the vouchers from the government for cash.

Assistance rendered through an education voucher is usually preferred to a straight cash payment to the family because, in this way, it is possible to ensure that the expenditure is in fact made on education instead of being used on (from the government's point of view) less desirable purchases. Thus the scheme does involve some restriction of consumer choice. This may be justified on the grounds that the government has better information about the benefits of education than the individual parent. Alternatively, it may wish to encourage people to obtain more education than they would choose freely because of external benefits. Finally, it may be that government takes a paternalistic view and encourages individuals to obtain at least the minimum quantity of education because it feels that it is good for them whether they agree or not.

There are a number of variants of the basic voucher scheme. In a flat-rate scheme every family would receive a standard voucher for each child of school age equal in value to the average cost of a year's schooling. Alternatively, an income-related scheme would link the value of the voucher to the family's income, with higher valued vouchers being provided for lower income households. Another variant allows a family to supplement the standard voucher allocation and thereby purchase more education than the government-specified minimum if it so chooses. In this way a voucher scheme could combine the guarantee of at least a minimum amount of education for everyone with the freedom for some to obtain more.

Interestingly, a comparison between an education voucher scheme and open enrolment suggests that they share many of the same features. Both aim to guarantee at least a minimum level of schooling to everyone, both are designed to offer more choice, and both seek to encourage greater efficiency in schools – and responsiveness to parents' preferences – by making schools' income dependent on their ability to attract pupils. At the same time, both attract similar criticisms. In particular, some people have argued that both open enrolment and a voucher scheme will fail to achieve equity and efficiency in the education system because of limitations on choice arising from imperfect information among parents, and because of the monopoly power possessed by many schools in the face of pupils' unwillingness or inability to travel long distances to rival schools.

To examine these criticisms, consider the voucher supporter's claim that it will offer wider choice through a diverse education system with a variety of curricula and methods of teaching catering for differing needs, in contrast to the present system which offers a more or less standard education to everyone irrespective of their particular preferences. A report on an education voucher demonstration scheme which took place in Alum Rock, California, expressed this view as follows:

> **Vouchers will overcome rigidities in the education system brought about by the public (i.e. state) schools' virtual monopoly of elementary and secondary education . . . The quality of schooling will improve because vouchers will promote educational innovation and diversity, parental interest in education, and school responsiveness to parent and student needs. (Weiller et al., 1974).**

However, there is no convincing theoretical reason why shifting the balance of control from teachers and educationalists to parents should necessarily produce a more diverse and varied school system which offers more choice. A feasibility study of a voucher scheme carried out in the UK for Kent County Council expressed a counter view.

> **It is possible . . . that parents would generally opt for the 'safety', as they perceived it, of a traditional curriculum and this would result in many schools following similar paths, all competing for the 'middle ground' of educational style. The idea of innovation tends to produce concern among a large number of parents. (Kent County Council Education Department, 1978, p.4).**

It might be thought that some evidence on the subject of diversity and choice could be provided by comparisons between the existing state and private sectors of schooling. Unfortunately, however, this evidence is inconclusive. Within the state school system there is a good deal of diversity of schools and courses, whereas numerous small private schools offer a more uniform, often examination-dominated type of education. On the other hand, however, there have been examples of exciting innovatory forms of education pioneered in the private sector while similar schemes have been strangled by temerity and bureaucracy in the public sector. At present both sides of the argument can find sufficient evidence favourable to their cases to continue to believe in their own veracity.

On the subject of choice and the ability of the school system to respond to parents' preferences, it is also important to point out that the responsiveness claimed for a voucher scheme, or for open enrolment, may well have been exaggerated. Schools with substantial investments in buildings and fixed plant would find it costly to expand or contract in response to short-run changes in parents' tastes. To illustrate the scale of the problem, the Kent study estimated that following the introduction of a voucher scheme between 20 and 46 per cent of the population of some secondary schools would move. They concluded that 'if most of the moves were to schools already most popular, this could produce an unmanageable situation'.

In an attempt to cope with short-run excess demand, some advocates of the voucher scheme suggest using the price mechanism – that is, schools for which there is excess demand could raise their fees. This, however, introduces the spectre of qualitative differences in the education received by different income groups on the basis of ability to pay. Indeed, one of the main fears of those opposed to a voucher system is that it would lead to a hierarchy of schools, based on fees, which would leave those who could not afford to supplement their vouchers receiving an inferior education at schools with poor facilities and less able teachers. According to this view, guaranteeing a minimum standard of education would not yield the social benefits or establish the genuine equality of access that society has set as its goals. Once again the Californian Report gives voice to these fears:

**Vouchers could foster segregation by race and class...and destroy the shared democratic values fostered by the traditional system of [state] schools.**

In reply to this charge supporters of a voucher scheme sometimes point out that the present system of state provision in Britain is already hierarchical and far from equitably distributed. There are gross inequalities in the amount and quality of education received by children from different socio-economic groups. Despite the widespread introduction of comprehensive schooling in recent years, children at schools located in middle- and higher-income catchment areas tend to be educated in better schools and stay at school longer (and hence receive more education) than the children from lower-income homes. Given this inequality, the relevant question becomes:

would the introduction of a voucher scheme reduce or increase inequality? Opponents of vouchers argue that in education – as in other areas – greater choice for the middle classes will place children from lower income groups at even more disadvantage. The extent of this disadvantage would depend upon how far better schools creamed off the more able pupils, leaving sink schools for the remainder.

## Subsidies: Student Grants or Loans?

Another area in which critics of the present system have suggested further reform is in connection with the subsidies offered to students in further and higher education through the grant system. At the moment most students in full-time further or higher education in Britain receive non-repayable grants which pay their tuition fees and make a substantial contribution towards their living expenses while they are studying. Although they are not usually described in such terms, these grants are a form of education voucher: they are allocated to students to enable them to buy education services at approved institutions, and these institutions – which, under the new funding arrangements, are increasingly dependent on fee income – are in competition for students. Unlike the voucher schemes described in the previous section, however, they are not available to every potential student, only those who obtain the educational qualifications necessary to gain admission to a college or university.

Government subsidies in further and higher education – as in other areas of policy dealt with in this book – can be justified on grounds of efficiency and/or equity. That is, they may be used to bring about a socially efficient level of provision and/or to make sure that it is distributed equitably. Concern that these and other objectives were not being met by the students' grants system has led the government to introduce the beginnings of a loan system. Before we discuss the details of this reform, however, we shall look at some of the general arguments in the grants versus loans debate.

The grant system is frequently defended on grounds of the need to equalise access to further and higher education by ensuring that students from poorer families are not discriminated against because of their limited ability to pay tuition fees and finance a period of study. But to what extent can the grant system – which has been in operation in its present form since 1962 – be said to have equalised access? A variety of approaches to this question are possible. One factor that is likely to influence the access of lower income groups is the overall size of the higher education sector. The bigger it is, the wider is the pool from which it can be expected to draw students. In this connection, however, it is relevant to note that overall participation rates in higher education have increased in recent years despite the fact that the real value of the grant has actually declined. International comparisons also provide some insights into the workings of different methods of finance. In the UK, approximately thirty per cent of the relevant age group enter some form of high education. While this is higher than in, for example, West Germany – where taxpayers meet far less of the costs – it is a substantially lower proportion than in Canada, Sweden and the United States, all of which have repayable loan schemes. Perhaps the most direct way of examining the question of access is to look at the percentage of students from lower socio-economic backgrounds who enter higher education in Britain. This is the group which requires assistance in order to ensure equality of access. Once again the figures do not suggest that grants have had a major equalising influence: approximately twenty five per cent of university entrants are from families where the head of the household is in a manual job, whereas such families represent around sixty per cent of the general population. Moreover, this percentage has remained fairly constant since the grant system was introduced (Verry, 1977, p.71). The majority of students still come from middle- or upper-income homes. This means that a policy ostensibly designed to assist those students who would otherwise be denied access to higher education on financial grounds is, in fact, allocating a large proportion of its budget to the sons and daughters of the relatively well-off. Admittedly there is a means test – operated through the parental contribution – which places restrictions on the amounts higher-income families may receive, but the dominant picture is still one of a large number of low-income tax payers – who do not use higher education facilities – subsidising those who are better off.

Critics of the grant system maintain that if the aim of the policy is really to provide equality of access, then financial assistance is being given at the wrong stage of the education process. Most students from lower income backgrounds drop out of education before the point of entry into higher education; thus the proportion of students from 'manual' backgrounds in full-time education between 16 and

18 years of age is approximately the same as that in higher education. This is clearly a crucial period for the low-income family, for it is at this stage that the student starts to forego income if she remains at school without receiving any general financial assistance. If grants are to be awarded it is likely that they would make a greater contribution towards the establishment of equality of access if they were given at this stage.

Unlike a grants system, which redistributes the costs of education between people (that is from taxpayers who do not receive higher education to students), a loans system requires the recipients of education to bear its cost but allows them to redistribute the burden over time. As we have seen, education expenditure is an investment which can be expected to yield returns in the form of increased future earnings, and a loan scheme requires some of these earnings to be used to repay the costs of education.

Supporters of loans schemes claim it could be both more equitable and efficient than the present grants system. Greater equity could be achieved because repayable loans would reduce lifetime income inequality: students who receive higher future incomes as a result of education would be required to bear its costs. Loans would not discriminate against students from low-income backgrounds because they, it is argued – in common with all students – would earn extra income in the future with which they could repay their debts. In addition, if loans were combined with grants to the 16–18 years age group which, as we have seen, is the one in which inequality of access to higher education seems to start, it would provide a major stimulus to greater equality. Moreover, increases in efficiency would result, so supporters of a loans scheme claim, from encouraging a more responsible attitude among students. They would be expected to make better use of their time if they were incurring private costs. Finally, by freeing higher education from constraints arising from dependence on general government revenues, the whole system could expand.

Set against these advantages, opponents of loan schemes have raised a number of objections. First, they argue that loans would exacerbate existing inequalities of access because they would deter students from low-income backgrounds whereas, in higher-income families, parents would tend to look upon education as a consumption expenditure which they would finance, thereby releasing their children from the burden of debt repayments. Second, loans would fail to release government expenditure for other uses for many years because student loans, like mortgage loans on housing, would only be repaid in the distant future. Third, they point out that the efficiency of higher education in Britain is already high as evidenced by the 'drop-out' rate, which is very low by international standards; this, they argue, is because students, freed by the grant system from financial concerns, can devote their full attention to their studies. Fourth, they maintain that loans would deter people from entering relatively low-paid, but nevertheless socially useful jobs. Fifth, they claim that they would discriminate against women or others who left the workforce for childrearing purposes (some people have even argued that an educated woman's prospects would be affected adversely because she would be carrying a 'negative dowry'!).

How does the actual loans scheme being introduced in the UK match up to these possible advantages and disadvantages? The first point to emphasise is that, in its early years, loans will be available to top-up grants and not to replace them completely. Over time the loan element is expected to increase until eventually it is of equal value to the grant. In terms of the objections to loans listed above, three are dealt with explicitly in the government's scheme. Graduates will be able to defer payments when their incomes are low; public expenditure reductions are expected because the private sector will provide loan finance that is underwritten by the government; and there will be no cross liability to spouses and hence no negative dowries.

On the issue of 'drop-out' rates and efficiency it is certainly true that wastage rates in Britain are low by international standards, but this is hardly surprising when one considers the demanding selection procedures applied to applicants – through A' level requirements – and the rationing of places. In countries such as the United States entry to college or university is open to nearly all applicants with basic qualifications. In consequence nearly seventy per cent of the relevant age groups are in some form of higher education. Inevitably this means that many more marginal students with high 'drop-out' risk are admitted to college in the US than in Britain. This is almost certainly a more important determinant of relative wastage rates than the grant system. Whether students will use their time more productively when they have the responsibility to repay loans, or whether this will distract them from the wider purposes of education is, at the moment, an open question.

On possibly the most important question, however, namely the danger of increased inequality of access, it is likely that the partial replacement of grants with loans – even loans at zero real rates of interest – will relatively disadvantage students from lower income backgrounds. This conclusion is based upon the simple theoretical prediction that any increase in the cost to the student will impact more heavily on those from lower income households. The government has argued that this effect will be more than offset by an expansion in the overall size of the higher education sector: an expansion expected to follow from the decreased reliance on public expenditure. This case assumes that the lower participation rates of students from lower income backgrounds owes more to existing methods of non-price rationing (for example, A' level requirements) than to the costs of education. If this is correct, it is unfortunate that the government's plans offer no additional assistance to 16–18 year old students.

Faced with these difficulties, some people have argued that a financing system based upon student repayments should be devised which moves away from the principle of the individual repaying her costs to one that is based upon graduates' collective repayments. One way of doing this would be through a graduate tax. This would involve graduates paying an extra tax throughout their working lives. The tax would be related to income so that higher earners paid more than those on lower incomes.

Under a graduate tax scheme students *as a group* would repay the costs of their education, although individual students would not repay the individual costs they incurred. Thus a student who went into a low-paying occupation would have some of her costs paid by a colleague entering a more highly paid job. Such a scheme would embody a risk-pooling insurance principle where all students agreed to protect any one of their members from the adverse consequences of low future earnings. It would also, of course, overcome the problem of discrimination against women who may want to leave the workforce temporarily or permanently. While the British government appears to have no plans to move in this direction, it is interesting to note that such a scheme has recently been introduced in Australia.

# Summary

The education system has both *efficiency* and *equity* objectives. Efficiency requires the adoption of a system that maximises net social benefits – that is, the greatest possible excess of benefits over costs. These benefits take two main forms: production benefits resulting from training of the future work force and a more diffuse range of social benefits. The equity objective requires the establishment of equality of access or the guarantee of a minimum standard in education.

Although a market system in education allows the expression of consumer freedom of choice and has certain other advantages, there are strong reasons for believing that it will not achieve either of these objectives. The attainment of efficiency is likely to be impeded because of capital market imperfections, imperfect information, externalities, and spatial monopoly elements in the supply of education. At the same time, equity is unlikely to be achieved when access to education is determined by ability to pay and income is distributed unequally. For these reasons some form of state intervention in education is necessary. But this does not establish the form it should take.

Dissatisfaction with existing forms of direct provision and subsidy have led to a number of policy changes during the 1980s. Most of these introduce market-type elements into education and therefore can be described as *quasi-market* reforms. These have been designed to increase choice and efficiency. However, some people question whether they have gone far enough and have suggested more radical change. One suggestion is for the introduction of education vouchers. Schemes based on vouchers would, it is claimed, retain the advantages of a market system while guaranteeing everyone at least a minimum standard of education – thereby overcoming problems facing low-income families. Disputes about the relative merits of a voucher scheme have been based on two main issues: the diversity of the school system it would produce and the fears that it would lead to segregation and vastly different standards of schooling. In higher education the government has introduced a student loan scheme which is designed to reduce subsidisation. This, it is argued, will produce a more equitable and efficient higher education system. Opponents argue that it will increase inequality, increase drop-out rates and deter women and others who would have difficulty repaying loans. Some of these disadvantages could be overcome with a graduate tax.

# Further Reading

The economics of education has not attracted much interest in recent years. Several of the key books in the area are now rather old and out of print; however, if a copy of Blaug (1972) can be found, it is probably among the best works to consult. More recent material can be found in Atkinson (1983), Blaug (1987) and Psacharopoulos (1987). There are discussions of education vouchers in Le Grand (1989a) and of the graduate tax in Barnes and Barr (1988) and Barr (1989). A detailed analysis of recent developments in British educational policy can be found in Glennerster and Low (1990).

# Questions for Discussion

1.  'The private rates of return on investment in higher education are sufficiently large for students from both poor and rich households to suggest that the introduction of student loans will not affect the social composition of students entering colleges and universities'. Discuss this claim.
2.  Do you think that the education system would be more equitable if grants to 16–18 year olds replaced grants to students in higher education?
3.  Examine the case for using different levels of student grant to encourage students to follow courses which the government deems socially desirable.
4.  'As the production benefits of education are more tangible than the social benefits, the latter tend to be undervalued in discussions of education planning'. Discuss.
5.  Explain how you would estimate the social rate of return on investment in medical education.
6.  Open enrolment provides parents with freedom of choice among schools; however, if some schools are over-subscribed authorities typically employ place of residence as a criterion for allocation to schools. Analyse this procedure.
7.  How would the operation and the consequences of a non-supplementable voucher scheme differ from a supplementable scheme?

8.  Private market provision of education emphasises private benefits whereas state provision is concerned with social benefits. Discuss this claim.

9.  What do you understand by the term 'equality of opportunity' within the education sector?

10. Do you think that education is a means of promoting social mobility or a means of preparing certain social groups for a predetermined place in the socio-economic system?

# Housing 4

Successive British governments have pursued the aim of ensuring 'a decent home for every family at a price within their means' (Department of the Environment, 1971). And yet in 1988, the number of households accepted by local authorities in England for rehousing because they were homeless was 116 000. This represented a rise of over 100 per cent since 1978. As far as the quality of housing is concerned, the English House Condition Survey of 1986 reported that one-quarter of the nation's housing stock was defective in some respect and that nearly 5 per cent of dwellings (that is, just under one million) were so bad as to be deemed unsuitable for human habitation (Hills and Mullings, 1990). On the subject of affordability, spiralling house prices during the 1980s – when there was an increase in real terms of over 90 per cent between 1982 and 1989 – placed home ownership beyond the means of many households. Thereafter stagnant or falling prices, and sharp prices in mortgage interest rates, placed many recent buyers in severe difficulties. An increasing number of borrowers fell into arrears with their mortgage payments and, in some cases, there were loan foreclosures and property repossessions.

Why is it that these problems have arisen despite numerous housing policy initiatives? What are the reasons for the discrepancy between successive governments' declared objectives and their achievements in the housing sector? In this chapter we shall endeavour to provide some answers to these questions. As in other chapters, we shall start by looking at the basic housing objectives of efficiency and equity. This is followed by a section which argues that there are certain special features (or failings) of a market system which can be expected to prevent it from achieving efficiency or equity in the allocation of housing resources. This fact has provided the rationale for various forms of government intervention. Some of the more important of these are described in the third section which looks at policies on regulation (rent control), direct provision (council housing) and subsidisation (tax incentives for owner occupiers). These have all been used in an attempt to overcome market failings. However, these policies have displayed failings of their own. Indeed many of the policy initiatives of the 1980s were designed specifically in order to address perceived failures resulting from earlier government intervention. Hence the third section also provides an account of these policies and an assessment of their impact. Finally, we discuss how policies may be developed in the future in order to draw on the strengths of both the government and the private sectors in an attempt to improve housing sector performance.

# Objectives

As in other social policy areas, society's main objectives can be specified in terms of efficiency and equity. However, in practice, the formulation of housing goals has tended to emphasise the equity objective, albeit in an indirect form. To appreciate this, consider the often made claim that housing is a *necessity*. Now while it is undoubtedly correct that some form of shelter is necessary to sustain life, it is by no means clear that this establishes the need for luxury penthouse flats in Mayfair and Knightsbridge or the mock-Tudor, double-garaged residences of Cheadle or Esher. What people usually mean when they speak of housing as a necessity is that there is some *minimum standard* of accommodation that is a necessity of life as we have come to expect it in 20th century Britain. This is undoubtedly the official view implicit in the concept of 'a decent home'; namely, that there is a minimum standard of housing below which no family should be allowed to fall. In our terms this is one interpretation of the equity objective.

Similarly, the equity objective can be shown to lie behind the formulation of housing construction targets. For most of this century the overall shortage of dwellings in relation to the number of households seeking accommodation has been viewed as *the* dominant housing problem. Accordingly, successive governments have set building targets and judged their performance in terms of the number of dwellings constructed each year. At first sight this concern with the size of the total stock might appear to be an example of the pursuit of an efficient level of housing production. But, in fact, it is not. Rather, building more houses has been the method chosen to try to achieve a minimum standard of provision for everyone. In the drive to encourage housing construction, little attention was paid to increases in the amount of housing consumed by those families above the minimum standard who were already adequately housed, with the result that some economists feel that there has been an overinvestment in housing at the expense of other forms of investment.

During the 1980s, however, the government's housing objectives have tended to emphasise efficiency considerations rather more than in earlier periods. In both the public and private rental sectors, moving rents towards market levels has been justified in terms of providing incentives for both consumers and producers to make better use of housing resources, while subsidies related to household incomes have been used in an attempt to meet equity aims. In the case of the most striking housing policy of recent years, however – namely, the encouragement of owner-occupation – the link with an efficiency objective has been less clear. Government statements have emphasised the advantages of personal property ownership, and the self reliance it is held to promote, rather than the efficient use of housing resources. We shall return to this and other issues surrounding government policy in a later section. But before doing so, we shall look at the operation of the market system.

## The Market System and Housing

The market system is the main means of allocating housing in Britain. It covers approximately 80 per cent of dwellings. As we saw in Chapter 1, this system has several distinct advantages, but it also has a number of serious shortcomings. These have manifested themselves in an failure to meet society's minimum standards and a failure to produce an efficient quantity of housing. In this section we shall examine some of the reasons for these failures.

## Equity: Income and Access to Housing

There is no reason to expect a market system to achieve the aim of a guaranteed minimum standard. This is because many families simply do not have enough purchasing power to buy, or in some cases even rent, good quality accommodation. Thus one of the main reasons for the persistence of substandard housing is the poverty of the families that occupy it. Recognition of this correlation between poor housing conditions and low income households has led some economists to argue that the problem is not really a *housing* problem at all. For them it is just one other manifestation of general poverty: just as, without assistance, the poor would not be able to afford adequate food or clothing so they cannot afford adequate housing.

According to this view, slum housing may be neither inequitable as such (although poverty is) nor even inefficient. Indeed some economists have argued that given low income demand for housing, slum housing represents an efficient response to these demands. But is this claim correct? Other economists claim that although general poverty may be an important contributory factor towards the persistence of sub-standard housing, it is not the only one. They point to additional features that can be expected to produce inefficiency. These are *capital market imperfections, imperfect information* and *discrimination*, and the existence of *externalities*. In addition, the housing market displays serious adjustment problems because of short run *supply inelasticity.*

## Capital Market Imperfections

Housing is an expensive commodity. Average house prices are typically between three and four times average incomes. In fact, during 1990, the average price of a house in England was, at over £60 000, more than four times average incomes. This means that very few people are in a position to buy a house outright from their income and accumulated savings. Most people need to borrow money. Moreover, because the size of the loan will be large in relation to the borrower's income, repayments will have to be spread over a long enough period of time to permit each monthly repayment to be small enough to be paid from the buyer's monthly wage or salary. To meet this demand, a number of institutions – the Building Societies – have grown up, specialising in long-term mortgage loans to house buyers.

One feature that distinguishes these societies from many other financial institutions is that they borrow short-term and lend long-term – the reverse of normal practice. Thus, while loans may be offered for over thirty years, depositors and shareholders are free to withdraw their money in days, weeks or months. This highly liquid nature of their liabilities, and the illiquidity of their assets (houses on which they have advanced loans cannot be readily converted into cash) has traditionally made the societies very cautious and unwilling to take risks that might lead to a loss of confidence on the part of their shareholders. This risk aversion has been noticeable in their lending policies, where they have operated a stringent set of rules governing the types of property on which they have been willing to lend money, the amounts they have been willing to lend and the people to whom they would lend.

These practices have been criticised on the grounds that they reflect excessive caution, or even discrimination against certain groups of the population and areas of housing, rather than the real risks associated with different types of loans. For example, it has been argued that building societies discriminate against manual workers because their requirements about prospective borrowers' incomes favour those in occupations with stable incremental scales at the expense of those in jobs where the earnings profile is more uneven and/or includes substantial overtime payments. Similarly, the traditional unwillingness of societies to lend on older properties, particularly the practice of 'redlining' which has been used to designate certain areas as 'no-loan' areas, has been cited as a reason for the accelerated decay of certain inner city areas into slum conditions.

In recent years clearing banks and certain other financial institutions have increasingly entered the mortgage market. In 1988, for example, banks accounted for over a quarter of mortgage loan lending. At the same time, there has been interest rate deregulation. This has led to the abolition of the practice whereby the Building Societies Association recommended an interest rate to its members. As a result the market had become far more competitive. This has probably led to some reduction in the incidence of discriminatory rationing of mortgage loans. However, interest rate deregulation has also contributed to a rise in the cost of credit with a resultant increase in the barriers to entry to owner occupation for many low to middle income households. House price inflation fuelled by a sudden increase in mortgage loan availability in the face of supply inelasticity (see below) has also contributed to this problem.

## Imperfect Information

When people go to buy food, they have a general idea of the prices they will need to pay for eggs, butter, tea, and so on. They will not necessarily buy their food at the cheapest foodshop because there may be other factors to take into account. The shop's location, its service standards and the quality of its goods will all be important. After considering all of these factors, most people tend to develop regular shopping habits. However, if the level of service at their chosen store deteriorates, or if its prices rise substantially in relation to other shops, we may expect some customers to shift their custom elsewhere. This possibility prevents any one store from getting seriously out of line with its competitors. This system is able to function because people go shopping frequently and are able to assess relative standards continuously. As a result, consumers are well informed.

Well-informed consumers are essential if a market is to operate efficiently. If consumers do not possess adequate information on the goods and prices available elsewhere in the market, some sellers may charge excessive prices and make abnormal profits. Unfortunately imperfect information is widespread throughout the housing market. Both renters and owner-occupiers are affected. In the latter case, the transaction costs of buying and selling a house and moving to a new location are sufficiently large to prevent people from changing homes as casually as they may change foodshops. Hence they will enter the market only infrequently. Any change in housing will often result from an extraneous factor, such as a change of job location or a change in family circumstances. For most of the time, however, a household will remain in a house for which the price was determined some time in the past. If the need to change houses arises and, as is often the case, the change involves moving to new neighbourhood or town, then variations in prices between areas is likely to mean that property prices in its existing location will be a poor guide to the prices it will find in the new area.

Of course, when a household decides to move, it will usually spend time acquiring information about housing in the area in which it wants to move. But the costs of search in terms of time, money and inconvenience can be high, especially if there is some urgency about housing requirements. The growth of an industry devoted to the dissemination of information on property for sale – namely, estate agency – has reduced these costs somewhat. But they remain substantial.

Imperfect information may pose even more serious problems for renters, especially if they have low incomes. Recent migrants to urban areas are often at a particular disadvantage. This may be because they have only recently arrived in an area and have not had sufficient time to acquire the necessary information; or it may be that their lack of education or familiarity with the housing system prevents them from understanding how to acquire it.

The information problems faced by new arrivals are often exacerbated by racial or other forms of discrimination which prevent them from obtaining housing outside narrowly defined areas. With their mobility restricted in this way, many households find themselves confined to low income, slum areas and susceptible to unscrupulous landlords. Sometimes they end up paying a higher price per unit of slum housing than other families pay for good quality housing in suburban areas.

## *Externalities*

If one family on a street allows the state of its house to deteriorate so that it becomes an eyesore to its neighbours, the level of satisfaction its neighbours obtain from their own housing will be reduced. For they will be concerned with the visual appearance of their neighbourhood as well as the characteristics of their own homes. Equally, if one resident in a street persists in holding noisy, late-night parties that disturb others in the vicinity, the benefit these residents derive from living in the area will be reduced. Conversely, a decision by one owner to renovate his property in an attractive manner is likely to increase the enjoyment his neighbours derive from living nearby. These examples demonstrate that the level of benefits a family derives from living in its own house will be affected by the way its neighbours choose to behave: that is, there are externalities in housing consumption. If a market system is used to allocate housing resources, we cannot be confident that individuals will take externalities into account when deciding upon their actions. The result may well be widespread external costs (or benefits) and inefficiency.

Let us return to the first example involving the neglect of maintenance and repair work to illustrate the importance of externalities in the housing market. This example demonstrates how the existence of externalities can play a key role in the development and spread of slum housing, and also shows how they can feature prominently in the improvement of such areas. To see how this works, consider a typical slum neighbourhood. Most of the housing will be sub-standard, with low-income families living at high densities in multi-occupied, over-crowded buildings. Interspersed with this housing will be various abandoned buildings that have become uninhabitable and subject to vandalism. The local environment will be poor, suffering from an absence of decent recreational and leisure facilities. Often the proximity of industrial, commercial or transport networks will be a source of pollution. In short, the area will be run down and depressed.

Now consider landlords who own buildings in such an area. Why do they not invest in maintenance and repair work to improve the quality and their property? Would not an improved building attract tenants who are willing to pay rents that would offer them an adequate return on their investments? It does not take much imagination to work out the answers to these questions. Landlords will be only too aware that any investment that they might make is almost certain to yield a poor return because the slum neighbourhood conditions will dominate any improvement that they might make to a single dwelling. That is, the existence of strong neighbourhood external costs would deter prospective tenants who would be willing and able to pay the rent levels that would make improvement worthwhile. Consequently, landlords are likely to decide against spending money on their property and will thereby contribute to the decline of the neighbourhood.

Only if landlords could be confident that other landlords in the neighbourhood were also going to improve their property are they likely to consider investments of their own. In this case it is possible that concerted action on the part of a number of landlords might result in a sufficient reduction in the level of external cost being imposed by one on another to make individual investments worth-while. However, mutual suspicion and uncertainty among landlords about each other's actions will usually mean that no one is willing to take the initiative. The essence of this problem – which is sometimes known as the 'prisoner's' dilemma – can be demonstrated in terms of the following simple example.

Suppose there are two landlords, Bert and Ernie, who own two adjoining properties on a certain street. Both buildings have become rather run-down and they are each trying to decide how much to spend on repairs and renovation. For purposes of illustration, let us assume that they have both decided to spent at least £10 000 and that they are each considering whether it would be worth upgrading the buildings through an additional £10 000 on top of this sum. Let us start by looking at the decision from Bert's point of view. He cannot be sure what Ernie is going to do and yet he knows that because of externalities the return he receives will depend to a certain extent on Ernie's actions. The factors that he will need to consider are summarised in the 'pay-off matrix' shown in Figure 4.1.

**FIGURE 4.1**
**Bert's Rates of Return**

|  | Ernie does *not* invest | Ernie does invest |
|---|---|---|
| Bert does *not* invest | 4% | 6% |
| Bert does invest | 2% | 5% |

The matrix shows that if Bert decides not to invest the extra £10 000 and Ernie decides likewise, he will receive a 4 per cent return on his original investment. If, however, Ernie does invest while Bert does not, Ernie's improved building will bestow an external benefit on his property and raise his return to 6 per cent. So if Bert *does not invest* he will receive either a 4 or a 6 per cent return. On the other hand, if Bert decides to invest while Ernie decides not to do so, Ernie's less well-kept building will impose an external cost on Bert's property and reduce his return to 2 per cent. Finally, if Ernie did invest at the same time, Bert would receive some external benefit and his return would rise to 5 per cent. Thus, if Bert decides to *invest*, he will receive either a 2 or a 5 per cent return. So which option will he choose?

It is likely that Bert will approach the problem in the following manner. First, he will ask himself what is the best strategy to adopt if he thinks that Ernie is not going to invest; the first column of the matrix in Figure 4.1 shows that he too would do better not to invest in these circumstances because then he would make a 4 per cent return instead of a 2 per cent return. Second, he will ask himself what is his best strategy if he thinks that Ernie is going to invest; the second column of the matrix shows that once again he would do better not to invest in this situation. In this way he would make a 6 per cent instead of a 5 per cent return. Thus, in both cases he will make a larger return by not investing. Because Ernie is faced with exactly the same uncertainties concerning Bert's behaviour, he can be expected to go through a similar decision-making process. If he does, he will reach the same conclusion; namely, that his best strategy is not to invest. Therefore neither Bert or Ernie will invest and they will both make a 4 per cent return. Notice, however, that if they had both invested the extra £10 000, they would both have been better off because they would each have earned a 5 per cent return! This is the essence of the 'prisoner's dilemma'.

The term 'prisoner's dilemma' derives from the supposed problems facing two prisoners arrested on a joint charge. When they are kept in separate cells, and therefore unsure about each other's willingness to collaborate with the police in return for favourable treatment, they are likely to end up with – from their point of view – a worse outcome than if they had been able to plan a joint defence. By acting independently in situations where they are unsure about each other's behaviour, decision makers reach an outcome that is less desirable to both of them than one they could have reached if they had collaborated. But collaboration between landlords of poor quality housing is unlikely to take place, especially as it is in any one landlord's interests to appear to collaborate – in order to get his neighbour to invest – and then to renege on the deal.

Of course, external effects are unlikely always to be strong enough to have these consequences, regardless of all circumstances. Nonetheless, their existence does cast considerable doubt on the ability of the market system to achieve an efficient allocation of housing resources. Certainly, governments that invest in environmental improvement schemes rely upon their efforts having a positive external effect and thereby stimulating private sector activity.

# Adjustment Problems: Supply Inelasticity

In Chapter 1 we described the way in which the market system copes with changes in demand. We showed that if the demand for a commodity increases there will be a rise in its price which can be expected to encourage some firms to produce more. This increase in supply will satisfy some of the additional demand. As supply increases there will be a tendency for the price to fall gradually from its immediate post-change level until a new equilibrium price is established. However, in some circumstances, there is very little opportunity to increase output in response to rising demand. In these circumstances, demand will remain unsatisfied while prices rise to – and remain at – the immediate post-change level. If these conditions apply we say that supply is *inelastic*.

The difference between a situation of inelastic supply and one in which the supply response is more flexible (elastic) is demonstrated in Figure 4.2. In both parts of the diagram the vertical axis records the price of housing (in terms of £s rent per week) while the horizontal axis records the number of dwellings demanded and supplied in this particular local market. In the first panel the point of intersection between the demand schedule (*DD*) and the supply schedule (*SS*), indicates an equilibrium price of £100 per week, at which 1000 dwellings are demanded/supplied. Now suppose that there is a sudden increase in demand following the migration of additional families into the area. This is depicted by the second demand schedule (*D'D'*). The increase in demand leads to a new equilibrium at which the price has risen to £120 per week and the supply has increased by 50 dwellings. Note that a substantial increase in price (20 per cent) has led to only a small increase in the supply of housing (5 per cent).

In contrast, the second panel of the diagram shows how an identical initial equilibrium position, followed by the same change in demand conditions, results in a far smaller price increase and a much larger increase in the supply of housing. Here the price rises to only £105 (5 per cent) whereas 100 more dwellings are supplied (10 per cent). Thus we can see that when supply is inelastic, the bulk of the adjustment to a change in demand conditions will take place through a change in price instead of a change in the quantity of the commodity offered for sale.

**FIGURE 4.2**
**Supply Elasticity, prices and dwellings**

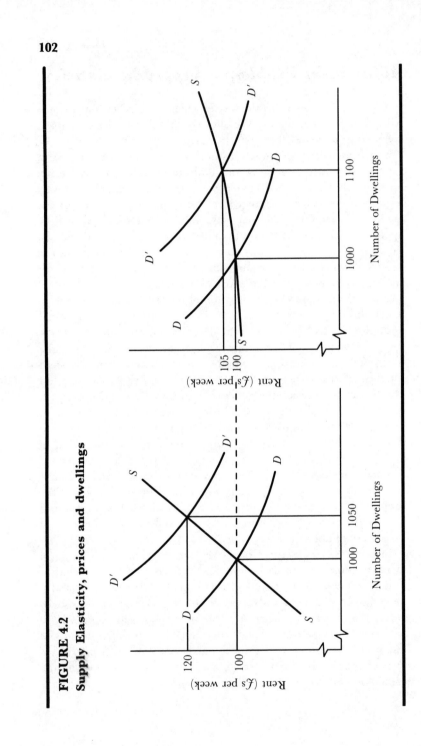

Although we have chosen to illustrate the concept of elasticity in relation to the rental housing market, it is also, of course, of relevance to the owner-occupier sector. In fact, periods of rapid house price inflation have often been caused by large volumes of mortgage loans being made available, and thereby increasing the level of demand, without the supply of housing being able to adjust quickly enough. Also note that although we have discussed supply elasticity under the heading of efficiency, it has important implications for the equity of the housing market. This is because when prices or rents rise, it is the existing owners of properties who benefit at the expense of their tenants or potential owner occupiers. As long as it is impossible to increase the supply of a commodity for which demand has risen, the owners of the existing stock will be in a monopoly position and will receive monopoly profits. Clearly this will affect the distribution of income, often in ways that penalise lower income groups who are less likely to be property owners. Given the importance of supply inelasticity, let us look at some of the factors which cause it.

## Fixed housing locations

So far we have spoken of housing as if there was a single market. In reality there are many different local markets. Because the existing stock of housing is fixed in location and cannot be moved from one place to another (with a few exceptions in the case of caravans, boats and tents!), the supply of housing services will be specific to a particular area. This contrasts with the supply conditions of most other goods. If there is a shortage of a particular model of car in Leeds, for example, but they are plentiful in Manchester, dealers can transport them from Manchester to Leeds. Such mobility is not possible in the case of housing and so supply shortages may persist in some areas while there are surpluses elsewhere. Of course, there will be linkages between different local markets. For example, if there is a shortage of housing in Leeds compared with Manchester, we may expect Leeds prices to be higher than those in Manchester. Lower Manchester prices may induce some people to move from Leeds to Manchester, and thus mobility of people may reduce some of the problems posed by immobility of housing. However, this type of mobility is likely to be limited because the decision to move from one town to another could involve a range of costs including a change of jobs or a longer journey to work, separation from friends, changes of schools for children and so on. The gains resulting from lower house prices would have to be quite substantial to bring about such movements.

Clearly, therefore, the location of housing is important. However, transport developments may increase the ease, and/or lower the cost of travel, and thereby increase the substitutability of housing at different locations. For example, the building of the M62 motorway obviously increased the ease of travel between Leeds and Manchester. Similarly, a suburban location may become an alternative to a central city one following the establishment of a fast commuting service. When the Victoria underground railway line was originally opened in London, it immediately gave greater access to Central London from a number of housing locations within the vicinity of stations on the line, thereby increasing the range of sites involving short commuting trips. More recently, the opening of the Docklands railway in London had a similar effect.

## Land shortages

Shortages of land have frequently placed limits on the supply of new housing. Apart from a few notable land-reclamation schemes, such as those involving the Polders in the Netherlands, the total supply of land in an area is fixed. The quantity cannot be increased year after year in the way that other factor inputs, such as the workforce or machines used in production, are increased. Often, however, the problem is not strictly one of a shortage of land in total, but rather a shortage of land available for house building in the areas in which it is required. Sometimes these shortages arise because of restrictions imposed by various land-use planning laws. Typically, these designate land for particular uses: for example, it may be reserved for recreational or agricultural use, in which case no building would be permitted. Restrictions on building on the Green Belt surrounding London, whatever their merits in terms of improving the environment, have the effect of restricting the supply of building land in an area where demand is increasing rapidly. Moreover, even if restrictions are relaxed in response to acute shortages, planning authorities are usually reluctant to take such decisions without lengthy deliberations. These can mean that supply inelasticity is maintained over a number of years.

## *Productivity in house building*

On average it takes between one and two years to build a house. One way in which dwellings could be constructed more quickly is through the wider use of industrialised building techniques. These involve the mass production of standardised building units that are either produced on-site or transported from the factory for erection on the site. However, the adoption of these production techniques has not been as widespread as might be expected. One reason for this is that the production of parts on a site requires substantial investment in capital equipment that will be specific to that site. Only if the development is really large will such investments be worthwhile. In situations where large-scale comprehensive development is taking place, or where certain types of dwellings – such as high rise flats – are being constructed, industrialised building methods may be appropriate. However, in the majority of cases, the size of the plot to be developed, and the type of housing, precludes the use of these methods. If, on the other hand, units are produced in a factory and transported to a site, the capital equipment that is used in their production can often by used on more than one project. However, high transport costs, and the difficulty of building to the higher specifications that are necessary when on-site adjustments are not possible, have usually meant that this approach is also uneconomical.

Another factor which has prevented the speed-up of construction times through the wider use of capital-intensive, mass-production techniques are the fluctuations in demand facing the building industry. When large amounts have been invested in plant and machinery, it is necessary to make sure that they are used to their full capacity. It is not possible to lay machines off when demand is slack in the same way that the workforce can be laid off or put on to short time. And machines standing idle incur capital costs even through they are not generating any income. Consequently, the typical house builder has been very cautious about investing in machinery.

A final factor militating against the use of mass production techniques is the need for a great deal of skilled specialist work not suited to such techniques. For example, bricklayers, carpenters, plumbers and electricians all work on tasks where the skill of the man is the a vital ingredient. There is only limited scope for increasing the speed of work by replacing these labour inputs by capital equipment.

# Government Policies

In the previous section we argued that housing problems arise because families have insufficient income to buy or rent decent housing; or because, even if they have sufficient income, there are various imperfections in the housing market that prevent it from functioning efficiently. Inadequate incomes lead to inequity, whereas imperfections result in inefficiency. Now the distinction between these two explanations is of some importance for housing policy. The view that housing problems arise because some families have inadequate incomes suggests that the problems could be tackled most effectively by supplementing the purchasing power of these families. According to this view, no specific intervention in the housing market is required. The market-imperfections view, on the other hand, suggests that specific policies aimed at removing the imperfections will be necessary.

Of course, we do not necessarily have to choose one theory and reject the other; it is quite possible that both factors have played a part in producing the problems described at the beginning of this chapter. In this case elements of both policies will be necessary in order to remove them. With this in mind, we shall look at three of the major policies that have been introduced in the United Kingdom. The first one – rent control – provides an example of government regulation of the private market. This is followed by a discussion of the direct provision of housing combined with subsidies by the government through council housing schemes. Finally, we shall examine the subsidisation of housing as it occurs in the owner-occupier sector through the tax system.

## *Regulation: Rent Control*

Rent control is a means of protecting tenants from high market rents that would otherwise result from shortages in the supply of rented accommodation. In essence, rent control involves specifying a maximum rent that a landlord may charge for a dwelling so that the tenant receives an implicit subsidy equal to the difference between the market rent and the controlled rent. To be effective, however, it is also necessary that a tenant should be guaranteed the right to occupy a dwelling at the designated rent. For this reason,

**FIGURE 4.3**
**Rent Control and Housing Supply**

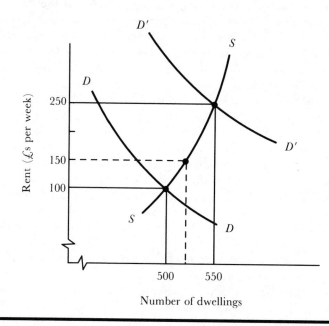

Number of dwellings

rent control has normally been accompanied by measures offering security of tenure.

A typical rent control situation is depicted in Figure 4.3. Suppose that initially the market is in equilibrium when 500 units of housing are rented at £100 per week. However, further suppose that there is a sudden arrival of a large number of additional families into the local housing market area and that this leads to an increase in the demand for rented accommodation. This is depicted by the demand curve $D'D'$ which is to the right of the original one. If the market is left to operate freely, a new market equilibrium will be established when 550 dwelling units are rented at £250 per week. However, the government may decide that rents of £250 per week are excessive and are only attainable because it has not been possible to increase the supply of housing to meet the influx of people. Legislation may therefore be passed to limit rents to a maximum of £150 per week. Thus tenants of controlled housing will receive a 'subsidy' of £100 per week because the controlled rent is £100 below the market rent.

The rationale for controlling rents in this way is the desire to protect tenants in situations where supply inelasticity will cause rents to rise sharply in the face of increased demand. (Note: if the supply curve in Figure 4.3 was more elastic, there would have been a smaller increase in rent and a larger increase in the supply of housing following the increase in demand). However, although the policy may alleviate the short-term hardship that would be suffered by some tenants, it will have long-term consequences that are against the interests of most tenants. This paradox arises because controlling rents makes investing in rented housing less profitable and can therefore be expected to reduce the supply. Even Figure 4.3 – which concentrates only on the short-run situation – shows that at the controlled rent only 520 units are available for renting compared with 550 at the market rent. However, it is the longer-term consequences of rent control that are likely to be more serious. Landlords who do not feel that they are earning acceptable levels of profit will be reluctant to make any further investments in housing. As a result, little new housing will come onto the market to meet growing demands or to replace housing that has become substandard through age, obsolescence, or for other reasons. The supply of existing rented housing is also likely to be depleted as dwellings are transferred to non-regulated sectors through, for example, sale into owner occupation. Moreover, the quality of the existing rent-controlled stock can be expected to suffer accelerated deterioration as landlords seek to reduce their costs by postponing repair and maintenance work. In terms of Figure 4.3, these longer-term reductions in supply will cause a leftward shift in the supply schedule *SS*, indicating that less housing is available at each rent level.

There is also a question mark over the equity of rent-control. As a result of the supply shortages it generates, those tenants who are lucky enough to obtain rent controlled accommodation, will benefit at the expense of new entrants to the market. Moreover, as we have seen, the policy effectively transfers income from landlords to tenants. Now, while it is likely that on average landlords will be more wealthy than tenants, it would be wrong to assume that all of them correspond to the prosperous, cigar-smoking caricature of popular mythology. Surveys indicate that many small landlords have other occupations and are drawn from the skilled, manual social class. As such, the equity basis of any income transfer policy based upon property ownership is likely to be highly imperfect.

The fact that a policy aimed at tenant protection has these adverse side effects is due to the unusual nature of the 'subsidy' involved in rent control. In most cases, when the government decides that a particular group merits assistance, it is the government itself that bears the cost, at least in the first instance. It usually does this by paying producers so that they can sell at a price below cost or by assisting consumers directly in cash or in kind. In the case of rent control, however, government regulatory policies determine the size of the subsidy but the cost is borne by landlords. Not surprisingly this reduces the incentive to become a landlord.

Faced with these adverse consequences of rent control, recent government policy has sought to restore incentives to private landlords through progressive deregulation of the sector. For most of the 1980s, rents were regulated through a 'fair rents' formula. This was designed to offer landlords a 'reasonable' profit while protecting tenants by excluding from rents any element attributable to extreme local shortages. It was also more flexible than earlier policies in that rents could be reviewed every two years. However, fair rent policy did little to stem the decline of the sector and, in 1988, was replaced by the more drastic provisions of the Housing Act of that year. Under the 1988 Act all new lettings are able to be let at market rents. Part of the equity aim of earlier policies is retained by guaranteeing tenants security of tenure as long as they meet their rent and other contractual commitments. However, the main form of tenant protection comes via income-based, housing cash benefits paid to tenants as part of the social security system. These are designed to increase their purchasing power in the market. In addition to these demand side subsidies, landlords may receive tax benefits under the Business Expansion Scheme.

Hence the new market-based approach is designed to protect low income tenants while offering incentives to landlords to expand the supply of private rental housing. The policy is clearly based on the assumption that problems resulting from supply inelasticity, externalities and other market failures can be overcome. Whether this is so, and a sector that has declined to less than 10 per cent of the total housing stock will be revitalised, remains to be seen.

## *Provision: Council Housing*

Council or Local Authority (LA) housing has traditionally sought to assist tenants, while avoiding the adverse supply effects of rent control, by combining the direct public sector provision of rented housing with rents below market levels. In terms of the objectives identified in this book, the direct provision of LA housing can be viewed as a means of overcoming inefficiency, particularly that arising from supply inelasticity, whereas the subsidy element addresses the equity objective. How successful has the policy been in pursuit of these objectives?

On the question of efficiency, we would expect an LA to be able to increase supply elasticity by undertaking building programmes that more risk-averse private developers might reject (although evidence on building times does suggest that private housing is built rather more quickly than council housing). Equally, we might also expect an LA to overcome the deterrence to repair and improvement posed by negative externalities because, as a large scale landlord, it is able to 'internalise' many of the costs and benefits involved. But even if LA housing does have these advantages, can we be confident that the public sector will produce the appropriate quantity and quality of housing when decisions are often made by politicians and bureaucrats and are not subject to consumer demand?

To answer this question, let us take a brief look at the recent experience of LA housing. At the outset, it is important to recognise that LA housing building programmes, often in the form of large estates, have played an important part in overcoming housing shortages in the past. This was particularly true in the post- World War II period. For those people who first came to live in them, council houses and flats represented a marked improvement on the cramped and often poor quality conditions in which they had lived previously. Acquiring a new council house was considered a step up the housing ladder. Over the last twenty years, however, a number of problems have manifested themselves. It has become clear that the design and layout of many large council housing estates has proved unpopular with the residents. High-rise flats, in particular, have posed difficulties for elderly people and families with children. The lack of adequate shopping and recreational facilities and other amenities has also been a problem, especially on estates located on the outskirts of urban areas. Moreover, in some cases, building construction has been faulty with inadequate insulation and defective heating systems leading to condensation and dampness. And more generally, a cumulative neglect of repair and maintenance expenditure has sometimes resulted in a serious problem of housing decay. The failure of LA housing departments to respond to residents' concerns over these problems has led to widespread dissatisfaction with old-style, centralised bureaucracies, and to search for more consumer-responsive methods of organisation.

As far as the equity of LA housing is concerned, it is necessary to consider the subsidies which tenants receive. These fall into two categories. First, there are the general subsidies that all tenants receive because rents are set below market levels. And second, there are housing benefits that are provided through the social security system and related to income. If the purpose of the subsidy is to assist low income households, the latter form is clearly more closely related to this objective than the former. During the 1980s, the government embarked upon a wide range of housing reforms which it claimed were designed to address the inefficiencies and inequities of council housing identified above. We shall look briefly at the two main ones; namely, the privatisation of council housing through sales to tenants and the reform of housing subsidies.

The most dramatic way of offering tenants a greater say over their housing conditions has been to sell their dwellings to them. This policy was pursued through the 1980 Housing Act which gave tenants a statutory right-to-buy. Moreover, the prices at which they were able to buy were set between 33 and 60 per cent below the market price. The policy has proved to be enormously popular with one and a quarter million dwellings sold to date; this represents about one fifth of the total LA housing stock. However, critics of the policy have argued that it is the more well-off tenants who have bought the better quality housing and that it will reduce the availability of decent accommodation for future generations of tenants in real need. It has also been argued that as better quality housing is sold, and better-off tenants become owner-occupiers, council housing is increasingly becoming a residual, welfare sector. This argument goes on to claim that this has led to increased inequality and the social polarisation of society between owners and renters. Polarisation has also been accentuated by recent government policy on subsidies to LA tenants. This has shifted the emphasis from general rent subsidies to subsidisation of tenants on low incomes through the social security system. It has been achieved by substantial LA rent increases – rents rose in real terms by nearly 50 per cent between 1980 and 1990 – and by placing heavier reliance on housing benefit payments. The combined effect of the chance to buy at discount prices, and reduced subsidies for better-off LA tenants has provided a powerful incentive for them to become owner-occupiers.

## Subsidies: Owner-Occupation

Owner-occupiers represent the largest tenure group in Britain. By 1990, approximately 65 per cent of dwellings were owner occupied compared with 55 per cent in 1979. Apart from the sale of council houses programme, the rapid expansion of this sector of the housing market has undoubtedly been encouraged by the favourable tax treatment of those households who choose to buy their homes in comparison with those who rent. To appreciate the nature of this preferential tax treatment, consider two people with identical incomes, one of whom decides to buy a house with the aid of a mortgage loan, and another who decides to rent from a landlord. Under existing tax law, the owner-occupier will pay less income tax because income earned to pay mortgage interest payments on loans (or portions of loans) up to £30 000 is not subject to taxation. No similar tax relief is, however, available to the renter.

The numerical example in Table 4.1 illustrates the way in which tax relief is computed. It shows that if an owner-occupier borrows £30 000 from a bank or building society and pays an interest rate of 15 per cent, approximately £4500 will be payable in interest during the first year. However, the income earned to make this payment will not be subject to taxation. Hence if this person is liable to an income tax rate of 25 per cent, the tax relief will be worth £1125 to her.

**TABLE 4.1**
**Mortgage Interest and Tax Relief**

| | | |
|---|---|---|
| Mortgage Interest: | £30 000 @ 15 per cent | = £4500 |
| Tax Relief: | £4500 @ 25 per cent | = £1125 |

The total sums of tax exemption given in this way each year are substantial; in 1989/90 over £5 thousand million was received in mortgage loan tax relief by owner-occupiers. With sums of this size involved, it is obviously of major importance to ask whether these tax subsidies are consistent with the housing objectives of efficiency and equity. The answer, unfortunately, is that they almost certainly are not.

On the question of efficiency, it has been argued by some economists that the favourable tax treatment of owner-occupiers has led to an over-investment in housing at the expense of other sectors of the economy. And as productivity in the housing sector tends to be lower than elsewhere, this tax-induced diversion of resources will have had a detrimental effect on the rate of growth of national output. On the question of equity, the relative treatment of households both within the owner occupier sector and between owner occupation and other tenures needs to be considered. On the first point, it should be borne in mind that the amount of tax relief that a person receives depends upon the size of her loan. The amount of tax relief will increase along with the size of the loan up to the ceiling entitlement of £30 000. Moreover, until recently, the amount of tax relief also depended upon a person's marginal tax rate: the higher the rate, the more tax relief was received. However, the 1991 budget withdrew the latter concession. None the less the tendency for better-off owner-occupiers to continue to receive larger amounts of tax relief has been widely criticised as being inequitable.

Similarly, the position of owner-occupiers in comparison with renters has also been criticised on grounds of fairness. For as we have seen in our discussion of the private rental and LA housing sectors, households in these tenure groups do not quality for tax relief in the same way as owner-occupiers. It seems therefore that there are strong grounds for believing that tax relief to owner-occupiers is both inefficient and inequitable. Given this conclusion, it is striking that this is the one area of housing policy where there has been only limited reform during the 1980s. Why is this? The answer is almost certainly that the government has wanted to promote owner occupation as a preferred form of tenure for political reasons. While this is a perfectly legitimate objective, economic analysis indicates that this has been achieved at a high cost in terms of efficiency and equity.

# The Market System and Government Policies

Our preceding discussion has suggested that, by themselves, neither the market system nor purely government based systems are likely to bring about an efficient and equitable allocation of housing resources. In the face of these limitations, future policy will need to search for that public/private mix of activity which yields the best achievable results. This should involve a careful assessment of the actual performance of alternative systems of organisation.

On the supply side, it is likely that both private and public sector providers will remain an important feature of the market. Private provision can be expected to dominate production for owner-occupation, whereas the public sector will have a larger role in the rental market. In the latter connection, however, it is worth noting that a third type of supplier has become an increasingly important part of the rental market in recent years. These are non-profit making, private sector organisations, known as Housing Associations, which receive government subsidies to enable them to let property at below market rents. Many people argue that, because of their generally smaller size, Housing Associations are able to be more flexible and responsive to tenants' choices than Local Authority landlords. As such, they provide a means for the government to meet its efficiency and equity objectives – by subsidising the supply of rental housing – without becoming involved directly in its provision.

On the demand side, our criticisms of existing policies suggest two basic elements that any housing policy for the future should incorporate: these are tenure-neutral treatment and income-related subsidies. A tenure neutral system would be one in which households receive equivalent tax and subsidy treatment irrespective of their tenure status. This would promote both greater efficiency and greater equity. However, because its main consequence is likely to be the withdrawal of tax relief for owner-occupiers, it would not be an easy policy to implement politically. On the question of subsidies, if their primary purpose is to ensure that every household obtains at least a socially defined minimum standard of housing, it is essential that payments should be targeted on low-income groups. The housing benefit system has already gone some way towards developing this element of the necessary strategy.

# Summary

The traditional housing objective of providing a decent home for every family at a price within their means is a long way from being met. The private market cannot be relied upon to meet this objective because of certain shortcomings. *Income limitations* prevent families from obtaining adequate housing and thereby lead to an *inequitable* distribution of housing resources. At the same time, *capital market imperfections, imperfect information, supply inelasticity* and *externalities* mean that the market will operate *inefficiently*. In an attempt to overcome these problems a variety of government policies have been introduced, but some of these have produced undesirable consequences of their own. *Rent control* keeps down housing costs for the tenant but reduces the supply of rental housing. In the face of this side effect, current policy is based upon *deregulation*. *Council housing* has overcome supply shortages and provided rental housing at affordable prices but in recent years has paid too little attention to tenants' preferences. During the 1980s over a fifth of the council stock has been sold to its tenants. Subsidies to *owner-occupiers* have been used to encourage the expansion of this sector but have led to major inefficiencies and inequities. Assessment of the experience of the recent past suggests that future policy should aim to encourage a mix of public and private providers on the supply side, while demand-side policies should be based upon *tenure-neutral treatment* and *income-related subsidies*.

# Further Reading

Maclennan (1982) contains a comprehensive treatment of the economics of housing. There are a number of works which examine recent housing policy reforms, including Black and Stafford (1988) and Hills and Mullings (1990). For those interested in an international perspective, OECD (1988c) offers an analysis of recent reforms in the major OECD countries. As far as specific policies are concerned, Albon and Stafford (1987) provide an in-depth economic analysis of rent control, and Hills (1991) provides an excellent discussion of current government policies towards housing subsidies.

# Questions for Discussion

1.  Who are the gainers and losers from the sale of council housing programme?
2.  Discuss the probable consequences of the removal of mortgage interest tax relief upon (i) the price of owner-occupier housing and (ii) its supply.
3.  'The price of housing is high because the price of land is high'. Discuss.
4.  What has been the effect upon the housing market of the increased willingness of clearing banks to make loans for house purchase?
5.  If the encouragement of owner occupation as the preferred form of tenure is accepted as a political objective, what is the most efficient way of pursuing this aim?
6.  What are the advantages of housing associations as suppliers of social housing?
7.  Discuss the possible consequences of the deregulation of the private rental sector.
8.  In Chapter 3 we discuss 'vouchers' in education. Do you think that these could have a role to play in the housing market?
9.  What effect is the replacement of domestic rates by the community charge likely to have on the price of housing?
10. Discuss, with examples, the effect that transport developments have had upon local property markets.

# Social Care

In any society there will be people who have difficulty looking after themselves, and who therefore need care and support from others. The most obvious examples of such people are children; but there are also many adults who find themselves in this position. The latter include some elderly people, those who misuse alcohol and other drugs, and people with physical disabilities, learning difficulties or mental health problems. Many people in these situations are looked after primarily by their families, or occasionally by friends or neighbours. This is sometimes termed 'informal' care and is a far larger source of care than is often realised; a recent study showed that one adult in seven provided such care (Evandrou, Falkingham and Glennerster, 1990, p.7). But other people in this situation are looked after by people outside the family or by institutions. This form of care is increasingly referred to as 'social', or sometimes 'community', care and it is that which will be the concern of this chapter.

Social care may come from a variety of sources, including private market operators, voluntary organisations and state, usually local government, agencies. It is of three main kinds: *residential care*, where the person concerned is cared for in a special home; *domiciliary care*, where people are provided with support in their own homes; and *day care*, where people are looked after during the day in centres or clubs. There is also another kind of activity often included under the heading of social care, although it is rather different from the other types of care described. This is *fieldwork*, where social workers counsel people on the kind of care they need and, if appropriate, help organise it. Sometimes this is undertaken with the active cooperation of the people concerned and their families; but on occasion field workers have to arrange for people to be taken compulsorily into formal care, when they are in danger themselves (as with child abuse cases) or when they might endanger others (as with some forms of mental disturbance).

In recent years, economists have been taking an increasing interest in the resource allocation questions posed by social care. What is the most efficient way to provide such care? What is the most equitable? Should it be left to families to support the individuals concerned as best they can, providing the care themselves or perhaps purchasing it in the private market? Or should the state intervene, either supporting the informal carers in a variety of ways, or by taking over the principal responsibility for care itself? What should be the role of charity or of voluntary agencies? Although, of course, economics on its own cannot provide the answers to all these questions, it can provide a useful framework in which they may be addressed.

In this chapter we explore the contribution of economics to these issues in the same fashion as we have treated other problem areas in this book. We begin with an examination of possible policy objectives in the realm of social care. We then discuss the ability of the market to achieve those objectives without any state intervention, considering the conditions necessary for it to do so and examining whether those conditions are likely to be fulfilled in most situations where social care is required. We conclude with a discussion of possible forms of government intervention in the area, and of the extent to which they might be expected to succeed where the market has failed.

# Objectives

As in other chapters, we may summarise society's principal objectives with respect to social care under the broad headings of efficiency and equity. In this section, we examine these in more detail. We also briefly consider the aim of 'community', as an issue that often arises in this area.

# *Efficiency*

Suppose we are trying to decide on the socially efficient level of a particular form of social care, the number of home helps, say, or of residential places for elderly people. If we could measure the benefits and the costs associated with each 'unit' of care (each home help or residential place), it would be easy to decide upon the efficient level by following the procedures described in the first chapter of the book. This would be the level where the extra or *marginal* social benefit from an additional unit of care equals the extra or *marginal* social cost of providing that unit. For to provide units of care beyond this level would mean providing units whose social costs were greater than their social benefits: a situation that would obviously be inefficient.

Now, although it is a useful theoretical construct, any attempt to apply this concept in practice would encounter major difficulties. The principal ones concern the measurement of social benefits. The benefits of social care are of two different kinds. First, and most obviously, they include any improvement in welfare of the individual in receipt of care. But, second, any comprehensive assessment of the benefits from a particular kind of social care should also include the benefits of that care to 'informal' carers: the saving of time and energy, the psychological relief from having the burden of care lifted, even if only partially, and so on.

The value of either of these benefits is not easy to measure. Those in receipt of care may find it hard to express or articulate their wants or needs and it may therefore be difficult to assess the extent to which those wants or needs are being met by any particular form of care. In such cases, it is possible to use the judgements of professionals such as social workers or doctors as to what a particular individual may need by way of social care. But professionals may be biased towards the form of care in which they are trained (doctors and medicine, for example). Moreover, at the end of the day, they are not the individual concerned and, even with their training, may not fully be able to ascertain precisely what really would contribute to his or her welfare.

The benefits to carers of alternative forms of care may also be difficult to ascertain. There are practical questions as to how to value any time or energy saved. More fundamentally, some informal carers may derive positive pleasure from looking after the person in need of care. Others may be driven, if not by pleasure, then by conceptions of duty or obligation that will only be properly satisfied if they actually provide the bulk of the care themselves. Such people may find themselves divided between the 'satisfaction' of providing care themselves and the desire to be released from the associated burden.

Given the difficulties involved in finding an inclusive measure of social benefits, and hence in specifying efficiency in terms of the relationship between social benefits and social costs, a more limited efficiency objective is to concentrate on the 'cost-effectiveness' of different ways of achieving the same level of benefit. This avoids the problem of measuring the level of benefit. Instead the question becomes: what is the cheapest, or most cost-effective, way of achieving a given level of benefit? This procedure (sometimes called the 'balance of care' model) is illustrated in Figure 5.1 for elderly people. Along the horizontal axis are measured some characteristics of elderly people that lead to their being in need of social care, such as their level of dependency: characteristics that lead to an increasing marginal social cost of care as they become more severe. Along the vertical axis are measured the marginal social costs of alternative forms of care, such as, for elderly people, hospital, residential or domiciliary care. The costs are those necessary for the elderly person concerned to achieve a given level of functioning: for instance, to perform (or to be assisted to perform) the tasks necessary for daily living.

If the diagram can be properly constructed, then the task of choosing the most efficient form of care for an elderly person, in this limited cost-effective sense of efficiency, is straightforward: the form of care with the lowest marginal cost is picked in each case. Thus in the diagram if the elderly person concerned has a degree of dependency in the range $OA$, then the most cost-effective mode of care is domiciliary care; for those in the range $AB$ the cost-effective mode is residential care; and for the range $B$ and beyond it is hospital care.

This balance of care model can be used to cover other client groups. For instance, for children the three care modes could be residential provision, a foster placement, or home under supervision; the characteristics could be level of disturbance or distress; and the benefit a given reduction in that stress. Of course the usefulness of the model in specific cases is dependent on the extent to which the necessary data are available, and so the extent to which the relevant

**FIGURE 5.1**
**The Balance of Care Model**

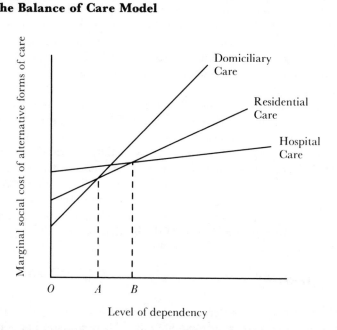

Marginal social cost of alternative forms of care

Domiciliary
Care

Residential
Care

Hospital
Care

*O          A     B*

Level of dependency

concepts can be measured. In particular. for every level of the
relevant characteristic, it is still necessary to find the costs of
attaining an equivalent level of benefit for each mode of care. The
difficulties of this should not be under-estimated. However, the task
is not impossible, and useful estimates can be obtained for key client
groups (see Davies and Knapp, 1988, for a useful summary).

## *Equity*

We can distinguish three interpretations of equity that are commonly
applied in the social care field: minimum standards; equal care for
equal need; and equality of access to care. The minimum standard
interpretation is simply the requirement that everyone in need of
social care should receive at least a minimum amount of it. Equal

care for equal need, and its corollary, unequal care for unequal need, is more ambitious; it requires that care should be distributed solely in relation to need, however the latter is defined. And, as in the case of health care, equality of access can be defined in terms of the costs of care: that everyone should face the same cost of care, where cost is interpreted not simply in financial terms but in the wider sense of including all opportunities forgone or sacrifices made.

However, the question of the cost of social care raises a further equity issue: the distribution of that cost. In practice, the cost or burden of social care rarely falls solely on the individuals in need of such care themselves. It also often devolves upon others, particularly informal carers, such as members of the family or friends. These informal carers on occasion have to make enormous sacrifices to meet the requirements of the person in their care: sacrifices whose equity or fairness is not always obvious. Given that most informal carers had little choice in determining their situation, equity would seem to require a more even distribution of the burden of care.

## *Community*

Finally we should consider an objective that is often raised in the context of social care: that of community. There are two opposing views concerning the aims of social care that could come under this heading. One emphasises the role of the family, arguing that policies towards social care should not undermine the family as the principal provider of care. The other regards the problem of people in need of care as one for the community as a whole to address, not simply the immediate family; moreover, for the community to take on this responsibility would strengthen it. Most people would probably adopt a middle position, acknowledging the importance of the family as a provider of care, but also seeing a role for the wider community in assisting the family, or, in cases where there is no family or the family cannot cope, providing the care itself.

## The Market and Social Care

Now that we have discussed some of the aims that policies concerned with resource allocation in the social care area might have, we must ask the question that has been asked about all the resource allocation problems discussed in this book: why not leave social care to the market to allocate? In particular, it will be recalled that in Chapter 1 we outlined the arguments as to why market allocation of many commodities would be efficient; the principal one was that competitive markets encourage suppliers to take account of the wants of their customers and clients, and the inefficient are driven out of business. Are there any reasons to suppose that markets in social care would be different in this or in other respects?

Critics of markets in social care cite a number of reasons why social care is indeed different. Three of these concern efficiency: *caring externalities*, *imperfect information*, and *irrationality*. Other problems concern *equity* and *community*; in the view of these critics, market allocations will be inequitable and individualistic. We shall look at each in turn.

## *Caring Externalities*

We encountered caring externalities in Chapter 2. Externalities, it will be recalled, arise when the activities of an individual in the market place, whether as producer or consumer, affect third parties who are otherwise in no way involved in the market transactions. A 'caring' externality arises when people feel concern for the care and treatment of others, even though they themselves are not directly affected. In the case of social care, caring externalities will arise if people are distressed either because an individual who needs such care is not receiving it, or because, although in receipt of care, she is unhappy. The provision, or the improvement, of care in such a situation will not only benefit the person concerned (the private or 'internal' benefit) but also the other people who care (the 'external' benefit). If caring externalities exist, then the market will tend to underprovide social care, relative to the socially efficient amount. This is because, when deciding how much care to consume, individuals will only take account of their own private benefit, and not that which accrues to others. For example, an elderly person may decide that, although she would like to, she cannot afford to go into a private residential home: for her, the marginal private cost exceeds the marginal private benefit. Now suppose that a number of her friends and relatives are concerned on her behalf; and the value of their satisfaction if she were to go into the home (the external benefit) and of her own satisfaction (the private benefit), if added together, would exceed the cost of her care in the home. In that case, the social benefit (the private benefit plus the external benefit) is greater than the social cost of residential care for her, and it would be socially efficient for her to enter the home; but under a pure market system this will not happen.

This conclusion could be challenged on the grounds that it ignores the possibility of charity. In this example, would not the people who are concerned about her welfare club together to help the elderly person to buy the necessary care? If they did so, everyone would be better off; the old lady because she was receiving the care she wanted and her friends and relatives because, although they were financially out of pocket, this was more than compensated for by their satisfaction at her being properly looked after.

However, relying on charity as a means of coping with caring externalities (or indeed with any kind of externality) has its own problems. The chief of these is the so-called *free-rider effect*. In our example, each of the relatives or friends may wait to see what others do before committing him- or herself to help: that is, everyone may be tempted to 'free-ride' on some-one else's charitable impulses, with the consequence that no-one actually comes forward to help.

Whether the free-rider effect is a significant problem in practice depends on a number of factors. The greater the numbers of people involved, the more likely it is that there will be free-riders since it becomes easier to conceal any failure to contribute. On the other hand, some people may derive pleasure from the *act* of helping, rather simply from the outcome of that help. Such people will not be tempted to free-ride. There is very little evidence concerning the extent of free-riding in practice; but most social care analysts would consider it doubtful whether charity can be relied upon exclusively as a mechanism for overcoming the inefficiencies of a market with caring externalities.

## Imperfect Information

For a market to function efficiently, all the consumers in that market should be 'perfectly' informed. In particular, they should know what constitutes quality for the good or service concerned, and which providers are offering the best service in terms of quality in relation to price. Further, if they find that the service being offered by a particular supplier is of low quality, they should be able to 'voice' their dissatisfaction with it; and if that is ineffective, they should be able to choose an alternative – that is, to 'exit' from the situation if they so wish. In other words it should be simple to protest about low quality service and/or to switch business away from the suppliers concerned.

But in many areas of social care none of these conditions are fulfilled. The best way to acquire information about the quality of a service being offered is to shop around: that is, to try the services provided by different suppliers and to decide for oneself which is the most appropriate for one's wants or needs. But someone who is elderly and frail, or for someone who is otherwise physically disabled, for instance, shopping around is likely to be at best extremely difficult and at worst quite impossible. More generally, the very reasons why people may be in need of care, their inability to perform the tasks of daily living, may prevent them from being able to obtain the information necessary for them to make an appropriate choice of market-provided care.

This problem is particularly acute in the case of residential care. It is very difficult to discover the quality of care being offered in a residential establishment except by actually living there; and by then it may be too late seriously to explore alternatives. 'Voicing' a protest may be ineffective, unless it is accompanied by a real threat to take one's business elsewhere: that is, to 'exit'. But to exit from a residential establishment without having fully researched possible alternatives is a dangerous thing to do.

## *Irrationality*

Even if people in need of social care *were* perfectly informed about the choices available to them in the market, some of them may not be able to act on that information in a rational manner. This might be the case, for example, for people with mental health problems or with various forms of learning difficulties.

In the absence of any government intervention, what usually happens in such situations is that the relevant decisions are taken by someone else, such as a close relative or friend. However, although this may resolve the problem in some cases, it will not do so in all. In some cases, there may be no relative or friend available. Even if there is, the relative or friend concerned cannot always be relied upon to put the interests of the person on whose behalf they are taking the decisions above their own. They will have their own interests and agendas to pursue; sometimes these may coincide with those of the person in need of care; but sometimes they will not. In such cases the outcome of their decisions may not be the best way of meeting the needs and wants of the individual concerned.

## Equity and Community

We discussed three possible definitions of equity in the social care context: minimum standards, equal care for equal need and equality of access to care. We also drew attention to the issue of the distribution of the cost or burden of care, and argued that equity may require a broad distribution of that burden. There is no real reason to suppose that market allocation will achieve equity in any of these interpretations of the term. Individuals on low incomes will often find it difficult either to purchase social care for themselves or their relatives, or to find the time to provide the care themselves; and, even if they did, there is no guarantee that they could purchase enough, or provide enough themselves, to meet some specified minimum. Differences in purchasing power are also likely to create differences in the amount of care purchased despite similar needs; and, even though a perfectly competitive market should result in everyone facing the same price for different forms of care, the sacrifices involved in meeting that price will be larger for those with lower incomes. Nor is the burden of care likely to be equitably distributed. In a market system it will fall entirely on the person in need of care herself, or on someone, such as a close relative, who feels the duty or obligation to assume it. This does not seem to be necessarily an equitable outcome. In most of the situations where social care is required, the people concerned (or their relatives) have little choice in the matter. Few would choose to be disabled, either physically or mentally; few enjoy being elderly and infirm. Since in many cases the burden of care can be almost overwhelming, equity would seem to require a wider sharing of that burden: but, as we have seen, this is unlikely to be achieved by market allocation on its own.

Similar arguments apply to the aim of community. In markets, the burden of care falls on the individual or on the family. The extent to which this strengthens the family is debatable; the stress of caring for a heavily dependent person is a not infrequent cause of family break up. In the area of social care, as with equity aims, communitarian aims are probably not well served by markets.

# Government Policies

We have discussed a number of reasons why the market allocation of social care is likely to be inefficient or inequitable. However, this does not necessarily imply that government intervention is justified. It may be that in some cases the implementation of government policies creates inefficiencies or inequities of their own; failures which may be at least as great if not greater than the market ones that the policies concerned are trying to correct. In this section we look at some of the problems that might arise.

As in other areas discussed in the book, governments intervene in the market for social care in three ways: provision, subsidisation and regulation. They directly *provide* some of the care concerned, through, for instance, local authority residential homes for elderly people, home help services and meals-on-wheels. They also provide information, advice and counselling; much of the activities of field social workers is of this kind. They *subsidise* care, by using revenues from taxation to reduce any charges levied by 'formal' providers (market or non-market), or by making payments to informal carers (as in payments to foster parents). And they monitor or *regulate* the quantity, quality and price of care offered using inspectors, registration procedures, or, less formally, visits by field social workers.

## *Provision*

Government provision can be viewed as a way of coping with the problems for the market created by imperfect information and irrationality. As we have seen, the inability of people in care to gather the necessary information, or their inability to act on the information even if they have it, can create opportunities for exploitation by market providers of care. Hence a possible justification for the replacement of market providers by government providers is that the latter are not motivated by profit and therefore not subject to the temptation to exploit people's ignorance or irrationality to maximise profits. However, although government providers may not be motivated by profits they may nonetheless be motivated by considerations of their own interests. So, for instance, staff at a government-owned residential home may be tempted to organise the establishment for their own convenience, rather than that of the residents. And they may get away with this for exactly the same reason that market providers get away with exploitation for profit: that is, because the elderly people find it difficult to 'exit' into alternative forms of care. This problem could perhaps resolved if people who could not exit were given a 'voice': for instance, if there were a suitable complaints procedure that could be easily activated and acted upon. However, the same reasons why people are in care in the first place and hence find it difficult to exit, may make it difficult for them to complain effectively, especially if the relevant procedures are complex or energy-consuming.

It should be emphasised that such exploitation is not a *necessary* consequence of government intervention. Many state social workers and residential staff are dedicated solely to the welfare and interests of their clients. However, the danger that some are not is one to which social policy decison-makers have to be always alert. The extent to which this danger is actually realised in practice is a matter not of theoretical speculation, but of empirical investigation.

## Subsidies

Government subsidisation can be viewed as in part a response to the problem of caring externalities. Any good or service that generates externalities will be undersupplied in the market; a subsidy to that service will encourage extra supply and so, if correctly calculated, will correct the shortfall. So payments may be made to formal or informal carers in order to increase the supply of such care and hence promote efficiency.

However, government subsidy will increase the amount of care supplied only if suppliers respond to market incentives. But if they do not – as might happen, for instance, if the suppliers themselves were government owned – then there may be an excess of demand over supply. In that case it will be necessary to use rationing procedures of some kind, such as waiting lists or relying upon the judgement of social workers to decide who gets what. The problem with waiting lists is that the people at the top of the list may have got there by luck or by having the right contacts More generally, certain groups, such as the better educated or the more articulate, may be able to manipulate the system more effectively than others; but they may not be those who want or need the care the most. Delegating the decision to social workers does not necessarily overcome this problem, since they too can be influenced by articulate, confident clients. Even if they are not influenced in this way, in making the relevant decisions social workers may pursue their own interests – and these may not always coincide exactly with those in need of care.

Government subsidy can also be viewed as a mechanism for promoting equity and perhaps also contributing to a spirit of community. The use of revenues from taxation to subsidise the provision of social care is a way of spreading the burden of care so that it does not fall wholly on the individuals or their informal carers. In consequence the cost of care is distributed more evenly – and hence more equitably – throughout the commmunity. Again, however, if rationing procedures have to be used, further inequities may arise, since it will not be necessarily those who need the service most who receive it.

# Regulation

Government regulation can be seen as an alternative response to provision to the problems created for markets in social care by imperfect information and irrationality. Instead of replacing market providers by government ones, the market providers could be controlled by a strict system of monitoring undertaken by field social workers or by inspectors.

However, the motivations of the relevant employees is also a problem for government regulation. In particular, it may suffer from regulator 'capture'. Government regulators, having to deal on a day-to-day basis with the providers whom they are regulating, may establish friendly relationships with those providers, relationships that make it difficult for them to confront providers with any breach of the regulations. If this does occur, then the regulation is likely to end up operating in the interests of the providers rather than the public.

## *Quasi-Markets*

One response to some of the problems with both market allocation and government intervention outlined above is to introduce a system that tries to combine the best elements of both: a 'quasi' or internal market. Such a system has been proposed in the British context in a report by Sir Roy Griffiths (1988), much of which was endorsed in a subsequent White Paper (Department of Health, 1989). Under the Griffiths proposals a 'case-manager' would be appointed for each client whose task would be to construct a package of care for the client concerned. This package could include residential care; or it could be some combination of domiciliary care services (home helps, meals-on-wheels, day centres). In making up the package of care the case-manager would compare the costs and benefits of alternative suppliers of the services concerned, including private sector and voluntary agencies.

This system can be viewed as essentially a 'voucher' system, with each client having an ear-marked budget or voucher which the case-manager can spend on his or her behalf. The allocation of resources would be determined by client choice (as delegated to case-managers) instead of by bureaucratic procedures as at present. Under this system, suppliers would have to compete for custom. They would therefore have to demonstrate to the case-manager that they could offer a service that met the client's requirements (as interpreted by the case-manager) at an appropriate cost. Efficiency would be thereby enhanced.

For these efficiency gains to be realised, however, certain conditions have to be met. In particular, there have to be a sufficient number of actual or potential suppliers; and case-managers must always accurately interpret the needs and wants of their clients. Neither of these conditions will necessarily be fulfilled; the market may not be large enough to attract sufficient suppliers to come forward, and case-managers may follow their own concerns rather than those of their clients.

Quasi-markets in social care may also create problems for equity, especially if the latter is interpreted as requiring care to be related to need. Unless the payment they receive is geared exactly to the client's condition, suppliers will have little incentive to take on those who require large amounts of care. In other words, they may engage in *selection*: that is, faced with a flat payment per client, they will compete for clients who will need relatively little care, while ignoring those who need a lot. If selection of this kind occurs, those who need care the most will receive the least: an outcome that would hardly be equitable. This problem could be overcome if it were possible for clients to 'top-up' their voucher by payments from their own resources. But this creates an equity problem of its own, since the better-off would receive better care and there would again be unequal treatment for equal need.

Overall, quasi-markets in social care may overcome some of the problems for efficiency and equity associated with government intervention. But, as forms of markets, not surprisingly they suffer from some of the problems associated with markets. There is no easy solution to the problem of providing social care equitably or efficiently.

## Summary

The objectives of policies towards social care can be summarised under the headings of *efficiency*, *equity* and *community*. One interpretation of an efficient allocation of social care is where *the marginal social benefit* equals the *marginal social cost*. However, this may present problems in implementation, especially over the measurement of benefits. Hence it may be necessary to rely upon a less ambitious interpretation of efficiency such as that implicit in the *balance-of-care* model, where the aim is simply to minimise the cost of achieving a given level of social care.

Equity can be defined in terms of *minimum standards*, *equal care for equal need*, and *equality of access to care*. A further equity issue concerns the distribution of the cost or the *burden* of care; given that most of the people involved (those in need of care and their 'informal' carers) did not choose to be in their situation there is an equity case for a wider sharing of the burden. This may also foster a spirit of community.

Social care has certain characteristics which mean that market allocation is unlikely to be efficient. These include *caring externalities, imperfect information* and *irrationality*. Also, market allocations will in most cases be *inequitable* and *individualistic*; in particular, they are unlikely to result in an equitable sharing of the burden of care.

Government intervention can take the form of *provision*, *subsidisation* or *regulation*. All of these create problems of their own, however, chiefly arising from the fact that the relevant government agents, professionals, residential staff, or inspectors, do not always have the incentive to pursue the clients' interests instead of their own. This can create both inefficiency and inequity.

Competition may be introduced through some form of *quasi-market*, whereby case-managers purchase care on behalf of clients from a variety of different suppliers. However, again it has to be assumed that case-managers will always act on behalf of their clients and not in pursuit of their own interests. There may also be inequity due to the problem of *selection*.

# Further Reading

Very little has been written on the economics of social care. The only book devoted to the topic is Knapp (1984); luckily this is excellent, and should more than meet the needs of those who wish to pursue the topic further. The balance of care model is outlined and much of the recent empirical work on the costs of alternative forms of care is summarised in Davies and Knapp (1988). The same volume in which this appears (Sinclair, 1988) contains very useful background papers by non-economists on residential care for various client groups. A detailed quantitative analysis of recent developments in social care in Britain can be found in Evandrou, Falkingham and Glennerster (1990).

Among the specific issues mentioned in the text, some of the theoretical and empirical questions concerning the *free-rider effect* are discussed in Sugden (1984). The idea that people must have a real possibility of *exit* for markets to work efficiently was first put forward (although not in a social care context) by Hirschman (1970). 'Case-management' and other *quasi-market* reforms were proposed in the Griffiths report (1988) and in the subsequent Government White Paper (Department of Health, 1989). The development of quasi-markets in social care (and in other parts of the welfare state) has led to a growing interest in their advantages and disadvantages as methods of resource allocation; a preliminary discussion can be found in Le Grand (1989b, 1990).

# Questions for Discussion

1. 'Measuring the benefits from social care is quite impossible. Hence any attempt to define efficiency in terms of the relationship between social benefits and costs is a waste of time'. Do you agree?

2. How would you define an equitable distribution of social care? How would you define an equitable distribution of the *burden* of care?

3. Discuss the extent to which the conditions for markets to be efficient are met in the case of social care. Do you think there are significant differences in this respect between residential care and domiciliary care?

4. 'The best way to correct inequities in the distribution of social care is not to intervene in the market for such care. Rather it is to correct the inequities in the distribution of income that caused them in the first place.' Discuss.

5. What are the problems created by government subsidy for the efficient allocation of social care? What are the implications for equity?

6. 'The fact that people in need of social care are often irrational or ill-informed creates as many problems for the government provision of that care as for market allocation'. Do you agree?

7. Can quasi-markets in social care capture the advantages of market allocation while avoiding its problems?

# The Environment

Concern over the environment is not new. In the fourteenth century a royal document complained about the 'abominable and most filthy stinks' generated by the activities of London butchers in Seacoal Lane. In the sixteenth century laws were passed prohibiting the use of coal fires in London, and in the 1850s perfumed sheets were hung over the House of Commons' windows to try and reduce the smell of the Thames. In the United States a magazine commented in 1881 that 'no dumping ground, no sewer, no vault contains more filth . . . [than] the air in certain parts of [New York] City during the long season of drought'. Chicago's air was described by Rudyard Kipling in 1880 as 'dirt' and its river by another visitor as 'coated with grease so thick on its surface it seemed like a liquid rainbow' (quoted in Bettman, 1974).

More recently concern over the environment has increased. This partly reflects a growing awareness of the impact of pollution on health and welfare, such as that of lead from car exhausts on children living in urban areas. But it also arises from ecological concerns. To fish or swim in unpolluted rivers and seas; to prevent 'global warming'; to protect species endangered by indiscriminate dumping of waste: these and similar environmental considerations have acquired a more important place in society's scale of values in recent decades.

Corresponding to this increase in social concern, there has been an expansion of interest among economists in environmental problems, and in this chapter we shall consider some of their contributions. As in previous chapters we shall begin by examining society's objectives with respect to the environment and pollution in particular. Should

**134**

the aim be to eliminate pollution altogether, as some ecologists want? Should we ignore it as an overrated problem, as some industrialists imply? Or should we find some kind of balance? Obviously the answers to these questions are going to depend in part on basic value judgements concerning the quality of human life, the value to be placed on lives of persons not born and so on; judgements about which economists – in their role as economists – have little to say. But the application of economics can help to place these judgements within a coherent framework that is useful for the formulation of social policy, and this is the subject of the first section.

The next section concerns the role of the market system with respect to pollution. Will the market achieve society's objectives concerning the state of the environment on its own? Or is some form of government intervention necessary? It will become apparent that pollution as a problem arises from the structure of property rights that underlie the operations of the market; accordingly the third section investigates property rights in more detail. In the fourth, we examine government policies in relation to the environment. We consider not the technological methods of controlling pollution – these lie in the engineer's province – but the various tools of legal and fiscal policy that can be used to cope with the problem. For simplicity the discussion is generally confined to air and water pollution, but the arguments are general and can be applied to other environmental problems, such as noise, pesticides or the disposal of solid wastes.

# Objectives

As in other chapters, society's objectives concerning the environment can be usefully summarised in terms of efficiency and equity. Economists have tended to concentrate on the efficiency objective and this emphasis will inevitably be reflected in what follows, but equity issues will not be ignored.

## *Efficiency*

It may seem curious to apply the notion of 'efficiency' to something as obviously 'inefficient' as environmental damage and pollution.

Indeed, many people feel that the efficient level of pollution is none at all. But those who think this way have usually only considered the benefits from controlling pollution; they have not considered its costs. In a world where resources are scarce, resources that are devoted to restricting pollution will not be available for fulfilling other goals. For instance, consider a chemical firm using a nearby river as a convenient place to dump untreated waste products. If it were forced to treat its waste it would have to install pollution control equipment – the manufacture and operation of which would use up resources that could have been employed in the production of other commodities. It would charge higher prices for its products, thus imposing greater costs on its customers and, except in the most unlikely circumstances, reducing its profits. Indeed, if the treatment requirement were strict enough, it might be forced out of business altogether, thus creating unemployment and personal hardship for its workers. This is not to say that it might none the less be socially desirable to prevent the firm polluting the river; the harm done by the pollution might greatly outweigh the beneficial effects of the lower prices and greater employment. It is merely to illustrate the general point that pollution control has its costs: costs that cannot be ignored in any assessment of its overall desirability.

So how should these costs be taken into account when formulating the efficiency objective? To see how this might be done in a specific case, let us take the chemical firm mentioned above. Suppose that the principal effect of the pollution is to kill a large proportion of the river's otherwise thriving fish population; and suppose further that this is seriously affecting the business of a commercial fishery downstream. To simplify matters, let us make two other assumptions; first that no-one else is affected by the pollution, and second that the only way the chemical firm can reduce its pollution is by cutting back its production of chemicals.

Table 6.1 puts flesh on the bones of the example by providing some hypothetical numbers. The first column shows the amount of chemical produced by the upstream firm. (To keep the numbers manageable, this is given in units of a single ton. In practice the relevant numbers would be much larger; however, the principle will not be affected by the choice of units). The second column shows the price the firm receives for each ton it sells; we assume that it is in competition with other producers and therefore has to accept the going market price ($£40$). The third column shows the cost to the

**TABLE 6.1**
**Costs of Chemical Production**

| Tons of chemical produced (1) | Price per ton ($£$) (2) | Cost of firm of producing an extra ton ($£$) (3) | Pollution damage to fishery of an extra ton of production ($£$) (4) | Social cost of producing an extra ton ($£$) (5) = (4) + (3) |
|---|---|---|---|---|
| 1 | 40 | 34 | 3 | 37 |
| 2 | 40 | 35 | 3 | 38 |
| 3 | 40 | 37 | 3 | 40 |
| 4 | 40 | 40 | 3 | 43 |
| 5 | 40 | 44 | 3 | 47 |

firm of producing each extra ton. This cost increases with each ton produced, reflecting the fact that, say, the firm has to bring older machines into use as its scale of production increases (see the discussion of production costs in Chapter 1). The fourth column shows the damage to the downstream fishery's business that results from the extra waste dumped in the river every time the chemical firm increases its production by a ton; for simplicity, we assume this is constant although in practice it may well increase with each ton produced. The final column shows the combined cost to both the chemical firm and the fishery of producing an extra ton of chemical. Since no-one else is affected, this is the total cost to society of each ton: hence we shall call it the *social cost*.

What is the efficient level of chemical production? If we assume that the market price for the chemical ($£40$) reflects the value that the chemical's users place on it, then the social benefits – in terms of that value – derived from the production of the first ton exceeds its social cost ($£37$). The same is true for the second ton, despite the fact that the costs have increased slightly (to $£38$). The cost of producing the third ton ($£40$) equal the benefits from producing it; hence that ton is also (just) worth producing. However, the social costs of producing each of the fourth and fifth tons ($£43$ and $£47$ respectively) are greater than the social benefits from doing so. Hence the socially efficient level is three tons – the point where the extra social costs of further production begin to exceed the social benefits. Note that at this level there will still be some damage to the fishery; social efficiency does not necessarily require the total elimination of pollution, nor of the damage it creates.

In the example we have concentrated upon the increase in costs and benefits associated with each extra or *marginal* unit of production. In previous chapters we have called these marginal costs and benefits. Moreover, in the example there were two kinds of marginal cost – the cost of production to the factory, which we can term the marginal private cost (*mpc*), and the cost imposed on the fishery outside the factory, which we term the marginal external cost (*mec*). These combine to form the marginal social cost (*msc*) of production, or:

$$\text{marginal private cost } + \text{ marginal external cost } =$$
$$\text{marginal social cost}$$

On the benefits side, since there are no extra benefits accruing to third parties from the production of the chemical, we can assume that there is no difference between the marginal private benefit (*mpb*) and the marginal social benefit (*msb*): both are, in this case, equal to the price. Hence what the example has shown is that the efficient level of a pollution-generating activity is at the point where the marginal social benefit of the activity equals its marginal social cost.

A useful way of presenting the argument is through a diagram such as Figure 6.1. The horizontal axis shows different levels of a pollution-generating activity, and the vertical axis the marginal costs and benefits of the activity. The numbers used in constructing the diagram are taken from Table 6.1, but it should be emphasised that the diagram, and the point it illustrates, could refer to any activity that creates pollution, from private motoring to oil tankers flushing their tanks at sea. The *mpc* and *msc* curves show how marginal private and marginal social costs respectively increase with the scale of the activity; the difference between them at any point is equal to the marginal external cost at that level of the activity. The *msb* curve shows the marginal social benefit for each level of activity. In this case it is a straight line because in the example the marginal social benefit was equal to price and therefore constant; however, there is no reason to suppose it will be so in all cases.

## FIGURE 6.1
## Costs and Benefits of Chemical Production

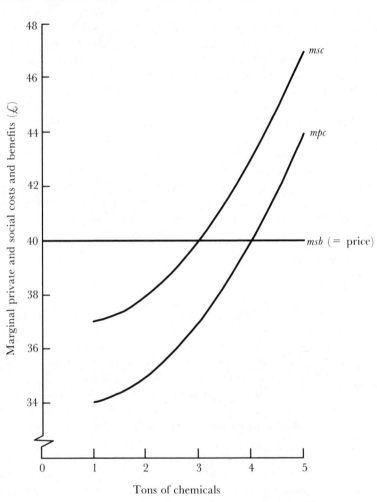

Now the efficient level of activity will be that corresponding to the intersection of the *msb* and *msc* curves. For at any level below this the extra benefit from increasing the scale of the activity will be greater than the costs from doing so; and at any level above it, the extra costs will be greater than the benefits. Note, however, that there is a range of activity beyond the socially efficient point (from 3 to 4 in the diagram) where the *msb* curve lies above the *mpc* curve; this is an important point to which we shall return in the next section.

We have thus found a suitable definition for the efficient level of a pollution-generating activity – the point at which the sum of the marginal private and marginal external costs of the activity begin to exceed its marginal social benefits. Although we will see later that implementing this definition in practice presents some severe difficulties, it is none the less an important conceptual idea that is useful for clarifying discussion. But efficiency is not the only objective a society may have with respect to pollution control. Others, in particular the promotion of equity, may also be important.

## *Equity*

Equity issues arise when the question of who should pay for pollution control is considered. At first sight this might seem simple; since it is the polluter who creates the problem, it should be the polluter who pays. But is this always the equitable solution? Suppose a factory making inexpensive clothes for the poor was polluting a particular river, and a group of rich boat owners wanted the river cleaned up so that they could sail their boats on it. Making the factory pay would raise the prices of the clothes it produces so making the poor worse off; would this be fair? It might be more equitable to make the boat owners – who, after all, are going to be the ones who benefit – pay for the river to be cleaned. More generally, the question as to who should pay will depend on the situations of the parties involved. The issue may be particularly relevant in the case of global pollution, where polluters are often third world countries with very low incomes per capita. In general the equity of a particular system of pollution control cannot be resolved by simple rules such as 'the polluter should always pay': rather, the judgement will vary with the situation.

# The Market System and the Environment

It is a demonstrable fact in our society that environmental damage and the market system coexist. But pollution in some form or other exists in almost all societies regardless of their economic organisation. No society has reduced environmental damage to zero, and it is unlikely that any ever will. So the question we must ask ourselves about the market system is whether environmental damage as a problem is inherent within the market system. An activity, almost by definition, becomes a problem when society's objectives with respect to it are not being attained. In this particular case we shall concentrate on efficiency and ask whether it is likely to be attained in the market. In the terms developed in the previous section, does the market system result in the marginal social benefit of a pollution-generating activity being equal to its marginal social cost?

The chief characteristic of a market system, as emphasised in Chapter 1, is that it consists of many individuals and firms, all making separate decisions on the basis of the costs and benefits to themselves of those decisions. Thus they are largely concerned with the private costs and benefits of undertaking certain activities and do not necessarily consider all the social costs and benefits. For instance, a mining company trying to decide whether to start operations in an area of outstanding natural beauty will consider only its own costs; it will not take account of the cost to those using the area for recreation. Similarly an airline, in considering whether to start a new night service, will only consider the costs and benefits accruing to it from this operation; it will not consider the cost to the people who live under the proposed flight path of the aircraft. Since social efficiency will only be achieved if social costs, that is private plus external costs, are taken into account, we can conclude the market system will not – on its own – achieve efficiency.

This can be illustrated by reference to our example. In making the decision about how much chemical to produce, the chemical firm will compare the marginal private cost from each ton with the extra revenue it can obtain by selling it. In this case the extra revenue – termed the *marginal revenue* – is equal to the price. So if the price is greater than the marginal private cost, then the firm will make a profit on that ton; if it is less, the firm will make a loss. Now for each of the first four tons, the price is greater than (or, in the case of the fourth, equal to) the marginal private cost; hence it will be profitable to the firm to produce up to that level. In terms of Figure 6.1, the firm will produce up to the point at which the *mpc* curve intersects the price line. However, as we saw in the last section, the efficient level of production is only three tons: the point at which the *msc* curve intersects the price line. Hence the actual level of production will be greater than the efficient level.

Now it could be argued that, in cases such as this where there are only two parties involved, this conclusion is incorrect. For it assumes that the party affected by the pollution will not react in any way to the fact its business is being damaged by the other party's activities. But it is equally plausible to suppose that the fishery will take steps to try to persuade the chemical firm to reduce its pollution. For instance, it might offer a deal to the chemical firm: reduce chemical output in return for some compensation for any loss in profits that would occur. Now the maximum compensation that the fishery would be prepared to offer would be £3 per ton of chemical output reduced; if it offered more than that, the gain it would make from the reduction in pollution would be more than offset by the amount it had to pay in compensation. Suppose it does in fact offer up to £3 per ton reduced. Then the chemical firm has to take account of the fact that for each ton of output it produces, it loses up to £3 worth of possible compensation from the fishery. In other words, its 'costs' of producing each ton have risen by £3. Reference to Table 6.1 will quickly reveal that, when this extra cost is taken into account, production of the first three tons remains profitable but production of the fourth does not. Hence the firm will reduce its production to three tons – the efficient level. In terms of Figure 6.1, the effect of the compensation offer is to push up the *mpc* curve until it lies along the *msc* curve: so the new *mpc* curve intersects the *msb* curve at the efficient level.

This conclusion is quite striking. It suggests that if bargaining of this kind can take place between the parties involved, an efficient level of pollution-generating activity will be achieved without the need for government intervention. If the chemical firm pollutes the river, the fishery, if it owns the rights to clean water, will demand compensation or sue. If it does not own the right to clean water, it will bribe the chemical firm to reduce the pollution. This approach, associated most closely with Coase (1960), who advocated using the legal system to deal with the problem of externalities, has strong implications for policy. It suggests the emphasis on the polluter paying is not necessarily valid from an efficiency perspective. It is as appropriate that the injured party, or indeed the government, pay subsidies to the polluter to reduce pollution to the efficient level.

In practice, however, this approach suffers from a number of problems. First, the example outlined above assumed one polluter and one 'pollutee'. Most cases of pollution involve large numbers of firms or individuals. The striking of private bargains in this case would be very costly. In some cases it might not be possible to reach a private deal – for example if there were opportunities for certain parties to *free-ride* on others, bearing none of the costs but gaining from the actions of others. Second, the model assumes that property rights are clearly defined, so that it is clear who should be paying whom. If property rights are not clearly defined, bargaining may be extremely costly or not possible at all. (We examine property rights in more detail in the next section). Finally, many cases of pollution affect the next generation. For example, while the extent of destruction of the ozone layer by carbon emissions is not known precisely at present, its occurrence will affect future generations more than those currently causing the emissions. In this case, it is not clear who will bargain on behalf of the next generation. The Coase solution, while it may not be possible to implement in practice, does shed light on the reason for the divergence between private and social costs. Externalities arise because markets are incomplete; certain assets, such as clean air or water, are not owned by anyone. To understand this, let us look in more detail at property ownership and externalities.

# Property Rights and Pollution

For you to 'own' a piece of property means simply that you have certain rights over the use of that property. For instance, if you own a car you have the right to drive it when you want, and the right to prevent other people driving it. If you own a house you have the right to live in it or to rent it out for someone else to live in. However, very rarely will you have the right to do anything you please with your property. In most societies, for instance, you will not have the right to knock people down with your car or to drive it at top speed through urban areas. Nor if you are a house owner are you likely to have the right to use your house for a brothel or bomb factory. Thus the owners of property have conferred on them, by virtue of their ownership, a carefully restricted set of rights as to the use of that property. Ownership of property means nothing more and nothing less than the ownership of certain rights.

Now one of the most important rights that property owners have in market economies is the right to sell their property. They can transfer all the rights they possess with reference to a particular piece of property to another person and obtain some compensation in return. Thus if you own a ton of steel, you have the right to sell this steel to a car firm and to receive a payment in return. In fact, given the structure of property rights, the only way the car firm can ensure that it has obtained the appropriate rights over the use of the steel is by buying it from you. It does not have the right, for example, simply to use the steel as if it were its own. The trading of property rights is the essential feature of a market economy.

However, there are some resources over which no private individual has any rights. Air is one and water (in most cases) is another. If motorists use the atmosphere as a dumping ground for the waste gases from their cars, they do not have to pay any compensation. If they did have to pay, then the cost would become an internal or private cost, and one they would have to take into account when making decisions about driving. Or consider the chemical firm and the fishery. Suppose there were fishing rights associated with the river and the fishery owned those rights. Then the chemical firm would have to pay the fishery for the use of the river and the external cost would become a private one.

The difference between private and external costs or benefits thus derives from the existence or non-existence of certain property rights. Individuals or firms will incur private costs when they have to pay compensation in order to obtain rights over certain pieces of property; they will create external costs when they use pieces of property and are not required to compensate those adversely affected.

As a consequence of this kind of argument, a remedy for the pollution problem of a fundamental kind has been put forward by Mishan (1969). He suggests that property rights should be extended to cover environmental features. When someone purchases a piece of land, for example, the bundle of property rights obtained by virtue of the purchase should include a set of 'amenity' rights. These might include the rights that any air or water in the vicinity of the property should be of reasonable quality, that the owner should not be disturbed unduly by noise, and that the view should not be disfigured. If property owners did possess such rights, argues Mishan, then they could demand compensation when those rights were infringed. In that case, the hitherto external costs for the polluters would become internal ones (in that they would now be forced to pay for them) and they would have to make their production decisions accordingly. As a result, they would produce an efficient level of pollution.

This solution is along the lines of the Coase approach and involves the use of the legal system to internalise externalities by creating new property rights. It deals with the problem of externalities in a fundamental way. But for it to work a number of conditions must be met. First, it must be possible to clearly allocate rights to amenities. However, the very nature of those amenities is such that it is generally not possible to allocate exclusive property rights. Take the rights to clean air. If one person were given the rights to clean air, it would not be possible to exclude non-payers from using the air. Thus allocation of rights would not be feasible. In those cases in which it was possible to grant exclusive rights (for example over a river or fishery) this allocation of hitherto shared resources would have implications for equity. Those granted the rights would either have the right to pollute or would receive money for not polluting. If those granted the rights got them because they had power to influence the division of amenity rights and those who did not were not powerful, this allocation might contravene equity considerations. Such issues might be important in an international context – for example, certain powerful nations may be able to claim rights over the sea round their countries and to defend these while poorer nations would be unable to prevent other countries intruding on their allocation of the sea.

Second, in order to set compensation it must be possible to identify how much pollution is occurring. However, typically we lack precise information on both the nature of externalities and the costs and benefits of alternative methods of dealing with them. Indeed, uncertainty is a pervasive characteristic of environmental problems. It will be at least a decade before we can be establishing whether global warming is really occurring, or whether climatic change we are currently experiencing is merely part of a cycle unrelated to emissions of carbon gases into the atmosphere. Even if this were known, the precise relationship between the emission of carbon gases and the extent of damage to the environment may not be possible to establish. Thus to set an appropriate level of compensation would be very difficult, if not impossible.

Third, even if it were possible to clearly establish rights, unless only two parties were involved, all the bargaining problems outlined in our discussion of the Coase proposals would be present. Finally, the allocation of property rights has implications for equity; the owner of the resource will have the right to use the amenity as they wish or may receive payment from others for not using it. Decisions over who has what rights could therefore be extremely contentious, involve very high legal (transactions) costs and may lead to a distribution of resources judged to be inequitable.

# Government Policies

Environmental problems and pollution arise directly from certain features of the market system. Governments have a number of options to try and remedy market failure; as in other markets, they can intervene through provision, regulation and taxes or subsidies. In addition, governments can create marketable property rights. All these methods have associated advantages and disadvantages and in this context of environmental damage, some are more likely to be more useful in the achievement of efficiency and equity goals than others. We now examine each in turn.

## *Provision*

Direct provision would involve the government taking over pollution-generating activities. For efficiency, it would run them at a level at which the net social costs of output of each good produced was equal to net social benefits, where social costs include pollution and damage to current and future generations. Government ownership of modes of transportation (for example, trains and buses) and of utilities (electricity and water) has been justified on the grounds that government provision may bring the level of output closer to the efficient level. However, the success of these enterprises in achieving an efficient level of output is far from clearly established. To achieve efficient levels of output, governments must first have knowledge of the relationship between output and pollution and second, government production must not result in inefficiencies. In practice, neither requirement is likely to be met.

With respect to the first factor, a common characteristic associated with environmental damage is uncertainty. It is not known how the output of certain substances is linked to environmental damage. While governments may know more than private individuals, they do not have the information required to choose efficient levels of production. With regard to the second, government provision of goods and services may be associated with efficiency failure. These types of failure are discussed at length elsewhere in the book (see especially Chapter 10) and therefore will not be further discussed here; all we need to note here is that government provision of goods and services which cause associated environmental damage is unlikely to be efficient and in some instances, for example in Eastern Europe, government production has been associated with very high levels of pollution.

## *Regulation*

In practice, regulation is the most common form of controlling pollution. Most countries have restrictions on the smoke emissions from private homes and manufacturing industry, they require vehicle exhausts to meet certain standards and they (usually) regulate the waste that can be dumped into rivers or the sea. Now regulation of the right kind can produce an efficient level of pollution control. If the government has sufficient information concerning all pollution-generating activities, it can work out the efficient level of each activity (and hence the socially efficient level of pollution control) and pass laws compelling individuals and firms to operate at that level. But the amount of information required would be enormous. For instance, in Figure 6.1, the government would need to know the exact positions of the *msb* and *msc* curves; to find these, it would need to know full details of chemical prices, of the chemical firm's private costs and of the external costs to the fishery. Multiply these requirements by the number of actual instances of pollution in modern society, and it will be apparent that the task of collecting the relevant information would be enormous. In practice, no government undertakes this task; instead, regulations are usually set in a fairly arbitrary, and hence inefficient, manner.

It is possible to imagine a system of regulation that would achieve a given pollution standard at minimum cost. If the government possessed information concerning the costs of pollution control for all the polluters concerned, it could identify those for whom such control was cheapest and legislate for them to be compelled to undertake the required amount of control. However, the information requirements to do this properly are again impossibly large. Hence, in practice, most governments using pollution regulation (and most governments do so most of the time) simply pass laws that are uniform in application, for example, that all polluters should cut back by a certain percentage, or that no polluter should emit more than a specific amount of untreated waste. This is obviously not efficient, as it means the extent of reduction is not related to the cost of cutting back. In addition, there is no incentive for the firm to cut levels of emissions to below the regulated level.

Regulation is also associated with the problem of *regulator capture*. Those being regulated may be able to persuade the regulator to act in their interests, rather than those of society as a whole. It has been argued that regulator capture may be less of a problem when the government does not own the polluter. If the polluter is in the public sector (that is, the state is also the provider), the representatives of the electors, the politicians, are answerable for the performance of the firm. They may be more interested in keeping down costs than raising costs by spending more on maintaining environmental standards. In the case of the UK water industry, it has been argued (Helm and Pearce, 1990) that government ministers frequently acted as apologists for the low standards of water quality when water was publicly owned. Now the industry is privatised, governments are still responsible for water quality but have no responsibility to the shareholders of water companies. On the other hand, private ownership means the government has less access to information and thus regulation may be less effective.

## Taxes and Subsidies

One way to achieve the same end as regulation but which requires less information is to use taxation or, as it is more commonly known in the pollution context, charging. If the costs of the pollution and the relationship between the production of a good and the production of pollution were known, a tax or charge could be levied on the emission of pollution itself. It could be set in such a way as to achieve efficiency. This is often termed an effluent charge.

We shall illustrate how these kinds of taxes or charges could be used by considering the effect of imposing an effluent charge on the chemical firm in our example. Suppose that it is known that for each ton of chemical produced, one thousandth of a ton of effluent flows into the river. From Table 6.1 it is known that this causes £3 of damage to the fishery. Then let us impose a charge of £3 for each thousandth of a ton of effluent. Then the costs to the firm of producing chemicals would rise by £3 per ton (since each ton of chemical output results in 1/1000th of a ton of effluent). Not only would the cost of producing a ton of chemicals rise, but it would rise by exactly the amount of the external cost imposed by that production. The external costs would thus become internalised; that is, they would become part of the private costs that the firm considers when making its production decisions. In terms of Figure 6.1, the effect of the charge would be to shift up the *mpc* curve until it occupied the same position as the *msc* curve. The firm would now find that, at the old level of production, its marginal private costs including the charge were greater than the price. Hence it would reduce production to the point where they were equal to one another again. Since marginal private costs including the charge are equal to marginal social costs, this will also be the point where marginal social cost equals the price – the efficient level.

Now the significant feature of this result is that all the government has to know to impose the charge is the value of the damage done to the fishery. To achieve the same end by regulation, the government needs to know not only the value of the damage but also full details of the chemical firms' costs and revenues, a much more demanding requirement. Hence, in this case, to achieve a socially efficient level of pollution-generating activity by charging requires far less information than by regulation. Effluent charging means pollution standards may be met at lowest cost. If, say, an effluent charge is levied on untreated waste then those polluters for whom the charge is greater than the cost of treating their effluent will cut back; those who face expensive treatment costs will prefer to continue polluting and pay the charge, Setting the charge at a carefully chosen level will ensure that the 'right' amount of pollution control is undertaken, and this control will be undertaken by those who find it cheapest to do so. Hence, in contrast to the situation under uniform regulation, the pollution standard will be achieved at minimum cost. A further advantage of this kind of scheme is that it offers a continuing incentive for polluters to cut their pollution. Under regulation, once polluters have met the regulation, they have no incentive to reduce their discharge any further. Under a taxation scheme, however, each unit of untreated waste that they discharge carries a price tag – an inducement to attempt to cut the costs of treatment.

Perhaps surprisingly, it is possible to devise a system of subsidy that has the same advantage over regulation as a system of charging. Suppose a subsidy is paid to the chemical firm to reduce its output below the level at which it would operate if there was no government intervention. Suppose further that the subsidy took the form of an amount for each unit of output reduced that was equal to the value of the damage caused by that unit to the fishery. In that case, for every extra ton of chemical produced by the firm, it would forego a subsidy equal to £3. This foregoing of subsidy becomes part of the firm's costs of production, for the production of each ton of chemicals not only incurs the usual costs of raw materials, labour and so on, but also loses it £3. Hence the effect of the subsidy is to raise the firm's *mpc* curve in exactly the same way as the output charge did! (In effect the subsidy is operating in a similar fashion to the compensation offered by the fishery in our earlier discussion of bargaining). The outcome will therefore be the same. The firm will produce at the point where the price it obtains for its product equals its marginal private cost of production, including the foregoing of subsidy, a point which, since the new *mpc* equals the *msc*, will be the socially efficient level. And again the only information required by the government will be the value of the damage to the fishery.

Subsidies and taxes do have different effects on the incentives to enter an industry. Profits in a polluting industry are higher under subsidies than under taxes. Hence, a subsidy scheme will encourage entrants into an industry while taxes will discourage entrants. If there are alternative ways of producing a good which have lower associated negative effects on the environment (say wind production instead of coal production of energy), then taxes will be preferable to subsidies. Taxes and subsidies also have different equity implications. If subsidies are used, taxpayers pay to limit environmental damage while polluters do not; under a tax system, the polluters pay whilst taxpayers benefit. Which is more equitable depends on judgements about the relative position of the polluters and those paying the subsidy. If the polluters were poor and the tax payers rich, a subsidy system might be preferred. Such a situation could well occur in the international area, where rich countries pay poor countries to reduce their emissions of ozone damaging CFCs. Tax receipts can also be used to promote equity; for example, an environmental tax on rich countries could be used to subsidise poor countries to reduce their pollution. Taxes and subsidies can also be used in conjunction to lower pollution; for example the producers of energy produced from fossil fuels could be taxed and the proceeds used for research into non-polluting energy production.

Taxes and subsidies are clearly superior to regulation but the information costs are nevertheless still high. Certain types of pollution – that from motor vehicles, for example – come from an enormous number of separate sources; in such cases it is impossible to attribute one particular piece of damage to one particular polluter. Even when this can be done it is often very difficult, if not impossible, to place a monetary value on the damage caused. What is the cost to a child of a reduction in intelligence due to lead pollution? What is the value of a beautiful valley destroyed by strip mining? Or of a river poisoned by pesticides run off from adjacent farmland? Attempts have been made to place money values on these kinds of damage (usually based on how much people are prepared to pay to avoid them), but the methods involved are controversial and expensive.

Given that it is often impossible to design a tax which precisely reflects the cost of pollution at the margin, two proxy solutions are often adopted. The first is to tax inputs to an industry which has caused environmental damage. An example would be a tax on carbon-producing fuels, on the basis of their approximate carbon pollution potential. This increases the price of these inputs and encourages substitution towards fuels with lower pollution potential (for example, gas for coal) and encourages production of energy using non-fossil fuels (for example, nuclear or wind). The disadvantage is that all users of the input would be treated the same and the most efficient plants in pollution reduction face the same increase in input price as the least efficient. A second option is to tax the output of a good which is associated with the production of pollution. An example would be a tax on electricity. This will reduce electricity consumption, and so pollution, provided consumers are responsive to price changes, and lower their purchase of electricity. However, an output charge has the disadvantage that all industries producing electricity are penalised and not just those which are polluters. So for example, if electricity were produced by both coal fired power stations, which caused environmental damage, and wind powered stations which did not, both types of producer would be equally penalised. However, if the tax revenues from the output tax were used to subsidise the non-polluting industries, this problem could be overcome.

Sometimes taxes may have perverse effects. The example of the wind powered versus the coal fired power station is one – society may not want to penalise the wind producer but would do so with a output tax on electricity. Problems may be particularly severe in the international arena. Much damage to the environment affects a number of countries, some affects all countries. A tax in one country, say the UK, on users of energy would increase the price of the UK goods traded on the world market. This would encourage the production of these goods by countries with no energy taxes, so possibly increasing, rather than decreasing, global pollution. As noted above, there will be equity implications. Imposition of either an input or an output tax will reduce production in the polluting industries and so employment. The tax on outputs will also affect the price of the good being taxed. In the case where the responsiveness of demand to price changes is small, the effect of this increase in price will be to reduce the disposable income of the consumers of the good. If the good is heavily consumed by the poor, this may be regarded as undesirable. Despite all these drawbacks, taxes, however crude, may provide an attractive alternative to regulation.

## Pollution Rights

Pollution taxes regulate the emission of pollutants by means of changing prices. But if individuals are not responsive to price changes, prices may be a poor way to change behaviour. In addition, as we have seen, considerable information, some of which may not even exist, is needed to set taxes to achieve socially optimal levels of output. An alternative, suggested by Dales (1968) is to market pollution rights; pollution quotas which can be traded. Under this scheme the government would sell to polluters a number of 'rights to pollute', the number of which would be limited by the level of environmental quality desired in the area. Potential polluters would have to bid for these rights as the number of rights they owned would determine how much pollution they could undertake. Those who found pollution control expensive would be prepared to bid more to obtain these rights than those who found it cheap; hence the former would obtain the rights and the latter would not. The result would be that polluters with high treatment costs would continue to pollute, but would have to pay the authority for the right to do so, while polluters with low costs would have to treat their discharge. The end effect, therefore, is exactly the same as in the case of charging, but with one important difference: the 'charge' has been set by the firms themselves by bidding against one another. Thus the authority need have no information concerning the firms' costs, nor does it need to engage in clumsy trial-and-error procedures. All it has to do is to issue the rights and arrange for their sale. Pollution abatement will be concentrated in the low-cost polluters (because they will not need to buy so many pollution rights) and this will minimise the compliance costs of the scheme. This scheme has been used under the US Clean Air Act. Some debate exists as to whether improvements in air quality have been achieved but it does not appear to have deteriorated. In addition, the costs of achieving this level of quality have been considerably lower than under regulatory schemes (Hahn and Hester, 1989).

# Summary

Any assessment of the *efficient* level of pollution control must take account of the fact that it involves *costs* as well as *benefits*. Given the existence of such costs, we can define the socially efficient level of pollution-generating activity as the point at which the *marginal social benefit of the activity equals its marginal social cost*. In general, the market system will not achieve this level because in such a system decisions are made on the basis of private costs and benefits which, in the absence of the relevant property rights, diverge from social costs and benefits.

Government intervention can take the form of *provision, regulation,* taxation or *charges,* and *subsidy.* Of these, provision raises issues well beyond the question of pollution control and is therefore rarely considered in that context. Regulation, charging and subsidy can all achieve efficient levels of pollution-generating activity, but regulation requires far more *information* than the other two. However, the implementation of an efficient charging or subsidy scheme requires more information than is generally available.

Given the information difficulties, governments generally do not try to achieve perfect social efficiency in practice but simply set pollution *standards* on a fairly arbitrary basis. These can be attained in a variety of ways; the two most commonly debated are *regulation* and *taxes.* In principle *regulations* that are specific to individual polluters can achieve pollution standards at *minimum* cost, but in practice the lack of relevant information means that uniform regulations are applied. *Charging* schemes may be applied to inputs or outputs. They can generally achieve a given degree of pollution control at less cost than uniform regulation, but they may have considerable implementation problems. They may also have perverse side effects. One method of overcoming these problems is to auction pollution 'rights' to potential polluters, the number of rights for sale being determined by the relevant pollution standard.

# Further Reading

The literature on the economics of the environment is growing rapidly. A comprehensive introduction to this is Baumol and Oates (1988) and another is Pearce and Turner (1990). An assessment of the use of economic tools in environmental management that is (just) accessible to the non-economist is given in Helm and Pearce (1990). For the reader familiar with economics, other articles in The Oxford Review of Economic Policy (1990a) consider various aspects of economic policy towards the environment. Pearson and Smith (1990) provides a detailed discussion of the costs and benefits of carbon taxation. Evidence on the effects of carbon emissions on the environment is provided in House of Commons Select Committee on Energy (1989). Dales (1968) discusses the relationship between property rights and pollution.

# Questions for Discussion

1. Should the optimum level of pollution be zero?
2. Does the fact that many of the benefits from pollution control are intangible mean that it is impossible to place a money value on them?
3. 'If property rights were properly defined, there could be no pollution problem'. Discuss.
4. 'Externalities can always be internalised by bargaining between the affected parties'. Do you agree?
5. Should polluters always pay?
6. Smoking imposes costs on non-smokers. Does this imply that:
    - non-smokers should pay smokers not to smoke?
    - smokers should carry on smoking but compensate non-smokers?
    - the government should ban smoking?
    - none of these?
7. Are output charges and effluent charges equally efficient?
8. 'The only difference between charges and subsidies as means of controlling pollution is in the long run'. Explain.
9. Why do you think governments generally favour direct regulation to control pollution, rather than charges or subsidies?
10. What are the practical problems involved in the use of charging systems to attain pollution standards? How might a system of 'pollution rights' overcome those problems?

# Transport 7

Transport plays a vital role in the lives of almost everyone. It is a necessity for most people's work and for social activities; those without transport can be isolated and lack the ability to participate in society. It is also a major component of economic activity. In 1988 in Britain, the total resources spent on transport accounted for 7 per cent of GDP. Expenditure on transport accounted for approximately 15 per cent of consumers' expenditure and 11.3 per cent was on motor vehicles alone. And concern over transport – its availability, quality, accessibility and price – is a major topic of social and political debate.

While transport is vital to daily life in an urban society such as Britain, travel is rarely valued in its own right, but is necessary to satisfy other demands. Hence the demand for travel is often termed a *derived demand* – derived from the 'final' demand for particular activities. For instance, in the case of business and commercial traffic, it is necessary to move raw materials and semi-finished goods to the factories where they will be incorporated into finished products ready for consumption, and also to move these finished goods to the shops from which they will be sold to customers. The demand for this transport is therefore derived from consumers' demand for final goods and services. Similarly, in the case of private traffic, a journey to work is necessary before one can earn income, watching a film requires a trip to the cinema, and so on. Of course, there are exceptions – taking a Sunday drive on a deserted road round a Scottish loch may be valued purely for itself – but for the most part individuals do not get direct utility or pleasure from time spent travelling. Transport is not of course unique in this – health care, discussed earlier in this book, has similar properties. People do not value painful medical intervention for itself; what they value is the gain in health status that will follow the treatment. Similarly, people do not value sitting in a car in a traffic jam; what they value is the activity, or the monetary reward of the activity, they are travelling to or away from.

In this chapter, we investigate the economics of transport. We begin, as in other chapters, with an examination of society's objectives. We then examine the extent to which the market is likely to be able to achieve these aims. Following this, we look at policies governments have adopted and assess whether these policies have been successful in bringing society closer to achieving its goals. We end by looking at some recent policy proposals.

# Objectives

We begin our analysis of objectives by examining the issue of efficiency, though this is by no means the sole concern in transport.

# *Efficiency*

In deciding how many resources to devote to transport and what type of transport should be provided, a society will need to consider all the benefits and costs that arise from transport. Accordingly, we begin with a brief discussion of these benefits and costs.

## *Benefits of transport*

Benefits arise from use of transport because transport is necessary to satisfy a wide range of work and leisure activities. As noted above, demand for travel is a derived demand. This association of travel with different activities means that the benefit individuals derive from a trip, and hence their demand for the trip, will be related to the benefit they derive from the final activity. Thus trips along the same stretch of road involving commercial deliveries to shops, private shopping trips, commuting journeys to work, and so on, will all yield different levels of benefit. This will need to be borne in mind when deciding on the way that demands on the limited resources that can be devoted to travel are met. A second factor that will affect the level of benefit that travellers obtain from a journey is the mode of transport they use. For example, if we look at the relative merits of car and bus travel we usually find that the car has the advantages of door-to-door travel, privacy, guarantee of a seat, a flexible route and, usually, a faster journey time; while the bus has the advantages of no parking problems, no frustrations of driving, and the option of undertaking other activities (for example reading) while travelling. The level of benefit travellers obtain from a journey will depend on their preferences regarding these characteristics. If they place a high value on door-to-door travel and hate depending on timetables, they will tend to value a car trip more highly; if, on the other hand, they enjoy reading a newspaper or magazine while travelling and become agitated by driving, they will prefer the bus.

## Costs of travel

The costs of travel can be divided into three broad categories. First, there are the *private* costs. These are paid directly by travellers or the firms employing them. For motorists, these include petrol costs and vehicle depreciation. For those on public transport, these are fares. For all travellers, there are also non-monetary costs, in particular, the costs of time spent on journeys. This last item is particularly important in the case of transport for these costs represent a major portion of private travel costs. At first sight it may seem strange to speak of time 'costs', for time is not bought and sold in the market in the normal way. But it is a scarce resource (there are only twenty-four hours in a day) and so has a distinct opportunity cost. For example, time spent on travel has an obvious cost as far as people travelling for business or commercial reasons are concerned, because time spent on a journey is usually far less productive than time spent in an office, factory, or shop. But time spent on travel also represents a cost to a person travelling to or from work or for non-business reasons; most people can probably think of more pleasant ways to spend the time they now use for travelling. Certainly most of us would prefer (and would therefore be willing to pay for) an extra half-hour in bed in the morning instead of fighting traffic on the way to work.

Second, there are costs that transport users impose on others. There may be *congestion* costs. For road users, these are the costs that one motorist imposes on another when the number of vehicles using a road reaches the point at which drivers start to impede each other's movement. This results in frequent stopping and starting and lower traffic speeds. The delays that occur cause higher journey costs both through higher vehicle operating costs (for example more brake and tyre wear, higher petrol consumption, and so on) and longer journey times. In the case of air travel, an airplane coming to land at an already crowded airport will delay take-off and landing for passengers in other planes.

Users also impose *environmental* costs on non-users, such as pedestrians and residents who live in the vicinity of roads and train lines or people who live under the approach paths to airports. Environmental costs include costs such as noise, air pollution, damage to the environment and increased risk of accidents. Most of these costs tend to increase as the level of transport increases. Notice that a crucial feature of both congestion and environmental costs is that although they result from an individual's journey, the individual does not bear them herself. She imposes them on other people. In the case of congestion costs they are imposed on other transport users, whereas in the case of environmental costs they are imposed primarily on wider society (and perhaps on future generations too). Because they costs are borne by people other than the traveller they are termed *external* costs.

Finally, there is a category of costs that in practice cannot be related, or are very costly to relate, to the amount of travel the individual undertakes. In the case of roads, there are the costs of maintenance, repair work, and so on. In the case of air travel, there are the costs of terminals, runways, and so forth. In the case of trains, there are the costs of track, of maintenance, of signalling equipment and so on. In most cases, these costs are *fixed costs*; their level is not directly related to the amount of travel undertaken (though there is obviously some relationship between the two).

## *The efficient level of travel*

As for other goods, the efficient level of travel occurs when the net benefit obtained from using transport (total benefits minus total costs) is maximised. Thus we need to take into account the level of benefit received by each traveller and the costs, both private and external, that result from her journey. If we consider a group of travellers, the sum of the individual benefits and costs associated with each one of them will indicate the total benefits and costs that arise for that particular volume of traffic. When the volume of travel that maximises net benefit is achieved, we have an efficient level of road use.

## *Equity*

As we noted above, access to transport is necessary if individuals are to participate in a modern society. Without travel facilities, most people would not be able to work, visit friends, buy goods or take holidays. For this reason, transport is sometimes designated as a *merit good*. The rationale for merit goods is based on the notion that there is a certain basic set of goods to which an individual requires access in order to sustain a minimum standard of living. A useful distinction can be made between *absolute* requirements, such as food, clothing, shelter and *participative* requirements, goods that allow individuals to participate in society. Such goods include education, opportunities for employment and mobility. Transport clearly falls into this second category. The idea that transport is necessary for participation can be used to justify the existence of a certain *minimum standard* or level of provision, access to which is open to all, irrespective of income, age, race or sex. Or it can be used to justify *equality of access costs* to this minimum. In contrast, ideas of *full equity* are not generally part of society's objectives with respect to transport; it is seldom argued, for example, that if one person has a Rolls Royce, all should have one – or that Rolls Royces should be shared equally between all members of society.

We turn now to an examination of the market and ask the question: Will market provision meet either society's efficiency or equity aims? The fact that there is government intervention in the transport sector might be some indication that the market has not been judged to meet society's objectives. However, the fact that government intervention may itself fail makes it important to identify the precise nature and sources of market failure.

## The Market System and Transport

We first focus on the level of travel undertaken relative to the efficient level. The first form of market failure we can identify arises from *externalities*, or more specifically, from *external costs*. To see this, we need to return to an examination of the costs and benefits of travel. For simplicity, we first examine road use by car commuters, though the argument can be generalised to other groups of travellers.

## *Externalities*

Let us look first at costs. As we have seen, there are a number of different categories of costs. In this instance we are particularly interested in the distinction between *private* and *external costs*. Moreover, to make our point as clear as possible, we shall restrict our consideration of external costs to congestion costs in the first instance. Suppose, near the beginning of a road, we set up an observation point that enables us to count the number of vehicles passing per minute. We may express this as a flow of vehicles per minute. When the flow is low each vehicle will be able to travel freely at its chosen speed – subject to speed restrictions – without impeding other vehicles. However, as the flow increases, a point will be reached at which vehicles begin to delay each other; the delays will tend to become greater as the flow continues to increase. The road becomes congested. As additional cars join the flow, they slow it down and impose costs on others. Typically, time costs form a large part of congestion costs. The simple numerical example shown in Table 7.1 indicates the nature of the problem.

The first column shows the flow of vehicles per minute. To keep the arithmetic simple, we have shown these in units of a single vehicle per minute. In practice such increases would probably have a negligible effect on costs; however, the principle is not affected by the unit of measurement adopted. The second column shows the time it takes for each vehicle to travel along the road at different levels of flow. This is the private time cost per vehicle for the journey. When there is no congestion, the journey time taken by each vehicle is ten minutes. This situation prevails up to a flow of four vehicles per minute. Beyond this point congestion begins and journey times become longer. At five vehicles per minute the journey takes eleven minutes, at seven vehicles it takes sixteen minutes, and at ten vehicles it takes over thirty minutes. The important point to note is that when additional vehicles join the stream, they slow down *all* the traffic. It is not just the additional vehicle that travels at the new, lower speed,

## TABLE 7.1
## Vehicle Flows and Time Costs

| Vehicle flow (cars per minute) (1) | Journey time per vehicle (minutes) (2) | Total journey time, all vehicles [(1) × (2)] (3) | Increase in total journey time as flow increases by one vehicle (4) | Extra journey time *imposed* but not *borne* last vehicle [(4) − (2)] (5) |
|---|---|---|---|---|
| 1 | 10 | 10 | | |
| 2 | 10 | 20 | 10 | 0 |
| 3 | 10 | 30 | 10 | 0 |
| 4 | 10 | 40 | 10 | 0 |
| 5 | 11 | 55 | 15 | 4 |
| 6 | 13 | 78 | 23 | 10 |
| 7 | 16 | 112 | 34 | 18 |
| 8 | 20 | 160 | 48 | 28 |
| 9 | 26 | 234 | 74 | 48 |
| 10 | 34 | 340 | 106 | 72 |

but also the traffic that was on the road before the increase in flow. For example, when the flow increases from four to five vehicles per minute the journey time for all motorists becomes eleven minutes. Hence we may say that the additional motorist has imposed a *congestion* cost upon the original motorists.

If we look at columns (3), (4) and (5) in Table 7.1 we can see the extent of congestion costs. Column (3) shows the total journey time taken by all vehicles. For example, at a flow of four vehicles per minute total journey time is forty minutes (4 × 10); at five vehicles it is fifty five minutes (5 × 11), and so on. Column (4) shows the increase in total journey time as the flow increases by one vehicle; for instance if we look at the row showing five vehicles per minute, we see that the increase from four to five vehicles adds fifteen minutes to the total journey time (55 − 40). This sum of fifteen minutes is attributable to the fifth vehicle that joins the flow. However, the fifth vehicle takes only eleven minutes to make the journey itself – column (2), so the difference between eleven and fifteen minutes – four minutes – represents the extra journey time it imposes on other motorists. This extra journey time is shown in column (5).

To this point we have been concentrating on the way that journey times change as *additional* vehicles join the flow; that is we have been looking at the change in journey time attributable to the *marginal* vehicle. If we can put a monetary value on the time spent travelling, then by multiplying the amount of time spent travelling by the per minute cost, we can express these journey times as costs. We can thus derive the additional cost attributable to each vehicle that joins the flow. This is termed the *marginal* cost. Moreover, at each level of flow the costs arising from the marginal vehicle can be broken down into two components: the private cost and the congestion (or external) cost. Together they comprise the social cost arising from the marginal motorist's journey, that is

$$\text{marginal private cost} + \text{marginal congestion cost} = \text{marginal social cost.}$$

An alternative way of presenting this information, which shows the distinction between private and social costs very clearly, is to depict it in the form of a diagram. This has been done in Figure 7.1. The horizontal axis shows the flow of vehicles per minute on the road. The vertical axis measures the marginal cost of using the road. In Table 7.1, we showed the travel times for each vehicle in minutes. To convert journey time into monetary costs, we have assumed each minute spent travelling costs each motorist 5p. (For the purpose of the example, we ignore any differences in value of time between different travellers. The two curves in the diagram show the way marginal private costs (*mpc*) and marginal social costs (*msc*) change as the vehicle flow on the road increases. Up to a flow of four vehicles per minute there is no congestion. Therefore the cost per vehicle journey is 50p (= 10 minutes at 5p per minute) for each of the first four vehicles. Because there is no congestion, marginal private cost equals marginal social cost. At a flow above four vehicles, congestion sets in and the marginal social cost associated with each vehicle becomes greater than the marginal private cost by an amount equal to the marginal congestion cost. For example, at a flow of eight vehicles, marginal private cost equals £1.00 (= 20 minutes at 5p per minute) whereas the marginal social cost equals £2.40. The marginal congestion cost thus equals £1.40. This means that the eighth vehicle to join the flow imposes a cost of £1.40 on all the other vehicles as well as incurring a cost of £1.00 itself. As can be seen from the figure, when the flow increases and congestion becomes more

**FIGURE 7.1**
**Vehicle Flow and Marginal Journey Cost**

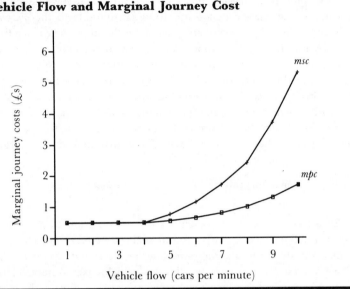

serious, the divergence between private and social costs becomes larger. Hence at a flow of ten vehicles per minute the marginal congestion cost equals £3.60.

So far we have restricted our attention to congestion costs but we can quite easily introduce other forms of external costs. For example, suppose the noise suffered by residents adjoining the highway become more acute as the level of congestion increases. This will mean that *environmental* costs are being incurred. If these can be valued, these could also be represented in our diagram by construction of a second marginal social cost schedule such as the *msc* curve above the previous one. In this case the discrepancy between the marginal private cost and marginal social cost will be greater than before because an additional category of external costs has been included. Similarly if the costs are known, we could add in damage to the environment caused by the emissions from each car per minute.

If we now turn to benefits, the benefit each potential motorist will derive from using the road for her journey to work will depend on the importance she places upon the particular journey: some will derive considerable benefit while others, who have access to alternative means of transport or places of employment, or can make the journey at a different time or by a different route, will derive less benefit. If we rank road users according to the level of benefit they obtain from a journey, we can see the extent of these variations. A typical pattern is portrayed in Figure 7.2.

On the bottom axis of the diagram we show the number of vehicles per minute travelling along a road. On the vertical axis we show the level of benefit that each motorist would derive from using the road. Once again, we have assumed that each motorist is able to express her level of benefit in terms of money and that the economist knows this monetary value. The curve *DD* expresses this information. For example, as individuals are ranked by the benefit they get from making the journey, *DD* shows that the fourth motorist to join the

**FIGURE 7.2**
**Vehicle Flow and Marginal Journey Benefit**

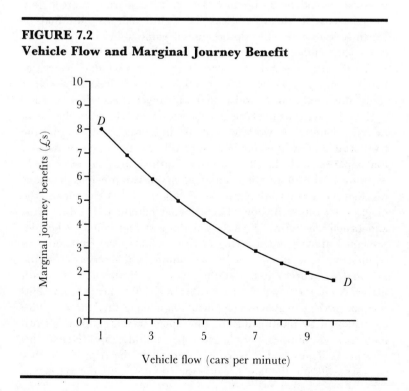

flow of traffic values the journey at £5.00 whereas the eighth road user attaches a value of only £2.40 to it. Thus each point on *DD* indicates the level of benefit received by the last motorist to join the flow. Therefore we can say that it indicates the level of benefit obtained by the *marginal* vehicle user or, put alternatively, it is a *marginal benefit* curve. As we have confined our attention to the benefits received by individual motorists, it is of course a marginal *private* benefit curve. However, as the incidence of externalities is not as widespread in the case of benefits as it is in the case of costs, at least as far as road users are concerned (drivers who enjoy travelling in convoys provide an exception!), we may assume that marginal private benefits (*mpb*) equal marginal social benefits (*msb*). Thus the *msb* associated with the eighth motorist's journey along the road is £2.40.

Notice that if the cost of travelling along the road was in fact £2.40, eight motorists would make the journey. The first seven motorists would do so because they value a journey more highly than its cost to them, whereas the eighth motorist just finds it worthwhile to make the trip because its value to her is equal to the cost. The ninth potential motorist would not travel because she values the trip at less than its cost. Thus we can see that, as well as being a marginal benefit curve, *DD* is a travel demand curve; it shows the number of motorists that will travel at each level of cost.

Having looked at the costs and benefits that arise from the use of roads for journeys to work, we are now in a position to see what the level of road use will be under existing allocation arrangements, and to compare it with the efficient level. This may be done more easily by bringing the information contained in our two previous diagrams together in a single diagram as in Figure 7.3. Once again the diagram measures the flow of vehicles per minute and records costs and benefits in terms of £s. Given the cost and benefit schedules presented above (and ignoring environmental costs) we expect an equilibrium flow of ten vehicles per minute. The intersection of the *DD* and *mpc* curves at this traffic volume indicates that the tenth driver to join the flow attaches a value of £1.70 to her journey. This is equal to the private costs she incurs in making the journey. (This cost is found by multiplying the time spent travelling for this tenth motorist, 34 minutes, by the cost per minute, 5p). Hence this traveller will just find it worthwhile to make the trip. No further car users will join the flow because they do not value the journey as

**FIGURE 7.3**
**Marginal Costs, Benefits and Road Use**

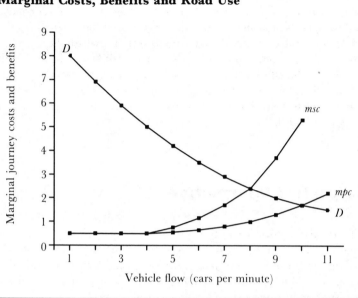

highly as the cost they would have to incur. However, we can see from the diagram that £1.70 is not the total addition to costs arising from the tenth vehicle's journey, since there are congestion costs that she imposes on others. These are depicted by the difference between the *msc* and *mpc* curves, that is £3.60. Thus the benefit that the tenth motorist obtains is less than the total costs (private plus external costs) of her journey. If the flow were reduced below ten vehicles the discrepancy between *mpb* ( = *msb*) and *msc* would be reduced, until at a flow of eight vehicles per minute *msb* would equal *msc*. At this traffic volume the benefit derived by the last motorist to enter the flow, £2.40, is equal to the sum of the costs she imposes both on herself and others. This is the efficient level of road use.

It would appear, therefore, that a system of road use that does not require the car user to take account of the external costs of her actions will lead to an excessive number of vehicles using the roads. Externalities are not only a feature of car travel. Buses also impose congestion costs, though the cost per passenger carried is lower than that of a car (and we return to this point later). Indeed external costs are a feature of all congested resources whether they are roads, railways, ports or airports. The same argument applies equally to the environmental costs associated with travel. Provided the traveller does not take these costs into account, her use will be too high relative to the efficient level. Heavy lorries, noisy trains and aircraft taking off and landing all impose environmental costs, some of which fall on a well-defined group of people (those who live near airports), some of which fall on wider groups.

## Imperfect Information

The regular occurrence of travel disasters – the capsizing of a cross-channel ferry, train crashes, aircraft accidents – highlights an important feature of transport – safety, or the lack of it. Safety is an area in which consumers are likely to be poorly informed. Safety information in transport is highly technical. Even if consumers could be given the safety facts about the mode of travel they wish to use, it would be difficult for them to interpret them. For example, even if every aircraft passenger were allowed to 'kick the tyres' of a plane, it is unlikely that they would learn much from this experience. Train travellers do not, in the main, have knowledge about the signalling systems on the track along which they travel. Ferry passengers cannot know whether the overall number of passengers on the ferry makes it more likely to sink. Thus the suppliers of transport – the airline, shipping, train companies and the car manufacturers – are likely to have considerably more information than the consumers. This is a case of *asymmetric information*.

In these circumstances suppliers have an incentive to under-supply safety because safety provision costs money. For example, in order to get passengers out of a plane quickly, airline companies have to fit fewer seats than an aircraft could technically hold, so forgoing revenue. Train service operators must spend more money on signalling systems and maintenance of track and rolling stock. When consumers have little information about safety, opportunities exist for companies to increase profits by reducing safety.

# *Monopoly*

A common feature of many transport modes is the existence of high entry costs. By entry costs we mean investment which is required before transport can be sold. In the case of motoring, a road must be built before anyone can drive on it. Similarly, if trains are to run, track must be laid, if aircraft are to fly, runways and terminals must be constructed. And the costs of constructing roads, track and terminals tend to be high relative to running costs. The presence of these entry costs allows the development of monopoly; once one company has made an investment in infrastructure such as track or airline runways, only firms with access to very large sums of capital can compete against the first firm. Thus in an unfettered market there tends to be a limited number of suppliers in the transport sector. This limited competition gives these suppliers the power to raise prices and/or cut quality below what it would be if more competition existed. Thus the consumer loses out.

# *Equity*

Will the market allocate transport services according to the concepts of equity discussed above? The answer is likely to be no. There is no mechanism in the market for the allocation of a basic minimum level of transport to all persons in society, nor are there any automatic mechanisms for ensuring that access costs are the same for all. For example, nothing in the market ensures access costs for those living in rural areas will be the same as that of those living in urban areas. In fact, as average incomes have risen, the position of certain groups with respect to transport may actually have deteriorated. The rapid expansion of public transport networks in the UK in the years around the Second World War provided a basis for dispersion of residential locations. As car ownership rose in the 1960s and 1970s, the financial viability of public transport services declined, leaving those with no car access with fewer transport services available to them. And because lack of car access is concentrated among certain groups in society – in particular, the elderly, the young, the poor and women – these groups have suffered more than others. Furthermore, the decline in available transport may, in some cases, have led to a reduction in land values, so groups without car access were left with fewer transport facilities and a reduction in the value of their housing assets.

# Government Policies

Prior to the twentieth century, many of the transport modes were conceived and constructed as private ventures with little regulation. However, as the sector developed, government intervention became widespread, taking the form of *regulation*, *provision* and *taxes* and *subsidies*. We shall first briefly look at the way the government has intervened. We then turn to an examination of the perceived failures of this intervention and recent measures that have been adopted to overcome these failures.

## *Regulation*

In the UK by the late 1970s government regulation of transport was widespread. Regulation of quality – safety regulations – included and still includes the compulsory wearing of safety belts in cars, maximum loads on lorries, limits on the speed of vehicles and on the number of passengers carried on ferries and airplanes. Such intervention is intended to overcome the market failure arising from consumer lack of information. The government also used regulation as a way of curbing the monopoly power of suppliers. Governments regulated the ownership of transport networks and the location, price and quantity of services provided. This latter type of regulation was frequently coupled with direct provision.

## *Provision*

Government has built and managed infrastructure, such as the road network, airports and seaports. Until recently, it has provided and managed bus, rail, air, ferry and coach services. Much of this activity was justified on the grounds that because of high entry costs these activities could only viably be undertaken by one operator. Direct government provision would thus prevent monopoly abuse. State provision has also been justified on equity grounds. So, for instance, the government has owned and managed local bus services in order to promote access goals.

## Taxes and Subsidies

Uses of taxes and subsidies has been – and remains – widespread in transport. For example, car owners are subject to vehicle duty, a differential rate of VAT on car purchase and taxes on petrol. In 1988 taxes on cars alone accounted for £12.7 thousand million of government revenue. Subsidies were introduced to increase use of transport by those with less access to private transport, who, given the association between car ownership and income, tended to be the less well off. Sometimes subsidies have been targetted to particular groups, particularly the elderly. Sometimes they have been used to lower fares on all routes, as under the fares policy implemented in South Yorkshire between 1975 and 1981, which reduced fares on all buses in the county for all travellers. Sometimes subsidies were used to persuade people to use one transport mode rather than another, on the grounds that the per traveller externality was smaller in one form of transport than another.

## Assessment

How successful have these policies been? We begin our assessment with a brief discussion of safety regulation. While few would argue that such regulations should be abandoned, it needs to be recognised that imposition of such regulations has a cost which will be borne by the traveller. Thus wearing a seat belt imposes disutility on the driver who believes strongly in individual freedom, drink-drive legislation prevents a driver from consuming as much alcohol as she might wish, seat limits on aircraft increase the cost per passenger. Establishing the efficient level of safety regulation, that is the level at which the marginal social cost of regulation equals the marginal social benefit, is extremely difficult. As is often the case in the types of markets examined in this book, the valuation of benefits is particularly difficult. In the case of transport safety regulations, valuing benefits requires both information on the *extent* of accident prevention and some *money valuation* of the accidents prevented. To do the latter generally involves putting a value on human life and serious injury. This is a contentious, but important valuation, for the value selected will determine the efficient level of safety regulation. If the value is high, regulations which save more lives will be more desirable. We have not the space to go further into this issue here, but the interested reader should look at Jones-Lee (1990).

We turn now to an examination of the consequences of other forms of government intervention. The 1980s saw a considerable reduction in the extent of regulation of ownership and management of public transport, a liberalisation of entry into transport markets, a reduction in subsidies to public transport and the sale of some public assets. This *deregulation* – accompanied in some cases by *privatisation* (the transfer of assets from the public to the private sector) – and the reduction in the level of subsidisation, has been a response to the charge that government intervention was itself inducing efficiency failures. The type of intervention in the UK transport industry, which generally licensed a monopoly supplier, often located in the state sector – so that there was regulation plus direct provision – was argued to lead to inefficiencies in production and lack of accountability. Regulations focused on the implementation of pricing and investment rules. Prices were set for equity reasons, investment was dictated by macro-economic and political concerns, such as the maintenance of cash limits on public expenditure. Financial performance of the state run enterprises was also largely ignored. The result was that *productive efficiency*, the minimisation of costs for a given quality of service, was not achieved. And the requirement that transport providers serve 'the public interest' meant that there was confusion between commercial and public service considerations and so a lack accountability for outcomes. While the aim of subsidisation was to increase access by the less well off and less mobile, in practice, subsidisation may have reduced costs for higher income groups more than for poorer groups, as a large proportion of public transport passengers are in fact drawn from the better-off – the result of high utilisation of public transport by rush-hour commuters.

The proponents of deregulation and reduced government intervention argued that exposure of regulated monopoly providers, whether in or out of the public sector, to competition would encourage productive efficiency. Competition would encourage providers to seek to bring down costs and increase innovation in order to attract passengers. Opponents of deregulation argued that the existence of high entry costs would make competition impossible. In those cases in which competition was feasible, deregulation would allow operators to cut safety margins and to drop unprofitable services provided to meet social objectives.

Evidence from the deregulations of the 1980s is mixed. For instance, in the case of deregulation of local bus services, a significant rise in number of operators has occurred in only a few areas. Many new entrants failed to maintain a position in the market and rapidly exited. Thus widespread competition has not occurred. Nevertheless there have been improvements in the financial preference of local bus companies. Product innovation – for instance, mini-buses rather than double deckers, new routes and new time-tables – has occurred, and presumably these changes have benefited the consumer. Similar changes followed the deregulation of long distance coach services. The changes are too recent for a complete assessment, but in some cases efficiency does appear to have been improved (Glaister *et al.*, 1990; Gwilliam, 1989), though there remain concerns over the existence of high entry costs. In air transport, deregulation has lowered fares and increased services (Vickers and Yarrow, 1988).

In cases where state ownership has been retained, attempts have been made to introduce competition between public and private suppliers. Thus public bus companies no longer receive blanket subsidies which would allow them to reduce fares on routes where a private operator could compete. Instead, subsidies are allocated to particular routes, targeted to achieve specific equity goals. The result has been to reduce the average level of subsidies and to improve efficiency.

# Proposals for Reform

The measures outlined above have been adopted to overcome government failure, in particular, the lack of productive efficiency which is argued to have resulted from the high degree of regulation. But none of the changes outlined above deal with the problem of externalities. In this final section we turn to policies which have been proposed as a means of dealing with the existence of external costs. At the heart of all these proposals is the use of the pricing mechanism. We focus mainly on measures to deal with the congestion externality, though similar measures can be applied to the environmental externalities and we look briefly at these.

## Congestion Taxes

Because congestion arises as a result of excess demand for a scarce resource, the problem could be remedied by the extension of the price mechanism to use of congested facilities. To see how this would work, consider our earlier discussion of costs and benefits of road use. It will be recalled that if motorists are left to their own devices, they will ignore the external costs imposed by their use of the road. However, if a congestion tax was introduced that raised the marginal private cost of a journey to the marginal social cost, this would ensure that only those drivers who valued their journey at or above its marginal social cost would use the road. In this way traffic could be reduced to produce an efficient level of road use. In terms of Figure 7.3, this would be achieved by levying a tax of £1.40 per vehicle if the flow were eight vehicles. This would mean that the private cost incurred by the eighth driver (that is, the one who, after ranking, is shown to value the journey least highly of the eight on the road) would be raised to its marginal social cost level of £2.40.

Hence, through the introduction of congestion taxes, road users would be made aware of the social costs of their actions. As rush-hour commuting became more expensive, traffic volumes would be reduced in a number of ways. Some drivers might form car pools. Others might shift to public transport where the tax per passenger on a bus could be substantially less. In the longer term, commuters might look for employment in less congested areas where they would not have to pay these taxes, while firms confronted by workers demanding higher wages to compensate for higher travel costs would also have an incentive to relocate in less congested areas.

Notice, however, that taxes would only need to be applied where a discrepancy existed between *mpc* and *msc* (that is where congestion occurs). If the *DD* curve in Figure 7.3 intersected the cost schedule at a traffic volume of four vehicles or less, where *msc* = *mpc*, no tax would be necessary. This point is significant because fluctuations in traffic flow throughout the day often mean that taxes will need to be applied on the same stretch of road at some times but not at others. Indeed, in practice, huge differences exist in congestion costs. Newbery (1990) estimated that urban centre areas at peak hours have an average congestion cost of ten times the average over all roads and more than one hundred times that of the average motorway or rural road. And this brings us to the issue of implementation. To introduce a congestion tax, policy makers would have to have knowledge of the marginal externality cost for different vehicles. Estimates of these now exist (Newbery 1990), but two problems remain: first, there is the question of how exactly to implement the tax, and second, there is the issue of equity.

On the question of implementation, car owners are already subject to a number of indirect taxes on road use – value-added tax on car sales, road fund licences and petrol taxes. Could these not be extended to deal with road congestion? Unfortunately, the answer is that none of them is ideally suited for this purpose.

Value-added taxes and vehicle licences are taxes on ownership rather than use; that is they are payable in full even if the car is driven on public roads for only one mile per year. Thus they are *fixed* costs, and are paid whether the car is used or not. However, what matters to the motorist when considering a particular journey, and to the government concerned with the social costs of that journey, is the extra cost the journey is going to incur – that is, its *marginal* cost. These taxes do not affect marginal costs. So while they may make some contribution to rationing road use – by reducing the demand for car ownership – they are not really suited to the purpose of reducing congestion. They do not vary according to how much a car is used and whether it travels in congested urban areas or in deserted rural areas.

Petrol taxes, on the other hand, are related to the amount of use made of the roads. They are also related to some extent to the level of congestion in an area, because journeys in congested conditions tend to increase petrol consumption. Also, larger vehicles that take up more road space than smaller cars tend to be heavier on petrol consumption. But there are two drawbacks to petrol taxes. First, the huge variation in congestion costs noted above means that unless it were possible to link petrol sales to where the petrol is used the tax paid will not be related to the amount of congestion caused. Second, petrol taxes will only reduce congestion if motorists know how much petrol they are using in congested traffic. Another option could be to extend parking taxes. Charges would be levied on parked vehicles in congested areas, the aim being to deter vehicles from entering. This tax has, however, the disadvantage that it is only levied on those vehicles that actually park; it would not deter traffic that travels though congested districts but does not stop in them.

In the main, the methods for extending current vehicle taxes to act as an externality tax all fail. In all cases there are theoretical or practical problems of relating them to the use made of the road system. What is required is a system that actually bases charges on the external costs that arise from the use made of particular sections of the road network. Three possibilities are electronic road pricing, charges to enter congested areas and supplementary licensing.

Under electronic road pricing vehicles would be fitted with recording devices when they enter an area subject to congestion. Charges would be made depending on the level of congestion prevailing at the time, and car owners billed, as for use of gas or electricity in their homes. An experimental scheme for electronic road pricing was demonstrated in Hong Kong (Hau 1990) and a large scale scheme has been initiated in Holland. In the case of London, a scheme has been worked out which it is estimated would reduce traffic levels by approximately forty per cent in Central London and thirty per cent in Inner London (Glaister *et al.*, 1990). The main drawback of such a scheme is political accept-ability. Much would depend on public perception of the benefits of such a monitoring schemes. In Hong Kong, plans for electronic pricing schemes had to be shelved because of political opposition. Charging vehicles at the point of entry to a congested area, and allowing the charge to reflect the level of congestion in an area, could be more politically acceptable. But in large cities, with many access roads, this option could be administratively very costly. It would also produce delays, possibly very large in some congested urban areas, with resultant time costs. In the face of these difficulties, this approach is probably not suitable in Britain. A final proposal is a supplementary license, which simply involves the purchase and display of a special license if the vehicle is to be used at a specified time and place. This is perhaps less intrusive than electronic charging – after all cars already have to display their road tax disks – and hence would be more acceptable. Such a charging system has been in operation in Singapore for a number of years. While the fee paid cannot be as closely related to congestion costs as in the case of electronic metering, the practical advantages of this scheme over electronic road pricing perhaps outweigh this disadvantage.

## Equity and congestion taxes

The purpose of levying a congestion tax is to reduce the number of vehicles on the roads. As a result, those people who continue to use the roads after the imposition of the tax will gain through shorter and more pleasant journeys. This will apply both to those people who previously travelled by car and those who travelled by other modes, such as bus and bicycle. However, the reduction in congestion will have been achieved by deterring some car users from making their original journeys. Some of them will now make the journey by a means in which the tax per person is lower (for example a bus or a train) while others will reschedule their trips at different times or by different routes (where congestion and the tax are lower). Some may cease to make the trip altogether, and others may seek alternative, less-congested work or shopping destinations. On balance, these people are likely to suffer a loss in benefit from the introduction of a congestion tax. This raises the question of equity. Will different groups bear the costs in different amounts?

Initially, the beneficiaries are those whose time savings from lower congestion outweigh the money cost of the congestion tax. The losers are those for whom the net costs of making the journey have risen. To identify gainers and losers we would need detailed knowledge of the incomes and preferences of different road users; only then could we forecast how each group would react to congestion taxes. So, for instance, we would need to know what the incomes of car and bus users at different times of day were and how current road users would react to an increase in the money costs of their journey. We cannot simply assert that all those who travel at peak hours would lose, since, for some individuals, the increase in costs would be outweighed by the value of the time saved. These might be rich car owners, but could also be poorer bus users. The tax would also have longer-term effects. It could be expected to affect the level of property prices in a city, as these will be partly dependent on the costs of transport. Land values would tend to rise at the centre and fall at the periphery. At the same time rural areas would face lower taxes than urban areas. Ultimately this would affect the whole price structure of goods produced in rural and urban locations. Indeed, the impact of changes in transport prices on land values is one of the reasons why equity concerns can be high in transport.

## Environmental taxes

The principle of relating charges to the source of damage discussed for congestion also applies to taxes intended to internalise environmental damage. But it will not necessarily be possible to use the same tax to internalise both congestion and environmental costs. For example, taxation on petrol may be limited as a way of dealing with congestion, but would be more suited to the externality of environmental damage if the latter damage is more closely related to miles driven. At present fifteen per cent of the world's emission of carbon dioxide is from motor vehicles. In developed countries this figure is forty per cent. Vehicle emissions are argued to be responsible for fifty per cent of nitrogen oxide, a precursor to acid rain. Some of these emissions are related to miles driven.

In general the chief problem in setting taxes to deal with environmental externalities is to get information on the costs. This measurement problem falls into two parts. The first involves measuring the extent of the externality. In some cases techniques are well established, such as the measurement of noise caused by aircraft take-off and landing. In other cases, such as the relationship between car emissions and environmental damage, information is much poorer. The second is to value these physical impacts. Some techniques exist, but again for environmental problems valuations remain very tentative. One US study suggests internalisation of the costs of noise, pollution and accidents would raise motoring costs by twenty to thirty-three per cent (Glaister *et al.*, 1990, p.11).

## Second Best Policies

It is clear that efficient taxation of transport may be difficult to achieve. In such cases, economists have sometimes advocated what are called *second best* policies. Under such policies, inefficiencies or distortions in one sector – such as car travel – are dealt with by introducing taxes or subsidies in another closely linked sector – such as public transport. Bus services are argued to be able to carry passengers with lower congestion costs per traveller than private car transport. (Buses are equivalent to three to four cars in terms of congestion generating capacity but can carry up to forty to fifty times the number of passengers). Would it not, therefore, be possible to reduce road congestion by subsidising transport fares on buses and thereby attract car users from the roads? Moreover, would it not also directly benefit low-income public transport users and low-to-middle income car users (who would transfer to public transport), and therefore be more equitable?

While such an argument has been used as a rationale for subsidisation of buses, second best pricing may not achieve the desired ends. Available evidence suggests that the demand for bus travel has an extremely low *price elasticity of demand*; that is, demand increases by only a small amount in response to fare reductions. For instance, in South Yorkshire between 1975 and 1981, as part of a policy to increase accessibilty, fares were decreased by fifty five per cent and service levels increased by four per cent. But use of the services by men rose by only 1.5 per cent and by women by 11.8 per cent. Therefore subsidies may not lead to much increase in usage. It has also been argued that even if bus subsidies did increase the number of passengers and so initially reduce road congestion, new motorists would then take to the roads and in the end traffic would rise to the point where congestion was equal to that prior to subsidisation. Hence even very large bus subsidies are unlikely to secure appreciable reductions in the level of congestion. Thus the subsidy may not be an effective way of reducing congestion costs. In addition, though less true for buses than for other forms of public transport, the users of public transport during peak hours are not generally those with low incomes. Thus a subsidy to peak hour public transport may not promote equity. Commentators on recent British experience in the bus industry have argued that a move away from subsidisation for second best reasons has led to an improvement in net social welfare. It is argued that the industry may have a better chance of competing with the car if it is market orientated, rather than if it is heavily subsidised and consequently encumbered by government regulation and constraint (Gomez-Ibanez and Meyer, 1990). By making public transport more attractive – by increasing quality rather than reducing price – use will rise, so reducing car usage and congestion costs.

In conclusion, the current dominant view in transport, in Britain as elsewhere, is to reduce regulation and increase reliance on the price mechanism as a means of dealing with inefficiencies. A pricing system, it is argued, enables users to state their intensity of preference by the price they are willing to pay to use a road. It thereby gives a means of distinguishing between essential and inessential traffic as determined by the users' preferences rather than by those of the traffic authorities. The flexibility of pricing enables travellers who value their journey at a price equal to, or greater than, the costs they impose on others to undertake the journey. (Note that there are strong similarities between the argument for preferring pricing to regulation in the transport case and the argument for preferring tax/ subsidies to regulation in the case of pollution control – see Chapter 6).

Against this view, others argue that this freedom of choice is so dependent on an individual's income, and the distribution of income is so unequal, that for all but a few people their preferences are dominated by income limitations. This is essentially an argument about the best way to deal with equity issues. Some would then argue that equity concerns should be dealt with by income transfers which will allow the poor to buy transport services. Others would argue that direct income transfers may not be high enough and so some method of lowering the price of transport for the poor will still be necessary.

# Summary

Transport is a vital component of everyday life, but as all other goods, uses scarce resources. We ask the question, how should we allocate resources to transport? Society's objectives can again be defined in terms of *efficiency* and *equity*. The efficient level of transport occurs when the marginal benefit of transport equals the marginal cost of producing it. In a free market, such a level is not likely to be achieved because of the *external (congestion and environmental)* costs imposed by users on others, lack of *information* on safety and the existence of *monopoly*. Equity goals of *participation* or of *equality of access costs* are also unlikely to be met. Accordingly, government intervention, in the form of regulation, provision subsidy and taxation is high. Recently, it has been argued that this intervention itself results in inefficiency and may not improve equity.

Regulation may help achieve efficient safety standards. But more widespread regulation of price and market structure – the latter associated with direct monopoly provision – may hinder the achievement of *productive efficiency*. Blanket subsidies to public transport may not achieve equity goals. Reduction of state intervention may improve productive efficiency and consumer choice. *Pricing policies* could be introduced to deal with externalities. Different types of tax (*petrol and parking charges*), direct *congestion tax*, and the *subsidisation of public transport* have been put forward. Of these, taxes related to use (and so to the creation of costs) are argued to be most efficient but the costs of implementing them (technical and political) may be high. *Second best* policies of subsidising transport services with lower external costs per passenger may not be desirable from either an efficiency or equity point of view.

# Further Reading

There are a number of textbooks devoted to the economics of transport. Button (1982) is for students with a background in economics, and Nash (1982) examines the economics of public transport. A detailed and technical study on the value of time of different transport users is MVA *et al.* (1988). The case for and against a wide range of types of government intervention is clearly surveyed in Glaister et al. (1990). The Oxford Review of Economic Policy, 6, No. 2, (Summer 1990) contains several articles dealing with issues of efficiency and equity, though some are only accessible to economists. Jones-Lee in that issue deals with valuation of safety. The Journal of Transport Economics and Policy contains many articles on deregulation; Gwilliam (1989) assesses the effects of bus deregulation in the UK. Vickers and Yarrow (1988) provide an excellent discussion of privatisation and deregulation of transport industries. The use of public transport and equity is discussed in Le Grand (1982), and some evidence is provided in Bramley *et al.* (1989).

# Questions for Discussion

1. How might a system of road pricing be used to assist investment decisions on new road building?

2.  Because the external congestion costs that one road user imposes upon another are borne, in total, by road users as a group and do not affect non road users, they do not imply an inefficient use of resources. Do you agree?

3.  Consider the case for and against selling licences which would be necessary for a vehicle to gain entry to the present congested central areas of large cities.

4.  Is queuing a more equitable means of dealing with congestion than using a pricing policy.

5.  If public transport in cities was free it would solve the problem of traffic congestion. Do you agree?

6.  Consider the arguments for and against abolishing road fund taxation and replacing it by additional taxes on petrol and diesel oil.

7.  Time savings are a major benefit of most transport improvements. How do you think economists might go about valuing these savings?

8.  It is sometimes argued by anti-road-building campaigners that building new roads does not solve traffic congestion because new roads generate additional traffic. Show how this possibility would affect the analysis carried out in this chapter.

9.  Is there a case for removal of all subsidies to public transport?

# The Distribution of Income and Wealth

# 8

The distribution of resources is a concern common to most societies. Despite sustained economic growth, inequality and poverty remain issues even in rich countries. In the UK in 1987 the richest fifth of households received 42 per cent of post-tax income and the bottom fifth 7.2 per cent. The government's low income statistics showed that in 1985 over four million families were receiving government assistance because of low incomes and a further 2.5 million families had incomes below 110 per cent of the official poverty level. Much government activity has been directed towards the reduction of poverty or inequality in income. Many of the equity concerns discussed elsewhere in the book have at their base a concern over the unequal distribution of resources in a market economy. Indeed, some argue that equity concerns over access to specific goods, such as education, social care or transport, are best met by altering the distribution of the means to purchase those goods and services. To understand why an unequal distribution emerges and what actions a government might take to ameliorate this problem, it is necessary to examine how rewards are determined by the market.

We begin this chapter with a discussion of the distribution of wealth, of poverty and inequality, and of how each may be measured. We then examine possible objectives society may hold with respect to the distribution of income and wealth. We follow this with an examination of the operation of the market in the determination of this distribution of resources and assess whether market allocation will meet society's objectives. In the next chapter, we turn to an examination of government intervention.

# Measuring Income and Wealth

Before we can look at the distribution of income and wealth, we must distinguish between the two and consider how they are measured. Both are measures of an individual's purchasing power – her ability to buy goods and services. However, income is the increase in purchasing power over a given period of time, while wealth is the amount of purchasing power at any given moment. In other words, wealth is a stock and income is the flow from that stock. For example, an individual with £10 000 invested in a bank at an annual interest rate of 10 per cent would have a stock of wealth of £10 000 and a flow of income from that wealth of £1000 per year.

We can distinguish between three types of wealth. The first is physical wealth, consisting of the physical assets an individual may hold – for instance, houses and consumer durables. The second is financial wealth, which includes bank accounts and shares. The third is human capital, embodied in an individual as a result of skills and training. It is generally a mixture of innate talent – such as that possessed by a great opera singer – and investment in education and training. (A discussion of the acquisition of human capital is given in Chapter 3). Each type of wealth yields a flow of income. In theory, all these flows could be measured and added up to derive an estimate of an individual's annual total income. However, doing this is extremely difficult. For example, what is the correct measure of the income a person could derive from a physical asset such as a house? or a painting they own? or from their stock of skills? For these reasons, only money income is generally used as a measure of an individual's income.

Our examination of the distribution of income can be split into an examination of poverty and an examination of inequality. Both are based on information about incomes and both involve value judgements, but they are two different concepts. Poverty is concerned with the definition and measurement of the numbers and extent of the poor in society. Inequality is concerned with differences between individuals in income and access to resources.

# Measuring Poverty

The first problem involved in measuring poverty is to define what is meant by the term. This is not as easy it might appear. The official poverty line in the United States is over fifty times the *average* income in India. The American poor are thus extremely well off in comparison to the majority of Indians. Does this imply that poverty is not a problem in the United States – or indeed anywhere in the Western world including Britain?

The answer to this question will depend on whether one adopts an *absolute* or a *relative* definition of poverty. An absolute definition is one that could be applied at all times in all societies such as, for instance, the level of income necessary for bare subsistence. A relative definition relates the living standards of the poor to the standards that prevail elsewhere in the society in which they live. Thus, for instance, the poor could be defined as those whose incomes fall below half the average income, or those whose income means they cannot afford to engage in the normal activities of individuals in wider society.

Both interpretations have their problems. It is remarkably difficult to find an absolute definition of poverty that is quite independent of social norms; scientists from different cultures disagree on even basic nutritional requirements for subsistence, let alone on the requirements for warmth, shelter and so on. On the other hand, to adopt a strictly relative definition is to imply that the poor in India are no worse off than the poor in Britain, which is clearly absurd. Ideally poverty should be defined in some way that takes account of both considerations.

In practice most experts in the field define poverty relative to their own society. However even once this has been decided problems remain. First, there is the problem of which measure of resources should be used as the indicator of poverty. Possible candidates for indicators include income, expenditure, housing conditions, education attainment and employment status. In practice, because the data is easily available and because it generally correlates well with other indicators, income is preferred, though as noted above, it does not necessarily reflect income from all sources of wealth. Second, there is the question of the choice of the appropriate income unit. Should we consider only the individual's, or should the measure of poverty take into account the fact that people live in families and households and they may have access to resources other than their own? The choice of unit of the analysis can make considerable difference to the number of persons defined as living in poverty. Consider a family with a single male earner, a woman and two children with an income of £10 000. Regarded as a family, the adults and children share the £10 000 and so here may fall below the poverty line. However, if the man is regarded as a separate unit then the woman and children have no income and so will be defined as poor. From a theoretical point of view a family or household is the appropriate unit if there is sharing within families and households; the problem in practice is ascertaining the degree of sharing and applying a common standard to all persons. Third, there is the problem of deciding what point on the indicator of poverty divides the poor from the rest of the population. One measure is the minimum level as specified in government social security pro- grammes. The principal problem with this measure is that when the level of payment under the social security programme is raised, the number of persons defined as being in poverty will also rise (assuming no other changes in incomes occurs). Use of such a threshold also makes it difficult to compare across countries or across time as it is impossible to distinguish differences in the generosity of income support schemes from underlying differences in extent of low income.

Others would prefer to see the indicator set to reflect an individual's ability to participate in society. While such an aim would seem an appropriate objective for a relative poverty mea- sure, it is difficult to define those activities on which participation should be evaluated. For example, participation could be defined, in the UK, as being able to eat meat four times a week. However the rich person who is a vegetarian will not consume meat, but it would be incorrect to classify them as poor. Even when the indicator of poverty and the cut-off point have been selected there remains a further problem: should we measure simply the *numbers* of persons or families in poverty or should we try to get some measure of the *degree* to which they are poor? The first is often termed the *head-count* measure. An example of the second is the *poverty-gap* measure, where the total amount of money necessary to fill up the gap between poor people's incomes and the poverty line is calculated.

Both concepts involve value judgements. And as the absolute and relative measures of poverty, these two summary statistics are complements rather than substitutes. The first provides a summary of the total numbers in poverty, but gives no measure of the extent of poverty. Moreover, it has the unfortunate property that a sufficient transfer of income from the poorest person in society to the person just below the poverty line will be recorded as a reduction in poverty.

The second is an estimate of costs required to remove poverty. Both measures have the defect that they take no account of duration of poverty. However, for those concerned to alleviate poverty the length of time an individual is in poverty may be as important as its occurrence. If most people experience poverty for a short period only, the problem is less severe than if a small number of people experience poverty for most of their lives. This last issue is linked to the analysis of why people are poor, and one to which we will return once we have reviewed some measures of inequality.

# Measuring Inequality

Poverty and inequality, though their causes may be linked, are separate concepts. Poverty refers to a standard of living below which individuals are defined to be 'poor'. Inequality is concerned with the distribution of resources between different individuals, not with the definition of what constitutes poverty.

The income distribution of a particular country is frequently presented in summary form, as in Table 8.1.

**TABLE 8.1**
**Distribution of Total Income, West Germany, USA, UK, and Sweden**

| Group | Share of Total Income (%) | | | |
| --- | --- | --- | --- | --- |
| | West Germany | USA | UK | Sweden |
| Bottom 20 per cent | 6.5 | 4.5 | 5.7 | 8.1 |
| Next 20 per cent | 11.9 | 11.3 | 11.3 | 13.3 |
| Middle 20 per cent | 16.1 | 17.8 | 18.2 | 17.4 |
| Next 20 per cent | 21.9 | 25.5 | 25.0 | 24.5 |
| Top 20 per cent | 43.6 | 40.9 | 39.8 | 36.7 |

Source: Calculated from data in Atkinson (1989b).

The data in such tables may also be presented graphically. One method of doing this is to draw a Lorenz curve. Figure 8.1 shows the Lorenz curve for the UK data. It was constructed by plotting the percentages of the national income received by different percentages of the population when the latter are cumulated from the bottom. That is, it plots the percentage of income received by the bottom twenty per cent, the percentage received by the bottom forty per cent, the bottom sixty per cent and so on. Now if there were full equality – such that the bottom sixty per cent of the population received sixty per cent of the national income, or the bottom eighty per cent received eighty per cent – then the Lorenz curve would lie along the diagonal of the diagram. Hence, the further the curve is away from the diagonal, the further is the distribution from full equality and therefore the greater the inequality. We can therefore obtain an indicator of the extent of inequality in a distribution by observing the position of the Lorenz curve.

**FIGURE 8.1**
**Lorenz Curve of Income Distribution (UK)**

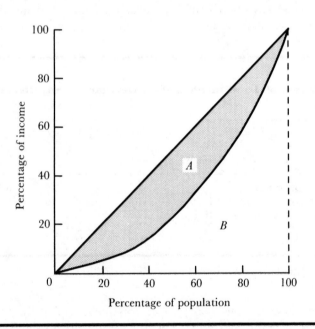

Source: Atkinson (1989b).

A summary measure of the amount of inequality implicit in a Lorenz curve can be obtained by use of the *Gini coefficient*. This is calculated by dividing the area between the Lorenz curve and the diagonal by the area of the triangle formed by the diagonal and the axes. In Figure 8.1, it is the area *A* divided by *A* plus *B* (the non-shaded area). As the Lorenz curve moves further from the diagonal, area *A* gets larger relative to *A* + *B*, and the Gini coefficient approaches one, indicating greater inequality; as the Lorenz curve moves closer to the diagonal, *A* gets smaller relative to *A* + *B*, and the Gini coefficient approaches zero, indicating greater equality. If we calculate Gini coefficients for the USA, West Germany and Sweden for the data in Table 8.1, we find them to be 0.368, 0.377 and 0.292 respectively, suggesting greater equality in Sweden than in West Germany and the USA.

However, one has to be careful in interpreting numbers such as these. The Gini coefficient is one of several 'summary statistics' that are used to measure inequality; others include the standard deviation, the coefficient of variation and Atkinson's index (the methods by which these can be calculated can be found in Cowell, 1977, pp. 152–4). All of these statistics are attempts to summarise a vast amount of information concerning differences in peoples' incomes by compressing that information into one number. In the process of this compression, inevitably, some pieces of information get emphasised while others get ignored. For instance, it is not apparent from the Gini coefficient (nor indeed from Table 8.1) what is the income share of the top *one* per cent in each country. If we were solely concerned with the welfare of the least advantaged group, say the bottom 20 per cent, then we might wish to compare across countries the proportion of income received by just this group across countries. For the data presented in Table 8.1, the USA heads the inequality league, followed by the UK. West Germany is now not the 'most unequal' member of the table. More generally, the choice of summary statistic (or indeed of all methods of summarising information concerning inequality, such as tables or graphs) will depend on one's values; there is no objective method of measuring the extent of inequality.

Finally, as in measures of poverty, there is the issue of which definition of income to use. Should income be defined as it is for income tax purposes; or should we use a broader conception that, for instance, takes account of capital gains or untaxed fringe benefits? Also, again, what is the appropriate unit of analysis – the individual, the 'tax unit' (the unit of assessment for income tax purposes) or the household? Are we interested only in differences in *annual* income, or ought we to concentrate more on differences in *life-time* income that people receive over the whole of their life? These are all important questions and ones over which there is not general agreement, in part because of technical difficulties, such as that of measuring lifetime income, but in part because all such measures involve value judgements about which there is not consensus.

# Objectives

The primary concern of policy aimed at the redistribution of income and wealth is likely to be to promote a fair or equitable distribution. But the definition of what is 'fair' or 'equitable' is one about which there may be considerable disagreement. As we have seen in Chapter 1 and in our discussion of other areas of social policy, a number of conflicting objectives may be present. Here we put forward four different types of objective and consider the arguments put forward in their defence.

## *Minimum Standards*

The minimum standards approach concerns itself only with people at the bottom end of the income scale, the poor. Its advocates argue that the interests of equity would be adequately served if society ensured that no-one's incomes fell below a given minimum. The wealth of the rich, or the more general pattern of inequality, are of no concern; all that is required is the elimination of poverty.

Most would accept that a concern for poverty is an essential part of any policy for redistribution. However, to argue that it should be the only concern would be more controversial. We have seen that it is very difficult to say what we mean by poverty without some reference to the rest of the income distribution. Further, it seems a little odd to apply considerations of equity only to those at one end of the income scale and not to those at the other. If a principle of equity is to be applied to judge the amounts that people receive in income, should it not be applied throughout the income distribution, not just to one part of it? It is not so clear that the problem of poverty can be so easily divorced from that of inequality.

## Equality

A more radical objective for redistribution policy is that of total equality. Every member of society, regardless of position or ability, should have the same income. To many this has a strong intuitive appeal. Our society cherishes equality of rights before the law and equal voting rights. Why should it not also be committed to economic equality: equality in economic resources?

If all individuals were identical in tastes and preferences, then full equality could be justified on utilitarian grounds. A utilitarian goal for society is that the sum of individuals' happiness or utilities should be as large as possible. Suppose that, as utilitarianism requires, we can compare peoples' levels of happiness or utility. Suppose further that, as seems reasonable, an extra pound's worth of income offers less utility to the rich than to the poor. Then taking money away from the rich and giving it to the poor will raise the sum of utilities, and as we continue to redistribute income from the rich to the poor, total utility in society will rise. It will be at its highest when all individuals have the same income.

However, this policy prescription can be challenged on several grounds. First, there are obvious difficulties in comparing peoples' levels of happiness or utility. Second, even if this can be done, it is not always obvious that an extra pound's worth of income is worth less to the rich than to the poor; as people's incomes rise they may develop more expensive tastes. More generally, we cannot assume that people have identical preferences and tastes. Third, taxing the rich and giving money to the poor may make both rich and poor work less hard, thus reducing total production and so total income and hence the total amount of utility that can be achieved.

## Inequality

Many believe there to be strong case for some members of a society to receive more by way of economic advantage than others. For instance, it is often argued that income should be distributed according to *need*. Equally often it is claimed that it should be distributed according to merit or *desert*. Precisely what constitutes a need or what makes one person more deserving than another will vary according to the values of whoever is putting forward the argument. As far as 'needs' are concerned, on different occasions it has been argued that the old need less than the young, the low-born less than the high-born (because the former have not been brought up with the latter's expensive tastes), the mentally ill less than the sane, the physically healthy less than the physically ill, the clerk less than the coalminer. On the 'desert' side, at various points in history it has been claimed that free people deserve more than slaves, aristocrats more than labourers, the hard worker more than the idler, the intelligent more than the unintelligent, men more than women, white more than black. In all these cases one or more of the features that distinguish one individual from another are isolated as the key factor or factors justifying an additional distinction in terms of a person's share in the distribution of economic resources.

In Western society, there has been more concentration on desert than on need. In particular, individuals are often considered to deserve any extra income they have acquired through their own efforts and sacrifices (from hard work, for example, or from savings). According to this view, income resulting from individuals' own efforts is justified; that which results from factors outside their control is not.

The desert view is implicit in another objective that often appears in discussions of redistribution: *equality of opportunity*. Under this conception a particular distribution of income is equitable if it is the outcome of a situation where everyone has the same opportunities open to them, the same chances of being rich or poor. A similar conception is that of *procedural justice*. If the income distribution is the result of a process, the rules of which everyone regards as fair, then the outcome is fair or just. An example might be a lottery; if everyone entering a lottery accepts the rules of the lottery, then the eventual distribution of the winnings from the lottery should be acceptable to all those participating, losers as well as winners.

The problem with the operationalisation of either of these two concepts is that value judgements about the equivalence of opportunity or procedure must be made. Extreme positions, say a society in which income depended only on an individual's parents, can easily be identified as lacking equality of opportunity. But situations in which the outcome may be procedurally fair but determined by differences in past actions, which may themselves be the result of discrimination in the past, are harder to define as either fair or unfair.

There are those who would reject the idea that there are intrinsic moral reasons why one individual 'needs' or 'deserves' more than another, but who would none the less argue that some inequality is necessary if some of society's other objectives are to be attained. Measures aimed at reducing inequality might, for instance, interfere with individual liberty to an unacceptable extent. Also there may be substantial costs in terms of economic efficiency. For instance, equality of income would greatly reduce people's incentive to work, for they would receive the same income however hard they worked, and indeed if they did not work at all. Moreover, people would have a reduced incentive to save; people would not save to receive an extra income from their savings because it would all be taken away, and they would not save for their old age because their retirement income would always be adjusted to be the same as everyone else's. Thus the supply of labour and of capital investment (financed out of people's savings) to the process of production would be severely reduced; and so, therefore, would production itself. The output of goods and services would fall heavily, and the net result of equalisation would be that everybody would be worse off.

This possibility can be illustrated by the diagram used in Chapter 1 to show the distribution of a commodity (butter) between two people (Adam and Eve). In Figure 8.2 the line $XY$ shows all the possible distributions of a fixed quantity of butter between Adam and Eve. Now suppose that the initial distribution is a point such as $B$, where Adam receives considerably more butter than Eve. A benevolent government observes this and decides to take some butter off Adam and give it to Eve. However, as a result, Adam, receiving less of the proceeds, begins to put less work into producing butter. The total amount of butter available therefore falls; the consumption frontier moves inwards, and they may end up at a position such as $C$ where they are both worse off.

In practice, the government does not take goods such as butter from people, but imposes taxes on their income or expenditures. Now the effect of taxation is not necessarily to make people work less (we look at this in more detail in Chapter 9) and people work for reasons other than money: for instance, enjoyment, self-esteem, status; so it is

**FIGURE 8.2**
**The Efficiency-Equity Trade-off**

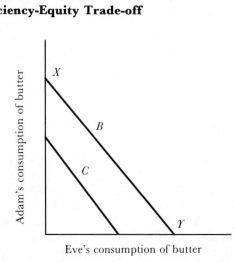

Eve's consumption of butter

difficult to assess the impact of taxation on work effort. However, it is likely that some disincentive effect of this kind exists and, that the greater the amount of redistribution the greater the disincentive. This fact, if true, implies that there is a trade-off between achieving greater efficiency (in the sense of producing greater national output) and achieving greater equality.

With this in mind it has been suggested that an appropriate social goal might be the achievement of the maximum degree of income equality compatible with a given rate of economic growth. A practical problem with this approach is that no-one as yet really knows to what degree incentives are important and therefore to what degree inequality contributes to economic growth. This ignorance can mean the growth argument is used to justify really high levels of inequality. During the late 1960s, for instance, Brazil grew at the rate of 10 per cent a year, and paid some of its higher executives at US income levels. Yet the calorie intake of peasants in the north-east of the country fell during that time to a level about one-half the United Nations' prescribed 'minimum' level of nutrition.

To counter this kind of difficulty, a refinement of the approach has been suggested by philosopher John Rawls (1972). He argues that inequality in a society is only justified if it works to the advantage of the least well-off member. Thus if some difference in incomes is necessary to induce people to increase the national output, and if as a result of the overall output increase the incomes of the poorest sections of the community are increased (even if the degree of inequality remains the same), then the initial difference in incomes is justified. The conclusion of this kind of argument is that society should permit that degree of inequality which maximises the economic position of those with the minimum resources; hence it is often termed the *maximin* objective. Adoption of this goal would have the advantage of enabling a society to avoid the kind of situation that existed in Brazil, for, under the maximin objective, the only inequality permitted would be that which maximised the welfare of the poorest peasant. A disadvantage of the objective is that it assumes society to be indifferent between varying degrees of inequality, all of which contribute to the same level of well-being for the least well-off, but which also contribute to considerable variations in well-being among other members of the community.

Such are some of the possible objectives that we might consider when deciding whether a given distribution of income is desirable. We must now examine the way in which incomes are determined in the market-place. We will then be able to analyse whether the resulting distribution can be described as desirable according to any of the criteria discussed above.

# The Market System and the Distribution of Income

Most governments intervene extensively in the market in order to redistribute income. But is such intervention really necessary? Could the market operating without government intervention meet any of the objectives discussed above? To answer these questions we must examine the way in which incomes are determined in the market-place. Note that we are not necessarily, as we have done in previous chapters, discussing market failure. Rather, we are examining the workings of the market and assessing whether the outcome is likely to fail to meet the equity objectives identified above.

Under a market system people derive incomes from selling the resources that they own. Many people own a range of resources, for instance, their homes, physical assets in the homes, some financial assets. For most people, one resource – their human capital – accounts for most of their wealth and their income. They sell this resource to the market, to be used in production, in return for wages. Those who own financial capital use it to participate in production in return for interest payments and profits. And those who own physical capital, such as land, sell the services of it in return for rent. The income that individuals receive will therefore depend on two things: the amount and type of capital (resources) they own and the price they can get for it. People owning large quantities of resources of the kind that command a high price will have high incomes; people with few resources or with resources that can be sold for only a low price will have low incomes, and hence be in poverty. We need therefore to examine two phenomena: the distribution of resources and the prices of those resources.

## *Differences in Resources*

Official statistics on the distribution of resource ownership concern the distribution of physical and financial wealth; that is, the value of peoples' holdings of land and financial assets. Some recent figures for the United Kingdom are summarised in Table 8.2. The first column shows the distribution of 'marketable' wealth; that is, the value of items that can be bought and sold (stocks, shares, property, and so on) among the adult population. The distribution is very unequal, with the top ten per cent owning half of all marketable wealth.

The second column shows the distribution of 'marketable' plus 'non-marketable' wealth. The latter category includes items such as private and state pension rights which, though arguably part of people's assets, are somewhat different from other items in that they cannot be marketed or sold by one person to another. Although more equal than the distribution of marketable wealth, this distribution is still quite unequal, with the top five per cent owning just under a quarter of all wealth.

What determines the distribution of wealth? There are basically two factors: inheritance and life-time accumulation. An individual may own non-human capital because she has accumulated it herself,

**TABLE 8.2**
**The Distribution of Wealth (UK 1987)**

| | Share of wealth (%) | |
| | Marketable | Marketable plus non-marketable |
| --- | --- | --- |
| Wealthiest 1 per cent | 18 | 11 |
| Wealthiest 5 per cent | 36 | 24 |
| Wealthiest 10 per cent | 50 | 35 |
| Remaining 90 per cent | 50 | 65 |

Source: Inland Revenue Statistics (1989): Series C and Series E.

for instance, saving it out of income; alternatively, she may have received it as an inheritance through a gift or legacy from someone else. The amount of labour an individual 'owns' will be dependent in part upon the physical strength and innate abilities that she inherited, and in part upon the skills she has accumulated during her life-time as a result of education and experience.

In practice, it is difficult to separate the different effects of accumulation and inheritance. How much of an individual's labour resources depend on her genetic make-up and how much on her education and environment is a question that has yet to be resolved. Perhaps the major factor affecting the quality of the labour resources owned by an individual is intelligence; but there is enormous controversy as to whether intelligence is inherited or acquired through environmental influence. Even in the case of non-human capital, it is not easy to specify what proportion of the wealthy at any point in time gained their wealth because of their own efforts at accumulation or because of inheritance.

Not only is it difficult to separate out the effects of inheritance and accumulation in practice, but it is also not always easy to separate them conceptually. For instance, consider the 'accumulation' of educational and other skills. Now it is commonplace in Western societies that the children of educated parents tend to do better in the educational system (and hence to accumulate more labour resources) than do the children from less-educated homes. This is because educated parents tend to introduce their children to reading and to other useful learning skills, and generally encourage a positive attitude towards school work in a way that less educated families do not. In a sense, the children of the former could therefore be said to have 'inherited' their superior skills from their parents – or at least to have inherited the ability to accumulate those skills.

A more detailed discussion of these issues is beyond our scope. However, it does appear that the ability to accumulate is to some extent dependent upon inheritance, and the importance of inheritance as a cause of differences in resource ownership must be thereby enhanced. Part of the inequalities in resource ownership in the present generation is thus the result of the inequalities in the previous one.

## *Differences in Prices*

The second reason why incomes differ is because people receive different prices for the resources they own. The price of a resource depends upon its productivity. The more productive a resource, the more profitable will be its use and so the higher the price its owner can command. As an example, let us consider a piece of waste land. If this land is located in the centre of a large city, potential buyers know they could charge high prices once they develop the land. They could build shops and offices and charge high rents, or build homes and sell them for high prices. Thus buyers will be willing to pay a high price to the land owner to acquire the land. In contrast, consider the same amount of land in a remote rural area. Here there are fewer opportunities to use the land. So the amount any developer would be prepared to pay is less, because any development on the land will reap only a small return. In some cases there may not even be any developers willing to buy the land.

Exactly the same argument can be applied to the demand for human capital. The more productive the employee, the more an employer will be willing to pay them for their time. So the wages people receive will depend on their productivity – on the quality of their human capital. Now human capital is a mixture of innate ability and training. To the extent that these differ (for whatever reasons) individuals will have different incomes. The fact that the rewards depend on productivity means not only will incomes differ across people, but within people's lifetimes their income will fluctuate. When first entering the labour market, their productivity will be low, for they have few skills. Once they have acquired skills their productivity will be higher. Finally, when older, their productivity may be lower, particularly if they work in a job requiring manual skills and a high degree of physical mobility.

In practice it is very difficult to establish how productive any one individual is, partly because an individual in one job may be more productive that the same individual in another. Thus to be a coalminer requires more stamina than to be a clerk. To be a singer requires less numerical ability than to be a computer programmer. What is clear is that other factors besides productivity can determine the rewards an individual gets. Some of these may be due to the actions of other *suppliers* of labour. For example, *professional associations* and *trade unions* act to raise the wages of their members. This they can do by closed-shop provisions, thus preventing non-members bidding down wages, or by extending training periods, so keeping out other workers. Both manual and non-manual occupations have 'restrictive practices'. It is argued, for example, that the training period of doctors is longer than necessary for obtaining the required standards. Indeed, for many professions, the standards themselves – which also have the effect of restricting competition – have been criticised as being too high for the bulk of activities undertaken.

Others are the result of actions of the *demanders* of labour. *Discrimination* may result in wage differentials for equally skilled workers. For example, if a group of employers in an area prefers to employ only white males, then black males and all women could not compete for the jobs offered. As a result, wages for the white males would remain higher than those for the rest. How long employers could maintain this preference for discrimination would depend on the competitive pressures they faced. Discrimination may also take place at the point of entry to training; this would prevent certain types of people from entering higher paid occupations and so act to maintain differentials in pay. One explanation for discrimination is asymmetric information between employer and employees. Because it is difficult for employers to tell how productive an employee will be, employers may use characteristics of the individuals as *signals* of higher productivity. Thus they may use the level of education as a signal of higher productivity and restrict entry to certain grades of work to those with, say, a degree. Or they may use gender as a signal and pay men more than women. If these signals are not perfect measures of productivity, then high productivity people with the signal that indicates low productivity may get paid less than their actual productivity.

Finally, because the demand for labour is a derived from the demand for final goods, the amount an employer is willing to pay will depend on the price of the good it produces. If demand for an employer's product is low, the value of an employee's work to an employer, no matter how skilled they are, will be low. Thus if demand falls employers will lay off workers or try to lower wages. If aggregate demand (demand in the whole economy) is low, some people may not be able to find a job, even though they would be willing to work at the going wage. In other cases, while demand in the economy as a whole may be high, employers may be located in one area of the country and the owners of human capital in another. If people are not in a position to move immediately they may be unemployed.

Thus we can see that the prices individuals receive for their capital (physical, financial or human) will depend on demand and supply. There will inequality of income between individuals. In addition, individuals' incomes from human capital will fluctuate over their lifetime, sometimes due to expected events – such as retirement – and sometimes due to unexpected events – such as a fall in aggregate demand. During these periods, unless individuals have access to large amounts of non-human capital, they may experience poverty. And because spells of unemployment tend to be concentrated among groups of people, some individuals will spend considerably longer in poverty or on low incomes than others. Policy to deal with the causes of movements in aggregate demand or labour market failure are outside the remit of this book. Policies to deal with inequality in the distribution of resources are discussed in other chapters. But does the market not provide ways for individuals to cope with fluctuations in income ? There does indeed exist a market response to deal with unexpected loss of income – insurance. So it could be possible to buy insurance against those fluctuations in income which result in inequality and poverty. But is it?

## *Insurance Failure*

Private insurance against disability, unemployment and old age was widespread prior to the 1930s in most European countries and in

North America. Since the 1930s, provision for these events has come to be viewed as one of the primary functions of government. There are several reasons why the private market may fail to provide insurance for all who want to buy it or may provide too low a level of cover.

## Social risks

Social risks are risks faced by society as a whole. Inflation is one such risk; all persons in society are affected by inflation. A fall in aggregate demand, resulting in an increase in unemployment, is another. Private insurance operates by pooling risks; insurers can provide cover provided the probability that one person makes a claim is not linked to the probability another will make a claim. In the situation of social risks, the private insurance market cannot pool risks because all their insured customers face the same risks. Technically the risks are not independent events. Thus, if private retirement policies provided indexation against inflation, in the event that inflation occurred, the insurance companies would face increases in payouts on all their policies and might well find they could not meet all these commitments at the same time. Many private insurers thus are not able to provide full cover for inflation. Government, on the other hand, can meet its pension obligations by raising taxes on the working population.

## Adverse selection

Adverse selection arises when insurance companies find it difficult to distinguish between high- and low-risk individuals and the high-risk group are more likely, at a given price, to demand more insurance than the low-risk group. With no way of telling a low from a high risk, insurance companies will set their premiums to reflect the average risk of all the insured. As a result, some of the low risk individuals may then not buy insurance, for the price will be higher than that they would be willing to pay, given their (low) riskiness. As a result of this, the ratio of high to low risks amongst the insured will rise, and so the cost of premiums will rise. More of the low risk group will not buy insurance. The end result will be fewer persons with insurance cover than would have been the case had the sellers of insurance been able to distinguish a low from a high risk person.

If individuals could conceal facts about their expected length of life, adverse selection could arise in the market for private pensions. Individuals who expected to live only a short time (the 'low' risks in this case) would find insurance unattractive.

### Moral hazard

Once an individual has taken out insurance she may reduce her efforts to avoid the event for which insurance cover has been purchased. This is called *moral hazard*. For example, if an individual has insurance against unemployment, she may be less likely to look for another job when made unemployed. Similarly, if she has a pension provided by her insurance policy, she may be more prepared to stop work than if she had no other form of income post-retirement. The effect of moral hazard is to increase the amount insurers have to pay out. This in turn will lead to an increase in premiums and as premiums increase, fewer people will want to take out insurance. Thus, as with adverse selection, the size and scope of the insurance market will fall; people will not be able to buy insurance at a price they are willing to pay and some people will be left uninsured against the costs of old age.

# The Market and Equity

Will the operation of a free market achieve any of the definitions of equity or justice discussed earlier? It is clear that the operations of the labour and capital markets will not ensure that all incomes remain above a certain minimum standard of living. Individuals with no resources (those without property, those unable to work) will not receive any income and hence will not attain a minimum standard. Of course, some of the individuals currently out of the labour market may have worked in the past (for example, the retired) and so may have savings, but in some cases these savings will not be sufficient to reach a society's minimum standards. Other individuals may have resources but receive unexpectedly low prices for them (for example, third world farmers whose income depends on world prices for their crops). Private insurance markets may not exist to cover these events. Thus in the absence of government intervention there are likely to be people whose incomes fall below a minimum standard.

The goal of full equality is highly unlikely to be met by a market system. Even if prices for all resources were the same, full equality would only arise if there was equality in resource ownership – for which there is no mechanism in a market system. *Need* and *desert* are socially defined concepts; there is no reason why the market mechanism should distribute according to these principles. While the market could create *equality of opportunity*, the existence of inheritance of financial and physical capital, which may in turn determine across to training, and so access to both labour and non-labour market rewards, is likely to prevent equal opportunity for all. Perhaps the only concept of equity to which a competitive market may conform is that of *procedural justice*, but the existence of monopoly and barriers to entry may limit the extent to which a market system can be seen as procedurally just.

Hence, under most interpretations of the term equity, there is a role for government intervention in the distribution of income to ensure goals are met. Such intervention has long been recognised by economists as a role for the state; however, it also has been long recognised that intervention may prevent the achievement of other goals of society, such as maximisation of economic output and freedom of the individual. Thus there exists, inevitably, a trade-off between efficiency and equity. In the next chapter we examine the type of policies adopted by governments to increase equity in income distribution, bearing in mind the impact of such policies on other goals held by society.

# Summary

Poverty may be measured in *absolute* or in *relative* terms. The problem with absolute definitions is to find one that can be applied at all times in all societies; the problem with purely relative definitions is that they create difficulties for comparisons between different societies. Either way it is necessary also to select the indicator of poverty (income, expenditure, education levels and so on), to select the poverty cut-off point, and to decide whether poverty should be measured in terms of a *head-count measure* or by a more comprehensive measure as the *poverty gap*. Degrees of inequality may be indicated by the construction of the relevant *Lorenz curves*, and measured by summary statistics such as the *Gini coefficient*, but the choice of inequality measure will depend on the values of the user.

The prime aim of distribution policy is likely to be justice or *equity*. It is not easy to define an equitable distribution of income. Possible interpretations include one where no-one falls below a *minimum standard*, where income is distributed *equally*, where it is distributed according to *need* or *desert*, and where it is the outcome of choices made under conditions of *equal opportunity* or *procedural justice*. Whatever interpretation is chosen, there is likely to be some *trade-off* between its attainment and that of efficiency; one possible 'combined' objective is for the economy to be organised in such a way as to maximise the welfare of the least well-off: the *maximin* objective.

Under a market system an individual's income depends on the *resources* she *inherits* and/or *accumulates*, and on the *price* she can obtain from selling those resources. The price for a resource is determined by the interaction of *supply* and *demand*. In the absence of any barriers to competition, this results in the *equalisation of net advantages* between occupations. However substantial barriers to competition do exist, particularly in the labour market. These include differences in *ability*, in *required training*, in *organisational strength*, and in the extent of *discrimination*. Private markets which provide insurance against fore-seen or unforeseen loss of income may fail due to *social risks*, *adverse selection* and *moral hazard*. Thus a purely market-determined distribu-tion of income is unlikely to be equitable, however the term is interpreted.

# Further Reading

Atkinson (1989a, Chapter 1) provides an excellent discussion of the conceptual issues in defining and measuring poverty. Other chapters in Part 1 of the same book contain more advanced technical or empirical material. For a discussion of broad measures of poverty and its extent in the UK in the 1970s, see Townsend (1979) and for a later approach in a similar spirit, Mack and Lansley (1985). For a discussion on the extent of poverty in Britain 1899–1983, see Piachaud (1988). Nolan (1989) provides a discussion of the measure-ment of poverty and the effect of changes in definition of the poverty line.

On inequality, a book well suited to non-economists is Atkinson (1983). A clear introductory discussion is provided in Barr (1987). Cowell (1977) is a textbook for economists. Atkinson (1980) provides a very useful set of readings, although some are too technical for those without economics training.

An often quoted and comprehensive discussion of need is provided in Bradshaw (1972). Begg *et al.* (1987) provide clear and introductory discussion of the economic theory of factor (labour) prices; other introductory (micro-) economic textbooks cover similar ground.

# Questions for Discussion

1.  In what sense, if any, can it be said that the lowest ten per cent of the income distribution in Britain are as poor as the lowest ten per cent in India?
2.  Is there an objective way of measuring inequality?
3.  'The poor will always be with us'. Discuss.
4.  Should we measure inequality in annual or in life-time incomes?
5.  Atkinson (1989b, p.4) gives the following figures for the income distribution in Sweden, UK and Germany. Construct the Lorenz Curve for each. Which is the more equal?

|  | *Share in Total Income* | | |
| --- | --- | --- | --- |
| *Group* | *West Germany* | *UK* | *Sweden* |
| Bottom 20 per cent | 6.5 | 5.7 | 8.1 |
| Next 20 per cent | 11.9 | 11.3 | 13.3 |
| Middle 20 per cent | 16.1 | 18.2 | 17.4 |
| Next 20 per cent | 21.9 | 25.0 | 24.5 |
| Top 20 per cent | 43.6 | 39.8 | 36.7 |

6.  Should miners be paid more than doctors?
7.  'Under the market system, the net advantages of different occupations are equalised. Hence the distribution of income is not only efficient; it is also fair.' Do you agree?
8.  'It is not in the long-run interest of employers to discriminate against women or blacks; hence discrimination in employment will eventually disappear'. Do you agree?

# The Redistribution of Income and Wealth

# 9

Most government policies aimed at redistribution of income and wealth can be classified either as transfers or regulation. Transfers can be divided into transfers from individuals – taxes – and transfers to individuals – subsidies. The income tax is an example of a transfer from taxpayers to the government, unemployment benefit is an example of a transfer from the government to individuals – in this case the unemployed. Regulatory activity includes legislative attempts to regulate the price individuals receive for the sale of their services; minimum wage legislation is an example. In this chapter we ask how effective these policies are in achieving redistribution, and what impact they have on efficiency of the economic system. We begin with an analysis of the current tax and the social security system. This is followed by an examination of proposals for integration of the two through a negative income tax scheme. We conclude with a discussion of minimum wages and the taxation of wealth.

## Taxation

The extent to which government taxes its citizens varies considerably, even within countries at similar levels of national income. In Sweden in 1987 taxes and social security contributions accounted for 67 per cent of GNP. In Switzerland and the United States the proportion was 32 per cent. The comparable figure for the UK was 44 per cent. Taxes on individuals can be classified into *direct* and *indirect* taxes. Broadly, direct taxes are taxes on income, and indirect taxes are taxes on the use of income. Income tax is an example of a direct tax; VAT, taxes on alcohol, cigarettes and petrol examples of indirect taxes. The proportion of government revenue which is accounted for by each type of tax also varies across countries. Table 9.1 gives some indication of this variability.

The mixture of taxes used in any one country may also change over time. Over the ten year span 1977 to 1987, government policy in the UK considerably altered the balance between direct and indirect taxation. In 1977 direct taxes accounted for 36 per cent of total taxes and social security contributions. Indirect taxes accounted for 38 per cent. By 1987 the figures were 28 and 43 per cent respectively. The redistributive effect of these taxes is in general different. To see this we need to look at how these taxes are used.

**TABLE 9.1**
**Composition of Total Tax and Social Security Contributions 1987 (%s)**

| Country | *Percentage of taxes and social security contributions derived from:* | | |
| | Direct Taxes on households | Indirect Taxation | Social Security Contributions |
| --- | --- | --- | --- |
| France | 15 | 35 | 43 |
| West Germany | 26 | 30 | 40 |
| Japan | 24 | 27 | 28 |
| Sweden | 38 | 31 | 24 |
| Switzerland | 39 | 23 | 31 |
| UK | 28 | 43 | 18 |
| USA | 37 | 28 | 24 |

Source: *Economic Trends* (1990a).

## Taxes and Redistribution

*Income tax*

The UK income tax is often thought to be highly progressive and hence to be an effective way of redistributing income. That is, it is supposed to take a higher proportion of income from the rich in tax than from the rest of the population and so reduce the share of the former in national income.

When considering the redistributive power of the income tax system it is important to distinguish between *average* and *marginal* tax rates. The average tax rate is the proportion of an individual's total income that goes in tax, whereas the marginal rate is the proportion of any extra income that goes in tax. To illustrate, consider an income tax system, not unlike the British one, where the first £3000 of income was exempt from tax and all income thereafter was taxed at a rate of 25 per cent. Then an individual with an income of £15 000 a year would pay £3000 in tax (25 per cent of £12 000), and hence would have an average tax rate of 20 per cent (£3000 as a percentage of £15 000). Any extra income, however, would be taxed not at 20 per cent but at 25 per cent; the individual's marginal rate.

Marginal tax rates in Britain are still progressive, despite cuts in tax rates in the 1980s. In 1988 the basic tax rate was 25 per cent, the tax rate on higher incomes was 40 per cent. But a high marginal rate on higher incomes does not necessarily imply a high average rate. For the average rate will depend on the allowances claimed; that is, on the amounts that can be deducted from income before it is assessed for tax. Under the British tax system one such allowance is the interest paid on mortgages. The allowance operates as follows. Consider an individual earning £20 000 per year who has interest payments of £3000 on her mortgage, and who is subject to 25 per cent income tax. With the personal and mortgage allowance, she will be able to deduct £6000 from her income before it is taxed. Her tax bill will therefore be £3500 (25 per cent of £14 000). She will thus have an average tax rate of 17.5 per cent; 3.5 percentage points lower than that faced by the £15 000 earner we considered earlier (assuming the latter does not have mortgage payments). Despite the operation of such allowances, the net effect of the UK income tax in 1987 was *progressive*. That is, the average tax rate rose with income. For non-retired households, income tax accounted for 4.3 per cent of the gross income of the households in the lowest quintile of the income distribution but for 17.7 of the gross income of those in the highest income quintile.

Income taxes may be paid on all sources of income – that is, income from wages and salaries and income from investments (though the rates on 'earned' and 'unearned' income may differ). But in many countries, a specific tax is imposed on wages and salaries to fund social security payments. These taxes are generally paid both by employees and employers and are often called *pay-roll taxes*.

## Social security taxes

In the UK the pay-roll tax is national insurance contributions, and is paid both by the employee and by her employer. The tax paid is related to the wage of the employee. The amount of National Insurance contributions paid by employees tends to be closely related to the amount of household gross income before tax at lower levels of the income range. However, since National Income contributions are paid only on wages up to a fixed ceiling (in 1987, the first £295 of weekly earnings), these tax payments are not progressive throughout the whole income range. In 1987, amongst non-retired households, households in the lowest quintile of the income distribution paid 2.5 per cent of their income in National Insurance contributions; households in the top quintile paid 4.5 per cent. But because of the ceiling, the proportion of income paid in national insurance contributions of the top quintile was less than the middle 60 per cent of non-retired households.

The combined impact of income tax and national insurance payments in 1987 was progressive – that is, higher income households paid a higher proportion of their incomes in income tax than lower income households. Looking at all households, those households in the bottom income quintile paid 13 per cent of their gross income in income tax and national insurance contributions. Households in the top quintile paid nearly 25 per cent of their gross income as tax. The effect was to reduce the inequality in gross incomes. Households in the bottom quintile had 7.5 per cent of total gross income, but 8.2 per cent of income after payment of direct taxes (including national insurance contributions). The shares for those households in the top quintile were 43 and 41 per cent respectively.

Since individuals in the UK are also taxed on their expenditure, these figures do not give the full effect of the tax system. To see what redistributive impact the tax system has as a whole we need to look at indirect taxes as well.

## Indirect Taxes

Indirect taxes are taxes levied on goods and services. The redistributive effect of such taxes depends on two factors, the *rate* at which tax is levied and the expenditure patterns of different income groups. For example, a good may be taxed at a very high rate, but if it is bought by only the rich the impact on redistribution of the tax will be very different than if it were bought only by the poor. In general, indirect taxation tends to be *regressive*. That is, the proportion of income paid in indirect taxes falls as income rises (though the absolute amount of tax paid by the rich may be greater than that paid by the poor). In the UK in 1987, for non-retired households, indirect taxes ranged from 28 per cent of income for households in the lowest quintile income group to 16 per cent in the highest, despite the fact that those in the highest quintile paid most in absolute terms. In addition, individual taxes have divergent effects – for example, the taxes on tobacco are more regressive than the taxes on motoring – a result of the different expenditure patterns of the rich and the poor.

The total effect of the tax side of the tax-benefit system in the UK was not strongly progressive, mainly because the regressive impact of the indirect taxes cancelled out the progressive effect of the income tax. In 1987 households in the lowest income quintile had average annual gross incomes (incomes after payment of cash benefits from the social security system) of £4400. Households in the highest income quintile had average gross incomes of £26 140. The ratio of these averages was in the order of 1:6. After taxes, the average income of households in the lowest quintile was £2780 and in the highest quintile was £16 560. The ratio of top to bottom incomes is again in the order of 1:6.

The often complex interactions between allowances, progressive marginal tax rate structures and taxes on different types of income have led some economists to call for the introduction of a *comprehensive income tax*. This would tax all income at the same rate regardless of source and would not have an elaborate system of tax allowances. Others have argued that the whole system should be replaced by an *expenditure tax*; that is a tax on people's outgoings rather than their incomings. Either of these could be made more progressive than the present system which uses both taxes on income and taxes on expenditure. Lack of space precludes our discussing these possible tax reforms here; however, it is worth noting that the introduction of these taxes would create large transitional costs as well as provoking considerable political opposition from those who lost tax advantages.

## Income Taxes and Efficiency

We now consider the effects of taxes on efficiency. Specifically, we shall look at the effect of income taxation on the incentive to work. An increase in the rate of income tax will affect an individual's desire to work in two ways. First, it will reduce the amount of income she receives from working an extra hour (from selling an extra unit of labour), and hence make working that extra hour, instead of using it for leisure, less attractive. Accordingly she might be inclined to reduce the number of hours she works; in other words, substitute hours spent in leisure activities for hours spent working. Economists call this the *substitution effect*. On the other hand, the reduction in an individual's income due to the tax may make her want to work more hours in order to regain the income levels she would have had prior to taxation. This is called the *income effect*. It works in the opposite direction from the substitution effect. The impact of an increase in the income tax rate is the net effect of the two.

Now it has been argued that an increase in the tax rates will always deter individuals from working harder. But if the income effect is greater than the substitution effect, then the effect of an increase in income tax rates will be to increase willingness to work, not reduce it. If the two are equal, then the net impact on work effort will be zero. Only if the substitution effect is greater than the income effect will the supply of labour be reduced. Thus we can make no statement a priori about the way income taxes might affect work; the matter can only be resolved by empirical investigation. A number of such investigations have been undertaken. Although there is still dispute over some of the findings, the broad pattern of results suggests that the total effect of tax changes on men aged between 25 and 65 is small, but the effect on other workers, particularly women with spouses or partners who work, may be quite large. An increase in income tax will tend to decrease hours worked for this group; indeed, in some cases it may lead to complete withdrawal from the labour market.

However, all these results ignore any impact taxation may have on the amount of effort an individual puts into work, or on the choice of job or on the timing of retirement or entry into the labour market. These long-run effects may be more important than changes in hours worked. At present we do not have enough evidence to draw any firm conclusions as to the effect of income tax on these decisions.

# Social Security

We have looked at the effect of taxes on individuals. We need now to look at the effect of benefits paid to individuals, most of which are paid under the social security system.

Social security benefits can be classified into *means-tested* and *categorical* benefits. To receive a means-tested benefit, a family has to show that its income – its means – falls below a certain level. In Britain Income Support is the primary means-tested benefit. It is paid to those with low incomes. Other means-tested benefits include Family Credit (paid to low income familites) and Housing Benefit. Categorical benefits, on the other hand, are paid to all those who fall within a particular social category – such as the elderly or families with children – regardless of their income. In Britain such benefits include child benefit, old age pensions and sickness benefit, paid to those with children, the retired and those who are out of work due to sickness respectively.

What are the effects of social security on redistribution and what are the consequences for the incentive to work? There is little argument that the social security system as a whole reduces poverty and it also reduces inequality. In 1987 contributory cash benefits including retirement pension, sickness/injury related payments, unemployment benefit – and non-contributory cash benefits – principally supplementary benefit and child benefit – substantially modified the UK income distribution. Cash benefits accounted for approximately seventy per cent of the gross income of the households in the lowest income quintile but less than three per cent of the gross income of households in the top income quintile. Households in the highest quintile group received fifty per cent of all income prior to the operation of the tax benefit systems. After taking into account cash benefits, this group's share fell to forty three per cent. At the other end of the scale the share of the lowest quintile group rose from 2.1 to 7.5 per cent. As a summary measure of the inequality of the distribution, the Gini coefficient (see Chapter 8) fell from 0.51 for original income to 0.36 after social security benefits.

While the system as a whole undoubtedly reduces inequality, the impact is not even across households. In the UK the reduction in inequality is most marked within retired households and a similar pattern has been found also in other systems, notably the USA. But there is growing concern about child poverty, especially children in single parent families. It is also the case that different benefits have different take-up rates and so different effects on redistribution.

Means-tested benefits are intended to target only those individuals deemed in need of support. Thus in principle they are cheaper than categorical benefits, which are paid to any person in the relevant category, regardless of income. So, for a given amount of government expenditure, more can be paid out to those in need. However, in practice, means-tested benefits have relatively low take up rates. People eligible for such benefits often do not apply for them. This may be due to lack of knowledge, because of perceived stigma of claiming a means-tested benefit, because of the complexity of the administrative procedure or because they do not expect their entitlement to be high – or, most likely, for a mixture of all these reasons. It is estimated that in 1984 the take up rates for supplementary benefit (an important means-tested benefit) was around eighty per cent and for Family Income Support (a benefit then paid to low income families) around fifty per cent (Fry and Stark, 1989). Indeed, in 1988 the government target take up for Family Credit (a means-tested benefit replacing Family Income Support) was only sixty per cent. Means-tested benefits also have the disadvantage of high administrative costs, because people's means must be assessed before they can receive benefits.

On the other hand, categorical benefits have lower administration costs and have take up rates which may often be close to 100 per cent. For this reason, some reformers have called for a 'Back-to-Beveridge' approach – called after the founder of UK modern social insurance, Sir William Beveridge. At the extreme, this would entail raising all categorical benefits to such a level that those in poverty who are in receipt of some form of categorical benefit (the majority of the poor) would be lifted out of poverty. However, while achieving this, benefits would also be paid to the non-poor. Thus in comparison with a means-tested system, a 'Back-to-Beveridge' approach would have lower administrative costs per benefit but would cost a great deal more in total as it would redistribute to both poor and non-poor.

Both types of benefit are argued to have effects on the incentive to work. That is, they have efficiency costs. Indeed all forms of social security create some disincentive to work. Benefit payments mean that recipients have to work less hard to obtain a given standard of living. In the terminology of the previous section, the benefits have an income effect which discourages work. Means-tested benefits, however, build in an additional disincentive, for they always involve a reduction in benefit if the individual concerned works harder and thus raises her 'means'. The gain from 'substituting' work for leisure is reduced; hence there is a substitution effect as well as an income effect discouraging work. Put another way, individuals face a *positive marginal tax rate* on their earnings; any increase in earnings is partly 'taxed away' through a reduction in social security payments. In some cases because of the interaction between the tax and social security systems, this tax rate can go above 100 per cent. In this case for every extra £1 earned, more than £1 is taken away in benefits. This state of affairs is often termed the *poverty trap*. In this situation there is no net financial gain to the individual from paid work. Thus, a priori, we might expect means-tested benefits to have a greater disincentive effect than categorical ones. In practice, things are not quite so simple, partly because some categorical benefits (for example, unemployment benefit) involve a reduction in benefit if the individual works.

In conclusion, in the short run, the receipt of social security benefits is likely to discourage work, whether or not payments are means-tested or categorical. It is more difficult to quantify the size of this effect as the precise effect will depend on the operation of both the tax and the benefit systems and on the group of people whose incentives are of interest. Minford (1988), for example, has argued that while the responsiveness of workers in the labour markets to income tax changes may be small, the effect of changes of the level of benefits on those on unemployment benefit may be larger because this group of workers have higher substitution effects (they are more willing to trade off money for leisure more than those in the labour markets).

Social security may also have longer-term disincentive effects. First, it is argued that the provision of state pensions has led to the widespread withdrawal of older workers from the labour force.

Throughout Europe, amongst these 65 and over, the proportion of income derived from employment has fallen since the early 1970s as the proportion derived from state transfers (including pensions) has risen. Second, it has been argued, particularly in the United States, but also in the UK, that the provision of social security creates a 'culture of dependency'. This argument, most closely associated with Murray (1984), states that the provision of social security may actually cause poverty. The operation of the benefit system makes working a less attractive option than not working. It may also lead to the break up of families because single mothers in the US can get benefits whilst mothers in households where there is a male adult cannot.

Finally, regardless of the impact on work, social security reduces an individual's incentive to save. Having savings often raise an individual's income above the eligibility level for receipt of benefit; public provision of pensions means individuals do not have to save for old age. If the rate of savings in the economy declines, economic growth may also fall. However, a fall in private savings does not necessarily mean a fall in public savings. If private savings for pensions were replaced by public savings, economic growth might not be affected by a decline in the private savings. This may influence the design of benefit instruments. For example, if state pension schemes were *fully funded* this would mean taxes on working individuals were paid into a fund, which was then paid out when these individuals retired. This would mean there was an accumulation of funds, which could replace private savings. In fact, in the UK, pensions are financed by a *pay-as-you-go* scheme, which basically transfer money from workers to the retired. Under this system, there is no accumulation of funds.

# The Negative Income Tax

The complexity of the social security system, the unintended interactions with the tax system and concern over the effect of social security on work effort have led to calls for reform of the social security system. Of these, the most radical proposal involves integrating the social security and income tax systems through a so-called 'negative' income tax.

The idea of a negative income tax is as follows. Under the existing income tax there is a basic income below which no one pays any tax (the 'allowance' level). If someone has income above the allowance level, then she pays a certain proportion of the difference between her actual income and that level in tax. It would seem logical, therefore, to make the arrangement symmetric; that is, if an individual has income below the allowance level, then she should receive a certain proportion of the difference between her income and the allowance level in the form of a 'negative' tax payment. Examples of how this might work for individuals at various levels of income are given in Table 9.1. The allowance level is £5000 and the proportion of the difference between this and the individual's income made up by the state (the negative 'tax rate') is 25 per cent. Column (a) gives each individual's income and column (b) her allowance which is the same at all levels of income. Column (c) shows the difference between her allowance and her income. Column (d) is the marginal tax rate (the same at all levels of income), and column (e) shows the amount of this difference that is made up by payments from the state under the scheme. Column (f) gives her total income after she has received the state payment. Note that the individual with an income above the allowance level (at £7000) is in the normal tax system; she has a negative amount 'received from' the state, which is simply another way of saying that she has to pay tax.

The negative income tax can be represented diagrammatically. In Figure 9.1 pre-tax income is represented on the horizontal axis and post-tax income on the vertical axis. The 45° line indicates where the two are equal. Under the negative income tax outlined in Table 9.2, this occurs at £5000. Below this point the individual receives tax. Above the threshold income, individuals pay tax. The amount of tax paid or received is the vertical distance between the 45° line and the line representing the relationship between pre- and post-tax income.

What are the advantages and disadvantages of replacing our present social security system with a negative income tax? Advocates of the negative income tax claim that it had three principal advantages over our present system. First, it is administratively simpler. By integrating the social security system into the tax system, considerable administrative savings could be made. Second, it would be a way of introducing more selectivity into the system, thus increasing its redistributive impact. But it would not suffer from the problem with other selective schemes; the low take-up

## Figure 9.1
## Operation of a Negative Income Tax System

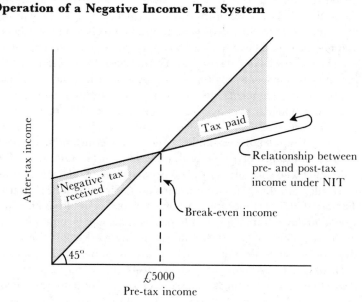

## TABLE 9.2
## A Negative Income Tax

|  | Income ($£$) (a) | Allowance ($£$) (b) | Allowance *minus* Income ($£$) (c) | Tax rate (per cent) (d) | Amount received (c) × (d) ($£$) (e) | After-tax income (a) + (e) ($£$) (f) |
|---|---|---|---|---|---|---|
| NEGATIVE TAX | 3000 | 5000 | 2000 | 25 | 500 | 3500 |
|  | 4000 | 5000 | 1000 | 25 | 250 | 4250 |
|  | 5000 | 5000 | 0 | 25 | 0 | 5000 |
| POSITIVE TAX | 7000 | 5000 | −2000 | 25 | −500 | 6500 |

of means-tested benefits. For every household in the country would fill out a tax return, and if their income was below or above the allowance level they would receive a payment from, or make a payment to, the state. Since everyone would be involved in the scheme, and no-one would have specially to apply, there would be less stigma attached to receiving payments. Third, the scheme preserves the incentive to work in a way that other social security schemes do not. Social security payments often cease as soon as an individual enters work. But under a negative income tax scheme some of any extra earnings are retained, and income can thereby be increased by working. Consider the example of the negative income tax scheme with an allowance of £5000 and a 25 per cent tax rate. Now if an individual who was earning £3000 per year from work increased her work effort, so that she was now earning £5000, it can be seen from Table 9.2 that her negative income tax payments from the state would go down from £500 to £0, but her after-tax income would go up from £3500 to £5000. By increasing her work effort she would therefore make a net gain, and she thus has an incentive to do so.

However, the scheme also has its problems. If the tax rate was lower than under existing social security and tax systems, the scheme might sacrifice equity for efficiency. It might not adequately provide for all those in need. For instance, in our example the amounts that even the poorest individual receives are not great; certainly not enough to lift her out of poverty. It would be possible to increase the amount received by the poor under the scheme by increasing the tax rate, say, to 40 per cent. However, this would increase the disincentive effects of the scheme for, with every extra pound earned, the individual would lose 40p (in tax payment). Moreover, this high tax rate would have to apply to all levels of income and it is argued that the disincentive effects this would cause would result in a larger loss in efficiency than the current system. Many of those currently in receipt of benefit may not be in the labour market at all (the retired, the disabled and chronically sick) and so the fact that they face a high marginal tax rate may affect their labour supply very little. On the other hand, it will raise the tax rate faced by those who are not currently in the benefit system but are in the labour market facing relatively low rates of income tax. They will therefore be discouraged from work.

Another way of coping with the poverty problem would be to raise the allowance level. But this would mean the scheme would provide substantial benefits to those not in need. For raising the allowance level sufficiently would take many people out of the positive income tax and into the negative one. As a result, large numbers of people could become eligible for payments who were, by any criterion, far from poor. In short, the negative income tax can create greater efficiency (by reducing work disincentives) only at the expense of equity.

Up to this point, we have looked at the types of taxes and subsidies the government use or could use to redistribute income. But the government can also intervene though direct regulation of prices of labour – for example through minimum wage legislation.

# A Minimum Wage

Many countries have a national minimum wage – the US and France among them – and its introduction has often been urged in the United Kingdom. We shall look at some of the economic consequences of introducing a minimum wage into a situation where there was none previously, and then use such conclusions as we might reach to evaluate its usefulness as a redistributive measure.

If a national minimum wage was to be introduced tomorrow, the first immediate consequence would be a rise in costs to those employers employing individuals whose wages were below the new minimum. Now the employer might try to pass these increased costs directly on to the consumer by increasing her prices. But unless demand for her product is totally unresponsive to changes in price, demand will fall as a result of the price increase. The employer will have to cut back production, reduce her labour force and accept a lower level of profit. Alternatively, she might try to maintain her level of production but lower her costs by replacing the now high-cost workers by previously uneconomic machines. These will be more expensive than the workers used to be, however, and hence her costs must still rise. Either way, therefore, there is likely to be a reduction in her work force, a rise in prices and a fall in her profits.

The extent of these effects, and their relative importance, will vary from industry to industry. In areas like the restaurant trade, which employ very low-paid labour and survive on low profit margins, the result might be a substantial increase in unemployment and in the number of bankruptcies. In others such as agriculture which again employs a large proportion of the low paid, but the demand for whose products is relatively unresponsive to price changes, the result might be simply a rise in prices and little increased unemployment. Whatever form the effects take, they will be compounded if higher-paid workers wish to maintain the differentials in pay between themselves and the low paid. For if they succeed in attaining their wish, a national minimum wage will result in *all* wages increasing so that the differentials are maintained. In that case, employment and/ or inflationary effects are likely to be far more severe.

We are now in a position to examine the possible redistributive effects of minimum wage legislation. Since the minimum wage is likely to make some workers unemployed, and to cause some prices to rise and some profits to fall, it will transfer income *to* the low paid who remain in employment *from* (a) those low paid who were in employment but are now unemployed, (b) the consumers of the products whose prices have risen, and/or (c) the profit earners whose profits are reduced. Now whether this will significantly reduce inequality in incomes is debatable. It would only do so if in the three groups (a), (b) and (c) there are more people with higher incomes than those of the low paid still in employment. Since those now unemployed are almost certainly worse off than those still employed, since products of industries which employ a large proportion of low-paid workers (such as agriculture and textiles) form a large portion of poor people's budgets and since many – although not all – profit-earners in low-paying industries have very low profit margins, it seems unlikely that this will be the case. Add to this the fact that the minimum wage only affects positively the incomes of those in work, and that, if differentials are maintained, even inequality within the labour force will not be reduced, it appears that the minimum wage will not be a very effective way of redistributing income.

In conclusion, so far as regulations of this kind are concerned, their principal advantage appears to lie in the fact that in some sense they tackle the root of the problem, and their principal disadvantage is their effects on the allocation of resources. Note that the latter are rather different from the effects of the tax and subsidy measures considered earlier. For the latter only affect the supply of resources, but legislative controls on the incomes that employers can offer will affect not only the supply but also the *demand* for those resources. Thus taxes and subsidies are not likely to cause 'involuntary' unemployment (although they may cause people to reduce their work effort voluntarily); whereas if legislative fixing of factor prices results in those prices being fixed above the demand and supply equilibrium price, the result might well be that some resources remain unused, despite the fact that their owners are willing to supply them to the productive process.

# Wealth Taxation

All of the policies considered so far have all been designed to affect individuals' *flows* of income. It is also possible to achieve redistribution by affecting individuals' *stocks* of wealth. In particular, wealth can be taxed. There are two kinds of wealth taxation: that designed to affect the *holding* of wealth, and that designed to affect its *transfer* from one person to another.

## *Taxation of Wealth Holding*

Many countries, such as Sweden and West Germany, have a tax on the holding of wealth. The theoretical workings of the tax are easy to grasp: every year the net assets of each individual or household (depending upon what is taken as the operational unit for tax purposes) are valued, and a tax levied on that value at a proportional or, more usually, progressive rate.

There have been two principal objections to a wealth tax in the UK: its *practicality* and its *effects on savings*. First, its practicality. It has been claimed that the problem of valuing households' assets on an annual basis would present enormous administrative difficulties. Many assets such as houses, or stocks and shares, are bought or sold on the open market, and hence a valuation could be relatively easily obtained for these. But how would the authorities value assets which have not recently been placed on the market? What of a unique work of art or a country house? Or, on a more mundane level, how would a household's assets in the form of consumer durables or furniture be valued?

The fact that, as noted earlier, several countries do operate a wealth tax already must mean that these problems are not insuperable. One rather appealing method of overcoming them is to allow each individual to set her own value on the asset concerned, and then to give the tax authorities the right to buy it if they wish at that value. Another alternative is to take insurance valuations. Either of these, or maybe both operating in conjunction, would seem to provide a reasonably satisfactory solution to the valuation problem.

Second, the question of savings. Many critics of a wealth tax have stated that its introduction would reduce savings. Now at first sight this might seem obvious. A wealth tax makes savings less attractive relative to spending money on consumption, since if it is saved it is taxed, whereas if it is consumed it is not. This effect (similar to the *substitution* effect discussed in the context of income taxes) would reduce savings. However, this is not the whole story. For the introduction of a tax would also reduce the post-tax amount of a given level of household savings. This might encourage households to save more in order to maintain their original levels of savings (in a manner similar to the 'income' effect in the income tax case). So we cannot say definitely without empirical investigation which of these two influences, operating in opposite directions, will predominate. There is no a priori case for the view that a wealth tax will automatically reduce savings.

## Taxing the Transfer of Wealth

The inter-generational transfer of wealth has been argued to be particularly important in the game of getting rich and so in maintaining inequality in the distribution of wealth. So it has been argued that wealth should be taxed when it is transferred from one person to another by means of a legacy or gift. Various types of such taxes exist or have been proposed and we shall now consider two.

The first type of tax is one on the *donor* of a gift or legacy. In the UK one form of such a tax was *estate duty*. This taxed all estates according to their size, and included within each estate all gifts made up to seven years prior to the death of the estate's owner. Its principal disadvantage was that it did not tax gifts or transfers of wealth made seven years before death. Accordingly individuals could arrange to transfer their wealth to whoever they wished, and not pay any tax on the transfer so long as they survived at least seven years after the transfer took place. The current UK tax on wealth transfer is the *inheritance tax*. The tax rate increases with the size of transfer and originally all transfers were subject to tax. However, recent modifications mean that now this tax is not dissimilar in its effect to estate duty.

A different type of tax is one which taxes the *recipient* of the transfer, under which the tax payment is assessed according to the size of an individual's inheritance. A more complicated version of this kind of tax is the *life-time capital receipts tax* which taxes all inheritance and gifts according to the amount of such transfers the individual has received in the past.

One of the principal differences between taxes on the donor and taxes on the recipient is the incentive the latter gives for donors to spread their wealth. This can be illustrated by an example. Suppose a wealthy parent has five children and £1 000 000 to give away to them either as a gift or as a legacy. Suppose further that one of the children (say the eldest) has already received a legacy of £500 000, whereas the other children have received none. Now if a tax on donors was in operation which taxed estates of £1 000 000 at, say, 40 per cent, it would not matter to whom the parent left her wealth; the tax would be the same (£400 000). But suppose a life-time capital receipts tax is introduced at the rates shown in Table 9.3. Now, if the parent left all her £1 000 000 to the eldest child, who has already had a legacy of £500 000, then, including this new legacy, the child would have £1 500 000 and the total tax would be 50 per cent of £1 500 000, or £750 000. If she spread it among her other four children – who have had no gifts or legacies – giving them £250 000 each, then the tax on each legacy would be 30 per cent of £250 000, or £75 000. The total tax bill on the estate would then be £600 000. Thus, by spreading her wealth among a larger number of people, each of whom have received little in the way of wealth transfers before, she can reduce the total tax to be paid from £750 000 to £600 000, a sizeable reduction.

It might be objected that, in practice, this wealth-spreading effect might be relatively small, since individuals are not so eager to avoid tax that they will change their whole pattern of legacies or donations. However, experience of the operation of estate duty and capital transfer tax suggests that people are prepared to go to considerable lengths to avoid paying tax: from the complete giving over of wealth seven years before death to the setting up of elaborate tax-avoidance trusts. The desire to avoid taxation in any form is a powerful force. The attractive feature of taxes on beneficiaries is that this force is harnessed to achieve (somewhat) more egalitarian ends.

**TABLE 9.3**
**A Life-time Capital Receipts Tax**

| If accumulated total of all legacies and gifts received by individual is | Then the rate to be applied to a new legacy or gift is |
| --- | --- |
| £250 000 | 30 per cent |
| £1 000 000 | 40 per cent |
| £1 500 000 | 50 per cent |

A further advantage concerns the effects on savings. If an individual's desire to save for her own future consumption is greater than her desire to save for others' consumption, and if there is a negative effect of wealth taxation on savings, then the effect is likely to be greater for a tax on wealth holdings than for a tax on transferring wealth (which does not tax the individual's own future consumption but only that of those who will receive her wealth). However, a disadvantage of transfer taxation is that it does nothing to reduce large concentrations of wealth accumulated during an individual's life-time; if such concentrations are considered as socially undesirable in and of themselves, then (among tax measures) they can only be affected directly by a wealth tax on holdings.

Finally, there is a point general to any type of tax on wealth. If taxation does discourage savings by those preparing to leave bequests, then because wealth holdings are concentrated among a few people, the taxation of wealth could have a large impact on the level of savings in the economy. This efficiency loss would have to be taken into account in the assessment of the introduction of any type of wealth taxation.

# Summary

*Income tax* is generally intended to redistribute income from the higher to lower income groups or individuals. The extent of redistribution depends on the *progressivity* of the tax and the system of *tax allowances*. The operation of tax allowances may mean the *average tax rate* (the proportion of income paid in tax) may be less than the *marginal tax rate* (the tax rate that applies to increases in income). The effects of income tax on the incentives to work (the *efficiency* effect of the tax) cannot be predicted from theory alone. An income tax has *substitution* and *income* effects which operate in opposite directions. Empirical evidence indicates that the short term response to income tax changes for many in the labour force could be quite small.

The *social security system* is an important redistributive tool. *Means-tested benefits* have the advantage that they go to the needy; they often have the disadvantage of relatively low take-up due to the stigma and to administrative complexity. *Categorical benefits*, including child benefit and forms of *social insurance*, such as unemployment benefit and old age pensions, have the advantage of a higher take-up, but the disadvantage of often helping the better off as much as the poor. Both types create some disincentive to work due to the income effect; however, means-tested benefits also have a substitution effect.

A negative *income tax* could create greater administrative simplicity, greater redistribution and reduce work disincentives. However, it is not possible to devise such schemes that do all three simultaneously. A *minimum wage* can raise the wages of low-paid workers who remain in employment; however, it can also create unemployment, higher prices and lower profits. Its redistributive consequences are therefore not clear.

Wealth taxation can either take the form of taxes on the *holding* of wealth or taxes on *transfer* of wealth. The former have practical disadvantages; moreover, they may discourage savings, although this cannot be predicted from theory alone. Taxes on the transfer of wealth are of two types: *taxes on donors*, such as estate duty or capital transfer tax, and *inheritance taxes*, that tax the recipients of wealth transfers. There are various forms of the latter, including a *life-time capital receipts tax*. These have the advantage that they encourage the spreading of wealth. The effect of taxes on the transfer of wealth on the incentive to save is uncertain, but is perhaps less than that of taxes on wealth holdings.

# Further Reading

There is a good, though at points a little technical, discussion of redistribution in Culyer (1980), and a more elementary discussion in

Atkinson (1983). A discussion of the effect of taxes on work effort is given in Stiglitz (1988) and can be found in other public finance textbooks and in economics textbooks, such as Begg *et al.* (1987). Kay and King (1986) provide a treatment of many issues in taxation.

There is much literature on recent changes in the tax-benefit system, though some can be rather technical. A brief summary of the main changes in taxes and benefits 1979–1989 is provided in Johnson and Stark (1989). Detailed analysis of the 1988 Social Security Reforms is provided in Dilnot and Walker (1989, Chapter 14); a detailed analysis of the budget each year is provided by the Institute of Fiscal Studies. A comprehensive collection of analyses of the effect of the tax and benefit system in the UK is provided in Dilnot and Walker (1989, Chapters 9,10,13,14). Chapter 9 examines the poverty trap. A summary of the redistributive effects of the 1987 tax and benefit system is given in Economic Trends, (1990b). Regular discussion of the effect of the tax and benefit systems is provided by articles in the journal *Fiscal Studies*, though most of the articles are aimed at readers familiar with economics. The implication of an ageing population for pension and other social security expenditure can be found in OECD (1988a and 1988b). A collection of essays on reforms of the social security system is provided by Atkinson (1989a), though some of the details are now of historical interest. Discussion of a negative income scheme is provided in Barr (1987). Classic works on wealth taxation are Meade (1964) and Atkinson (1972).

# Questions for Discussion

1. Does cutting income tax make people work harder?
2. The size of the substitution effect of the income tax depends on the marginal tax rate; the size of the income effect depends on the average tax rate. Explain this statement.
3. Discuss the case for a comprehensive income tax.
4. Assess the effects on equity and efficiency of a switch from income to indirect taxation.
5. How would you measure the effectiveness of a poverty programme?
6. What are the arguments for and against relying on categorical benefits as the principal form of social security?

7.  'Replacement of the social security system by a comprehensive negative income tax would create both greater efficiency and greater equality'. Discuss.

8.  'Since wages are largely determined by convention, the introduction of a national minimum wage would have little effect on unemployment and hence would be a desirable redistributive measure'. Do you agree?

9.  'An annual wealth tax is likely to be both inefficient and unfair'. Discuss.

# The Market and the Government

In the first chapter we discussed a number of possible objectives that society might have with respect to allocating scarce resources among its members. In subsequent chapters we saw how market and government systems can be used to allocate resources in various 'problem' areas and discussed whether their use can meet the relevant objectives in the area concerned. Throughout, certain key issues emerged repeatedly. Many of the difficulties involved in allocating resources within these areas have strong links with one another; indeed many are simply aspects of the same conceptual problem. It is the purpose of this final chapter to emphasise these links, and to draw out from the discussion some general lessons about different economic systems. More specifically, the chapter brings together material from previous chapters concerning the ability of markets and the government to achieve efficiency, equity and other objectives in the allocation of scarce resources. We begin with the market and efficiency, continue with the market and equity, and also briefly discuss the ability of the market to achieve other ends, such as freedom and community. We then consider the ability of the different forms of government intervention – namely, provision, tax and subsidy policies and regulation – to attain these objectives.

## The Market and Efficiency

In Chapter 1 we saw that under certain conditions the market allocation of a commodity will provide a socially efficient quantity of that commodity. Let us recapitulate the argument. Under conditions to be discussed shortly, the *market demand* curve will be identical to the *marginal social benefit*, or *msb*, curve. Also, under similar conditions, market supply reflects social cost; that is, the *market supply* curve is identical to the *marginal social cost*, or *msc*, curve. Now the socially efficient level of provision is the point where the marginal social cost equals the marginal social benefit; that is, where the *msb* and *msc* curves intersect. Under market allocation, the quantity of the commodity that is actually provided will be the point where demand equals supply; that is, where the demand and supply curves intersect. Since these curves are identical with the *msb* and *msc* curves, the points of intersection will be the same. Hence the quantity provided in the market will be the socially efficient quantity.

But what are the conditions that are required for this result to be achieved? We can now be more specific than was possible in Chapter 1. First, consider the identity of the *msb* and *market demand* curves. This requires the fulfilment of three conditions:

(1) that individuals in their roles as consumers are well informed: that they are able to judge the quality of the commodities they consume and are able to act on those judgments,

(2) that individuals are rational and the best judges of their own wants, and

(3) that the marginal private benefit equals the marginal social benefit.

If the first two conditions hold, then an individual's demand for a commodity will accurately reflect her marginal private benefit for that commodity. If the third condition holds, then the sum of the individual demands for a commodity (the market demand) will equal the marginal social benefit.

However, we have seen that for many of the commodities discussed in this book these conditions are not fulfilled. For instance, in markets for health and social care, education, housing and transport, there exists *imperfect information*. Prospective patients are in a poor position to evaluate different methods of medical treatment; elderly people living in residential accommodation find it difficult to find out about alternatives; parents may lack the essential information necessary to choose the right school for their children; the purchaser of a house may find it difficult to assess its faults before actually living in it. The lack of the relevant information means that consumers may not be able to assess accurately what will benefit them. If this is so, their demand for the commodity concerned will not reflect the benefit they actually derive from its consumption, and condition (1) will not be fulfilled.

It should be noted that the existence of imperfect information does not necessarily imply that markets will fail. Market institutions may arise that will provide the necessary information: estate agents or surveyors in the case of housing, for instance. But, for this to work, the consumers concerned have to be aware that they lack relevant information and to be prepared to pay for it, if necessary. Also, the very fact that they lack information means that they find it difficult to assess the quality of the information they purchase – which may lead to the market in information itself being inefficient.

Even if there is no obvious consumer ignorance, it is possible to challenge the view that individuals are always the best judges of their own wants: condition (2). In some cases consumers may be *irrational*, as in the case of people with a mental illness. More generally, some people believe that individuals are subject to such extensive social and economic conditioning that they cannot make rational decisions concerning their consumption – that, for instance, advertising and other pressures induce them to 'waste' their money on cigarettes or alcohol instead of buying proper food or housing. Others would view this as unacceptably paternalistic. They would argue that individuals have a right to have their desires respected, regardless of the origin of those desires. The ultimate authority as to what benefits individuals should be the individuals themselves; no one else is an appropriate judge.

The difference between people holding these two points of view is essentially a philosophical one concerning the nature of individual rights. However, there would be general agreement that if substantial consumer ignorance exists then individuals may not be the best judges of their own interests; and that there may be cases (such as the person with a mental illness) where even well-informed individuals' demands for a commodity may not accurately reflect their own long-term interests.

Condition (3) – that marginal private benefit equals marginal social benefit – is also unlikely to be met in many of the areas considered. For this requires that the commodity concerned has no *external benefits* associated with it; that individuals' consumption of the commodity benefits only themselves. But we have seen that health care, social care, education and housing all generate external benefits. For instance, the existence of infectious diseases means that the marginal private benefit of some forms of health care is less than the marginal social benefit. 'Caring' externalities also exist in health and social care. Education is not only of direct benefit to those receiving the education concerned but also can benefit those who work with them and with the community generally. House improvements can benefit not only the people who live in the house concerned but also those who live next door. All in all therefore, in each of these areas, market allocation is unlikely to result in an efficient level of provision.

Now let us look at the supply side. Three conditions are required to ensure that market supply accurately reflects social cost, or, more specifically, that the *market supply* curve is identical with the *msc* curve:

(4)  that producers are well informed,
(5)  that marginal private costs are identical with marginal social costs, and
(6)  that there are no monopolistic elements or barriers to competition in the relevant markets.

If conditions (4) and (5) are not met, then individual production and consumption decisions will not accurately reflect their social costs. If condition (6) is not met, then producers will be able to manipulate the prices their products receive to their own advantage.

Again these conditions are often not fulfilled in the areas discussed. Examples of condition (4) not being met are the phenomena of *moral hazard* and *adverse selection* that can affect insurance markets and that we encountered in Chapter 2 with respect to health and in Chapter 8 with respect to social security. Insurers cannot always know how their insurees are behaving (the problem of moral hazard) or their risk status (adverse selection); in consequence their premiums will often be higher than social efficiency would require. The production of many commodities generate *external costs*, driving a wedge between marginal private and marginal social costs and hence violating condition (5). Landlords or other house owners who let their property deteriorate impose external costs on their neighbours. The use of private cars can create congestion and air pollution. Much industrial activity, including the exploitation of energy resources, pollutes and despoils the natural environment. Indeed the whole environmental issue can be viewed as the quintessential case of market failure due to external costs.

As far as condition (6) is concerned (the absence of monopoly), we have seen that monopolistic elements exist in many of the areas discussed, including schools, hospitals and the markets for professionals (such as doctors). Whether such monopolies are an inevitable part of market allocation, or whether they are an aberration, is debatable. On the one hand, some of these monopolies arise because they are protected by government actions of various kinds: the monopoly to practise granted to certain professions, for example. On the other hand, government licensed monopolies are often at least in part a reaction to a particular form of market failure: that of imperfect information. So, for example, most countries restrict the practice of medicine to qualified doctors, thus giving them a degree of monopoly power; but this is mainly to protect potential patients against quacks exploiting their ignorance of medicine.

Moreover, there are some circumstances in which the forces that drive a competitive market are likely to encourage the development of a monopoly. These are situations where there are substantial fixed costs, or more precisely where *economies of scale* or *sunk costs* exist, such that the larger the firm, the more able it is to lower its average cost of production. In these circumstances, bigger firms will drive their smaller competitors out of business, until eventually the market is monopolised by one large firm. Economies of scale are not a particularly prominent feature of production in all the areas we have discussed in the book, but they are present in some of them: hospitals, for example, often have substantial fixed costs. To the extent that they exist, it may prove impossible for an initially competitive market to avoid degenerating into a monopolistic one.

So, in the areas reviewed in this book, some or all of conditions (1) to (6) are unlikely to be met. Consequently, market allocations are unlikely to be efficient. Will they also fail to achieve other objectives, such as equity?

## The Market and Equity

In the absence of any universally accepted definition of equity it is not easy to determine whether a particular method of resource allocation, such as the market system, achieves it. The best we can do is concentrate on the interpretations of the term that have emerged in our previous discussions. Most of these reflect either of two basic philosophies. The first emphasises the desirability of equality in the areas considered. Examples include the equal treatment for equal need objective of the National Health Service, educational policies designed to promote equality of opportunity, and policies aimed at reducing inequality in the distribution of income. The second philosophy concentrates only upon the attainment of minimum standards in each area. It is the philosophy underlying the concern that everyone should live in a 'decent home', and the perception of the poverty problem as one of simply bringing incomes of the poor above a specified level.

Whichever of those interpretations is preferred, it is unlikely that market allocation will achieve them. As we saw in Chapter 8, in a market system people's incomes – and hence their ability to purchase commodities – are determined by the resources they own and the prices they can obtain from selling those resources. Since the initial distribution of the ownership of resources is quite unequal, and since there are substantial barriers to competition in many resource markets (particularly that for labour), it would be remarkable if market processes produced an equal (or close to equal) distribution of income. Nor is there any reason to expect that minimum standards will necessarily be achieved; there will always be those with few resources and hence with levels of consumption below any reasonable minimum.

## The Market and Other Objectives

Although we have concentrated on efficiency and equity as the principal objectives that a society will wish to pursue, we have seen that other objectives may also be important. The promotion of freedom of choice and the fostering of a sense of community are two that have emerged in some of our discussions. How does the market system perform in relation to these aims?

Now it is often argued that competitive markets promote freedom of choice. The existence of large numbers of small producers, each vying for the consumer's business, ensures that even the most idiosyncratic of consumers will be satisfied. Freedom of choice could also be enhanced by injecting market type elements into areas where they do not currently exist. Under the education voucher scheme, for instance, parents would be free to choose whatever education they wished for their children, and not be compelled to accept the particular version provided by the government.

But, as we have seen, many markets contain considerable elements of monopoly. These, as well as impeding efficiency in the manner already described, also operate to limit freedom of choice. If, due to economies of scale, there is only one hospital in town, then choice is non-existent; if entry into a profession is limited, then freedom of choice of supplier is restricted. Overall, therefore, while there is a strong presumption that markets encourage freedom of choice, we cannot guarantee unequivocally that this will automatically occur in every situation.

Many people believe that markets are incompatible with the other objective mentioned, the promotion of a sense of community. They argue that the market fosters personal attributes, such as greed and a lack of concern for one's neighbour, that are incompatible with communal or cooperative behaviour. On the other hand, it could be claimed that since markets are means by which mutually profitable transactions take place, then they promote everyone's satisfaction and thereby promote a sense of communal well-being. For instance, street markets are usually pleasant places to stroll around; 'market' towns, so-called because they provide the market-place for their local areas, are often thought of as attractive places to live, with a strong sense of community.

In summary, we can say that market allocation without government intervention is unlikely completely to achieve either efficiency or equity, and may fail to meet certain other objectives as well. However, this does not necessarily imply that the government should therefore intervene. For it could be that such intervention may make things worse: it may create more inefficiency or more inequity than the market operating on its own. We need therefore to examine possible forms of government intervention and explore their ability to meet society's aims.

# Government Policy

In earlier chapters, we have distinguished between three forms of government intervention: *provision, tax and subsidy* policies and *regulation.* Under a system of government *provision* the government owns and operates the institutions that provide the good or service concerned, and employs the people involved in providing it. Examples that have appeared in this book include hospitals under the British National Health Service, state schools, the public road system, council housing and local authority residential and domiciliary facilities for people in need of social care.

The use of government *subsidy* is widespread in the areas that we have explored. Health care, education, residential care, domiciliary care, roads: all are provided free to the user or at subsidised prices. Much housing is also subsidised, either through direct subsidies to renters or through the tax system to owner occupiers. *Taxation* or charging policies may be used as an instrument for the control of environmental and congestion externalities. Taxation, together with social security, is of course, also used as a major tool of income redistribution. However, as most of the arguments concerning taxation as an instrument of social policy are similar to those concerning government subsidy, in what follows we concentrate on the latter.

Government *regulation* can take a number of forms. One is *quantity* regulation, where the government regulates the amount of the good or service being produced. An example of this is the control of polluting activities through regulations concerning the levels at which they may be undertaken. Another form of regulation concerns the *quality* of the good or service being produced: examples here are the qualification requirements necessary for practising medicine or the safety requirements for aircraft. A third is *price* regulation: examples that have appeared in this book are rent control, where the price of privately rented housing is regulated and the minimum wage, where the 'price' of labour is controlled.

As should be clear from the examples given, although all these forms of government intervention often accompany one another, there is no necessity for them to do so. Thus it is perfectly possible to have government provision without subsidy, taxes or regulation, subsidy without provision, regulation without subsidy and so on. moreover, one can substitute for the other. Indeed many of the current debates in several of the areas explored in this book involve just such a substitution. In health care and social care, education and prisons, for example, there are reforms at various stages of development that involve replacing the present systems of combined government provision and subsidy by some form of *quasi-market*. In quasi-market systems, government remains a subsidiser of services but ceases to provide them. Instead, by a variety of means, it finances independent suppliers to provide the service concerned, and, in order to ensure that its money is well-spent, expands its regulatory activities to monitor and regulate these suppliers. Quasi-markets are thus systems that combine government subsidy and regulation, while reducing, or in some cases, even eliminating the government's role as provider.

## Government and Efficiency

The arguments concerning the possible consequences of each kind of goverment intervention in terms of efficiency are rather different; it is important therefore to keep them distinct.

## *Provision*

There are a number of reasons for supposing that government provision will diverge from the socially efficient level of production. First, government providers are sometimes (although not always) monopolies; indeed their monopoly status is on occasion guaranteed by the government. Hence their market is not 'contestable': that is, it is difficult, if not impossible, for potential competitors to enter the market. Also, the fact that the monopolies are government owned means that, unlike private monopolies, there is no threat of bankruptcy; the management does not have to answer to shareholders; and managers are not under the threat of take-over if they are inefficient; hence all these incentives to efficiency are removed.

The absence of competition, either actual or threatened, and of the danger of take-over, reduces the incentive to keep costs to a minimum. Hence in these circumstances the marginal cost of government production will generally be higher than the marginal social cost of production. However, government providers do not always have to be monopolies. Following the recent quasi-market changes in the British education system, for example, government schools have to compete for pupils. Similarly, the implementation of the National Health Service reforms will result in government-owned hospitals having to compete for patients with private or voluntary hospitals.

The consequences of this competition for the efficiency of government providers will depend in part on the organisations with which they are competing. If the latter all have the objective of maximising their profits, as is likely to be the case if they were all private, then, unless the government provider concerned is subsidised, it will go out of business unless it also minimises its costs. If, on the other hand, its potential competitors are not profit-maximisers, if they were all voluntary organisations, for instance, then it only has to match their behaviour to survive. In that case, the marginal cost of provision (by all the organisations involved) may be higher than the actual social cost.

So there are two sets of circumstances where it is possible that government provision will be inefficient (where costs are not minimised): where the government provider is a monopoly, or where it is competing against other organisations whose principal concern is not the maximisation of profits. Now if the commodity concerned were being sold to consumers at a price that had to cover costs (that is, if there were no government subsidy), then the consequence of the cost of provision being above the marginal social cost would result in the price being too high for social efficiency. Demand would fall, and less would be consumed or provided than would be socially efficient.

However, government provided commodities are often not sold to consumers at cost-price, but are offered free or at a price below the costs of provision. In other words, government *provision* is often accompanied by government *subsidy*. What are the efficiency implications of the latter?

## *Taxes and subsidies*

If a commodity is provided free at the point of use to consumers with its provision being subsidised from taxation (and if there is no other cost to consumers such as time or travel) then the only cost to the consumer of consuming the commodity concerned is the perceived extra cost in terms of any extra tax she might have to pay as a result of her consumption. Since this is likely to be very small indeed, the amount demanded will be greater than the socially efficient level of demand. If the *msb* curve is the same as the market demand curve, and if the extra tax cost is assumed to be as near zero as makes no difference, the amount demanded will be given by the point at which the *msb* curve intersects the horizontal axis.

More generally, if a commodity is sold at a price below cost, there will be 'excess' demand (as compared with the level of demand that would prevail if the price were equal to cost). Faced with this excess demand the government has two choices. It can either meet all the demand, thus ensuring that more of the commodity is provided and consumed than is socially efficient. Or, if it knows the amount that is socially efficient (we shall discuss this assumption in a moment) it can simply provide this amount and use some other rationing device to decide who gets what. Such devices include queueing or waiting lists, or the delegating of the decision to the judgment of bureaucrats, managers or professionals, such as doctors in the case of health care or social workers in the case of social care.

The problem with queueing or waiting lists is that the people at the front of the queue or at the top of the waiting list may have got there by luck, by having plenty of free time or by having the right contacts. In such cases there is no guarantee that they are the people who really want or need the commodity the most. The problem with delegating the relevant decisions to professionals or bureaucrats is that, in making those decisions, the latter may pursue their own interests – and these may not coincide with those of either consumers or the government. Bureaucrats may be so-called 'budget-maximisers': that is, they may wish to promote their incomes and status by expanding their number of employees and hence their budget. Professionals are often self-employed, with their income therefore being directly related to the amount of the service they provide. In that case, they may try to increase their income and status by recommending that potential consumers use more services than they really need. On the other hand, if they are employees, so that their incomes are not directly related to the level of service provided, they may try to reduce their work-loads by under-providing the service. Both professionals and bureaucrats are usually bound by some commitment to the public interest or by professional ethics geared to the welfare of their clients, often formalised in a code of practice to prevent them exploiting their position; however, it is not clear that these are always as effective a restraint as they should be.

There is a yet more serious difficulty if the government through its taxation and subsidy policies forsakes the use of market prices as a means of allocating resources: that of *information*. As we saw in Chapter 1, movements in market prices provide information to producers. If there is a change in consumer preferences for a commodity such that there is an increase in the demand for it, its price will rise, thus conveying this information to producers; they will see that production of the commodity has become more profitable, and, if they are profit-maximisers they will increase supply to meet the increased demand. If they over-react by increasing supply too much, then this information will be conveyed to them again by a movement in prices, this time a fall.

Now it should be noted that at times prices will convey the wrong information. As we saw in Chapter 6, due to the absence of the relevant property rights, the price of many natural resources, including air and water, is zero. This conveys to consumers and producers the (incorrect) information that the supply of the resource is infinite: that there is no scarcity. Hence the resource is over-used, relative to the socially efficient level. In such cases, government tax or subsidy policies can be used to create a price where none existed and thus promote efficiency: the pollution charge discussed in Chapter 6 is an obvious example.

However, these cases aside, the effect of a government tax or subsidy policy can be to drive a wedge between prices, demand and supply such that the role of prices as conveyors of information is reduced or even eliminated. In the absence of market signals such as movements of prices, the government will find it very difficult to assess the overall efficient level of production of the commodity concerned. For, without a price mechanism, it has only very limited ways of assessing the social benefit of the commodity and relating that to its social cost.

The problem is particularly acute with respect to the assessment of social benefit. Essentially there are two mechanisms available to governments for this purpose: voting procedures and, again, delegation to bureaucrats or professionals. Now there are reasons for supposing that voting procedures might give a better indication of the 'true' social benefit of the production of a good than relying on market signals, such as the movement of prices. First, the mechanism of voting allows everyone who is affected by the consumption and production of a good to have a say in its level of provision. Hence, if there are external benefits or costs associated with its production or consumption, then, in theory at least, the political process will take these into account. Second, voting gives everyone an equal say, in the sense that everyone has only one vote; hence this overcomes the disadvantage of market demand that it gives a greater weight to those who are better off.

However, these advantages have to be set against a powerful set of disadvantages. First, under certain conditions it can be shown that majority voting gives greater weight to the preferences of certain groups than others. In particular, it can favour the 'median voter'. For instance, suppose there is a vote over how much of a commodity should be subsidised. Some voters will want a a large subsidy; some, a small one; some, none at all. If all voters preferences are ranked along a scale, there will be one voter who is the 'median': that is, half the electorate would vote for a subsidy larger than the one she wants, and half would vote for a subsidy smaller than the one she wants. If there are only two political parties, the one that offers a level of subsidy that is the one favoured by the median voter will win the election; for if it offers any other level of subsidy, by definition it will attract the votes of less than half the electorate. Hence both parties will compete for the median voter, whose preferences will therefore be given a disproportionate weight.

A second disadvantage of simple majority voting procedures derives from the very fact that everyone has only one vote. This means that it is impossible to gauge the depth of someone's preferences: how much she actually wants the commodity concerned relative to other possibilities. If she had many votes she could 'rank' alternatives according to how many votes she gave them; with only one vote, she can only vote for or against. There are more complex voting systems that do give some weight to preferences; but they can be cumbersome and difficult for the electorate to understand.

A third problem is that elections or referenda are expensive to arrange and organise. In consequence, in practice people do not have frequent votes over levels of subsidy or provision of particular goods and services; rather, they vote infrequently over broad packages offered by different political parties. This does not allow for 'fine-tuning' in the allocation of resources.

Fourth, when people vote they are rarely properly informed about either the benefits or costs of the various proposals with which they are confronted. Economists are divided as to whether they are likely to be better informed about the benefits or about the costs. Some argue that the activities of pressure groups favouring particular kinds of government expenditures will lead people to exaggerate the benefits from those expenditures, and to underestimate the costs; if this is correct they will vote for a level of provision that is higher than the socially efficient level. Others argue that the benefits from government spending are often very diffuse, while the costs, in terms of increased taxation, are very obvious; hence people will be tempted to vote for too little government spending. In either case it is unlikely that the amount they vote for will coincide with the socially efficient level.

Finally, there is an additional source of potential inefficiency that arises from government subsidy. This is the disincentives for work and savings created by the taxation necessary to finance the subsidy. As we saw in Chapter 9, taxation can create inefficiencies of these kinds; although again, the actual size of the loss in each case is a matter of empirical investigation.

## *Regulation*

In theory a perfectly informed government with suitably motivated civil servants could achieve an efficient allocation of a good or a service by using them to regulate its production. Thus if it knew the exact position of the *msb* and *msc* curves, and hence the point of intersection, it could compel the organisation concerned to produce (and price) at the appropriate level, in terms of both quantity and quality. However, in practice it will face two problems. First, it will find it very difficult to obtain the relevant information. We have already seen the difficulties involved in obtaining information concerning social *benefits* in the absence of a properly functioning market. But in addition in this case the government will need to obtain information from the organisations concerned on their *costs*, information that the latter will have little incentive to supply.

Second, and related, is the problem of 'regulator capture'. The regulators of the production of a commodity usually have to meet regularly with the representatives of the producers. Inevitably, there will be a tendency for them to develop personal relationships of various kinds which will perhaps lead them to be sympathetic to the interests of the producers. The eventual level of regulation might therefore correspond more to those interests than to those of the society as a whole (as represented by the socially efficient level).

Both of these phenomena create problems for each kind of regulation. The absence of perfect information means that quantity regulation can result in either too much or too little of the good being produced. Poor information and regulator capture can result in quality regulation being used to protect those being regulated from competition and thereby create inefficiency. And both can result in regulated prices being set either too high, thus creating excess demand and necessitating rationing as discussed above, or too low thus creating over-production or excess supply.

There may also be consequences of government regulation for efficiency over time. Too heavy regulation may stifle incentives for invention and innovation. It may also discourage potential suppliers from entering the market or encourage those already in it to leave (as with private landlords and rent control). Price regulation, in particular, impedes the information-role of price movements discussed above.

In short, all forms of government intervention may create inefficiency – inefficiency that may be less, equal to, or greater than the inefficiencies in the market that the interventions are intended to correct.

# Government and Equity

What of government's ability to achieve other objectives, such as equity? Again it will be useful to divide our discussion into the likely effects on equity of each of the three forms of government intervention: provision, tax or subsidy policies, and regulation. There seems to be no especial reason for supposing that government *provision* will be either equitable or inequitable *on its own* (that is, if it is not accompanied by subsidy or regulation) so far as the distribution of the good or service itself is concerned. However, there may be consequences for the distribution of income. For instance, the replacement of a monopoly private supplier by a monopoly government one may create a more equal distribution of income because (a) the latter would have less incentive to exploit its monopoly position and (b) the profits would accrue to taxpayers rather than to its shareholders (who, on average, are likely to be richer).

Government *subsidy* may achieve equity, if the latter is defined in terms of minimum standards. For subsidising a good or service will make it easier for poorer people to consume it and thereby help ensure that everyone has a minimum quantity. Here it is useful to distinguish between the effects of universal and means-tested subsidies. If the subsidy is means-tested – that is, if it is confined only to people on low incomes – then it may also promote equity in the sense of greater equality of consumption; for it will encourage poor people's consumption relative to that of the rich. However, this assumes that the means-test does not discourage poor people from consuming the good or service. Chapter 9 discussed some of the reasons why, in the case of cash benefits, means tests might deter take-up of the benefit concerned, including administrative complexity and possible social stigma. These problems also confront the use of means-tests in other areas, such as means-tested charges for social care.

A further problem with means tests, again discussed in Chapter 9, is their effect on the marginal tax rate faced by individuals and hence on their incentive to work. Those in receipt of a means-tested service may lose their entitlement if they increase their income, and hence may be discouraged from trying to do so by working harder. Given these difficulties, it has been argued that universal subsidies are preferable to means-tested ones. However, these have problems of their own. They encourage demand for the good or service by both rich and poor; hence, while this may result in everyone having at least a *minimum standard* of consumption, it will do little to promote greater *equality* of consumption. Indeed, in some cases it may make matters worse. As we saw earlier subsidies create excess demand, necessitating the use of non-price rationing devices, devices that may on occasion favour the better-off.

Finally, government *regulation*. Regulation that is designed to control prices, such as minimum wages or rent control, often has the explicit intention of promoting equity. However, again there may be perverse consequences. Minimum wages, for example, may reduce employment, making it more difficult for workers to get jobs; they may also push up costs and prices, thereby affecting consumers. Rent control may reduce the overall supply of rented housing, thus adversely affecting those who cannot afford to buy a house. Government regulation designed to promote quality may also have undesirable consequences for equity. Qualification requirements for professionals, for example, can be used to restrict entry into the profession and hence raise the incomes of the profession concerned.

Similarly, quality controls on products can be used to restrict competion to supply those products thus increasing the profits of existing suppliers.

Of course, none of these are *necessary* consequences of regulation. If the regulators are perfectly informed and truly impartial, then some of them may be avoided. But, as we have seen in the discussion of the consequences of government regulation for efficiency, the same market failures that provided the motivation for the government intervention in the first place militate against impartiality and perfect information.

# Government and Other Objectives

Perhaps the major criticism of government intervention with respect to objectives other than efficiency and equity is that it erodes individual liberty; perhaps its major justification is that it promotes a sense of community. These arguments raise issues that take us well beyond the confines of this book, and indeed beyond the normal province of economic analysis. However, a few brief comments are in order.

It would be hard to deny that societies with the most extensive government intervention, the old communist economies of Eastern Europe, were also illiberal, oppressive regimes. On the other hand, tyranny has also co-existed with capitalism (Nazi Germany, for example) and some highly interventionist societies have extensive political freedoms (Sweden, for example). The connection between government intervention and the erosion of individual liberties is thus far from automatic.

As the constitutional embodiment of the community, it might be expected that government intervention would promote a spirit of community. If a combination of government provision and subsidy, for example, can ensure that everyone uses a particular service, such as the government education system or the National Health Service, then fellow-feeling and a common sense of citizenship may be enhanced. However, again, the experience of Eastern Europe is instructive, where arguably the only communal response to the government's heavy-handed intervention was to unite its citizens against it.

# Conclusion

Both market and non-market systems of resource allocation thus have their advantages and disadvantages with respect to their ability to achieve social objectives. Which system one ultimately finds superior will depend on two factors: one's values concerning the relative weights that should be put upon society's various objectives, such as efficiency and equity; and the extent to which the final allocation under each system meets these objectives. The first is a matter of value judgements about which economists – in their role as economists – have little to say. The second, however, is an empirical question to which economists have a great deal to contribute. What is needed is more empirical investigation – by economists and others – to substantiate the competing claims of the different systems. If this book has succeeded in inducing any of its reader to pursue such investigations, one of its main objectives will have been achieved.

# Summary

There are a number of conditions necessary for the market allocation of a commodity to be *efficient*. Both consumers and producers are *perfectly informed*; consumers are *rational* and the best judge of their own wants; neither the consumption or production of the commodity generates *external benefits* or *external costs*; and there are no monopolistic elements or *barriers to competition* in the relevant markets. For each of the problem areas investigated in this book, most of these conditions are violated. Moreover, market allocation will generally not be *equitable* and, while it may promote *liberty* in the sense of freedom of choice, it is also likely to encourage self-interested behaviour and perhaps thereby affect the spirit of *community*.

However, the fact that market allocation may fail to achieve social objectives in a number of areas does not imply that government intervention will automatically succeed. Government *provision* may be inefficient, especially if the government provider is a monopoly. Although on occasion government *tax or subsidy* policy can be used to correct market failures, especially with respect to externalities, they can also drive a wedge between prices, demand and costs, thus damaging the role of prices as conveyors of information. Alternative methods of deriving information, such as voting mechanisms or reliance upon the judgement of bureaucrats or professionals, all have deficiencies of their own. Government *regulation* also suffers from information difficulties and from the associated problem of regulator capture.

Government provision has no necessary consequences with respect to *equity*. Means-tested government subsidy can help attain a minimum standard of consumption of a commodity, so long as the means test itself does not discourage consumption by the poor. Universal subsidy avoids the discouraging effects of means-tests, but does little to promote equality of consumption. Government regulation may have perverse consequences for equity, especially if those who are adversely affected by the regulations are poorer than those who benefit from them. Finally, government intervention may restrict individual *liberty*, but promote a sense of *community*. However, more empirical testing of these propositions, together with all the others discussed in this book, is required; for their truth cannot be established by theory alone.

# Further Reading

An excellent analysis of the reasons for market failure can be found in Barr (1987), although in places some knowledge of economics is required. Another useful exposition of market failure (and a defence of government intervention) is Heald (1983). A theory of government failure is put forward in Wolf (1988); it is criticised and an alternative theory put forward, along the lines of the second half of this chapter, in Le Grand (forthcoming). Quasi-markets are discussed in Le Grand (1989b, 1990).

Seldon (1990) provides an immensely readable account of the virtues of markets and the failures of governments. The issues are also extensively discussed from a rather different perspective by the contributors to Le Grand and Estrin (1989). Many of the criticisms of government, particularly with respect to efficiency, derive from the theory of 'public choice': useful, though at in places technical, reviews of the relevant literature are Cullis and Jones (1987) and Mueller (1989). Le Grand (1982) and Goodin, Le Grand *et al.* (1987) discuss some of the equity consequences of government intervention. Much factual information concerning the recent performance of British government policies with respect to efficiency, equity and other objectives in many of the areas discussed in this book (including education, health and social care, housing and social security) can be found in Hills (1990).

# Questions for Discussion

1.  'It is a happy coincidence that the form of economic organisation most likely to promote efficiency – perfect competition – is also that which involves the greatest decentralisation of power. The market is thus the cornerstone of liberty'. Do you agree?
2.  Discuss the problems that imperfect information (on both the demand and supply sides) creates for market allocations.
3.  Is the appropriate government response to externalities *always* to tax or subsidise the activity concerned?
4.  What are the similarities between rent control and minimum wages as instruments of social policy?
5.  'There are shortages of doctors, nurses, policeman, etc., but none of food, shirts, cars, etc., because the market is used in the second case but not in the first'. Discuss.
6.  Some argue that, while the pursuit of self-interest in the market generally promotes social welfare, its pursuit in government is invariably disastrous. Do you agree?
7.  'In all cases the comparison should be between an imperfect market and an imperfect [government], not some ideal abstraction' (Charles Schultze). Discuss.

# References

Albon, R. and Stafford, D.C. (1987) *Rent Control* (London: Croom Helm).

Arrow, K. (1963) 'Uncertainty and the welfare economics of medical care' *American Economic Review*, 53, 941–73.

Atkinson, A. B. (1972) *Unequal Shares* (Harmondsworth: Penguin).

Atkinson, A. B. (eds) (1980) *Wealth, Income and Inequality* (Oxford: Oxford University Press).

Atkinson, A. B. (1983) *The Economics of Inequality*, 2nd edn (Oxford: Oxford University Press).

Atkinson, A. B. (1989a) *Poverty and Social Security* (London: Harvester Wheatsheaf).

Atkinson, A. B. (1989b) 'Measuring inequality and different social judgements', *Working Paper TIDI/129*, STICERD, London School of Economics.

Atkinson, G. B. J. (1983) *The Economics of Education* (London: Hodder & Stoughton).

Barnes, J. and Barr, N. (1988) *Strategies for Higher Education: the Alternative White Paper*, David Hume Paper No. 10 (Aberdeen: Aberdeen University Press).

Barr, N. (1987) *The Economics of the Welfare State* (London: Weidenfeld & Nicolson).

Barr, N. (1989) *Student Loans: the Next Step*, David Hume Paper No. 15 (Aberdeen: Aberdeen University Press).

Baumol, W. and Oates, W. (1988) *The Theory of Environmental Policy*, 2nd edn (Cambridge: Cambridge University Press).

Begg, D., Fischer, S. and Dornbusch, R. (1987) *Economics*, 2nd edn (London: McGraw-Hill).

Bettman, O. (1974) *The Good Old Days – They were Terrible!* (New York: Random House).

Black, J. and Stafford D.C. (1988) *Housing Policy and Finance* (London: Routledge & Kegan Paul).

Blaug, M. (1972) *An Introduction to the Economics of Education* (Harmondsworth: Penguin).

Blaug, M. (1987) *The Economics of Education and the Education of an Economist* (New York: New York University Press).

Bradshaw, J. (1972) 'A taxonomy of social need' in G. McLachlan (ed) *Problems and Progress in Medical Care* (Oxford: Oxford University Press).

Bramley, G., Le Grand, J. and Low, W. (1989) 'How far is the poll tax a "community charge"? The implications of service usage evidence', *Policy and Politics*, 17, 3, 187–205.

Button, K. J. (1982) *Transport Economics* (London: Heinemann).

Coase, R. H. (1960) 'The Problem of Social Cost', *Journal of Law and Economics*, 3, 1–44.

Collard, D. (1978) *Altruism and Economy* (Oxford: Martin Robertson).

Cowell, F. (1977) *Measuring Inequality* (Oxford: Philip Allen).

Cullis, J. and Jones, P. (1987) *Microeconomics and the Public Economy: A Defence of Leviathan* (Oxford: Basil Blackwell).

Cullis, J. and West, P. (1979) *The Economics of Health* (Oxford: Martin Robertson).

Culyer, A. J. (1980) *The Political Economy of Social Policy* (Oxford: Martin Robertson).

Culyer, A. J. (1985) *Economics* (Oxford: Basil Blackwell).

Culyer, A., Maynard, A. and Posnett J. (eds) (1990) *Competition in Health Care: Reforming the NHS* (London: Macmillan).

Dales, J. H. (1968) *Pollution, Property and Prices* (Toronto: University of Toronto Press).

Davies, B. and Knapp, M. (1988) 'Costs and residential social care' in Sinclair (1988).

Department of Education and Science (1988) *Top-up Loans for Students*, Cm. 520 (London: HMSO).

Department of the Environment (1971) *Fair Deal for Housing*, Cmnd 4728 (London: HMSO).

Department of Health (1989) *Caring for People: Community Care in the Next Decade and Beyond*, Cm. 849 (London: HMSO).

Dilnot, A. and Walker, I. (eds) (1989), *The Economics of Social Security* (Oxford: Oxford University Press).

Economic Trends (1990a) 'International Comparisons of Taxes and Social Security in 20 OECD Countries 1977–1987' *Economic Trends*, 438 (April), 134–145 (London: HMSO).

Economic Trends (1990b) 'The Effects of Taxes and Benefits on Household Income 1987', *Economic Trends*, 439 (May), 84–118 (London: HMSO).

Enthoven, A. (1985) *Reflections on the Management of the National Health Service*, Nuffield Provincial Hospitals Trust Occasional Papers 5 (London: Nuffield Provincial Hospitals Trust).

Evandrou, M., Falkingham, J. and Glennerster, H. (1990) 'The personal social services: "everyone's poor relation, but nobody's baby" ', Chapter 6 in Hills (1990).

Fry, V. and Stark, G. (1989) in Dilnot, A. and Walker, I. (eds) *The Economics of Social Security* (Oxford: Oxford University Press).

Glaister, S. Starkie, D. and Thompson, D. (1990) 'The assessment of economic policy for transport', *Oxford Review of Economic Policy*, 6, 1–21.

Glennerster, H. and Low, W. (1990) 'Education and the welfare state: does it add up?', Chapter 3 in Hills (1990).

Gomez-Ibanez, J. A. and Meyer, J. R. (1990) 'Privatizing and deregulating local public services: lessons from Britain's buses', *Journal of American Planning Association*, 56, 9–21.

Goodin, R. and Le Grand, J. (1987) *Not Only the Poor: the Middle Classes and the Welfare State* (London: Allen and Unwin).

Griffiths, R. (1988) *Community Care: Agenda for Action* (London: HMSO).

Gwilliam, K.M. (1989) 'Setting the market free: deregulation of the bus industry', *Journal of Transport Economics and Policy*, XXXIII, 29–44.

Hahn, R. and Hester, G. (1989) 'Where did all the markets go? An analysis of EPA's Emissions Trading Program', *Yale Journal of Regulation*, 6, 109–53.

Hau, T. D. L. (1990) 'Electronic road pricing: developments in Hong Kong 1983–1989', *Journal of Transport Economics and Policy*, XXIV, 4.

Heald, D. (1983) *Public Expenditure: Its Defence and Reform* (Oxford: Martin Robertson).

Helm, D. and Pearce, D. (1990) 'Assessment: economic policy towards the environment', *Oxford Review of Economic Policy*, 6, 1–16.

Hills, J. and Mullings, B. 'Housing: A decent home for all at a price within their means', Ch. 5 in Hills (1990).

Hills, J. (1990) (ed.) *The State of Welfare: the Welfare State in Britain since 1974* (Oxford: Oxford University Press).

Hills, J. (1991) *Unravelling Housing Finance* (Oxford: Oxford University Press).

Hirschman, A. (1970) *Exit, Voice and Loyalty* (Cambridge, Mass: Harvard University Press).

House of Commons Select Committee on Energy (1989), 6th Report, *Implications of the Greenhouse Effect* (London: HMSO).

Johnson, P. and Stark, G. (1989) 'Taxation and Social Security 1979–1989: The Impact on Household Incomes' *IFS Commentary* (London: Institute for Fiscal Studies).

Jones-Lee, M. (1990) 'The value of transport safety' *Oxford Review of Economic Policy*, 6, 2, 47–74.

Kay, J. and King, M. (1986) *The British Tax System*, 4th edn (Oxford: Oxford University Press).

Kent County Council Education Department (1978) *Education Vouchers in Kent*.

Knapp, M. (1984) *The Economics of Social Care* (London: Macmillan).

Le Grand, J. (1982) *The Strategy of Equality* (London: Allen and Unwin).

Le Grand, J. (1989a) 'Markets, welfare and equality' in Le Grand and Estrin (1989).

Le Grand, J. (1989b) *Quasi-Markets in Public Policy*, Studies in Decentralisation and Quasi-Markets No. 1 (Bristol: School for Advanced Urban Studies).

Le Grand, J. (1990) 'The State of Welfare', Ch. 8 in Hills (1990)

Le Grand, J. (1991) *Equity and Choice* (London: Routledge).

Le Grand, J. (forthcoming) 'The theory of government failure', *British Journal of Political Science*.

Le Grand, J. and Estrin, S. (eds) (1989) *Market Socialism* (Oxford: Oxford University Press).

Le Grand, J. and Robinson, R. (1984) (eds) *Privatisation and the Welfare State* (London: George Allen & Unwin).

Le Grand, J., Winter, D. and Woolley, F. (1990) 'The National Health Service: safe in whose hands?', Ch. 4 in Hills (1990).

Loewry, E. (1980) 'Cost should not be a factor in medical care', *New England Journal of Medicine*, 302, 697.

Mack, J. and Lansley, S. (1985) *Poor Britain* (London: George Allen & Unwin).

Maclennan, D. (1982) *Housing Economics* (London: Longman).

Marshall, A. (1890) *Principles of Economics*, 8th edn (London: Macmillan, 1961).

McGuire, A., Henderson, J. and Mooney, G. (1988) *The Economics of Health Care: an Introductory Text* (London: Routledge & Kegan Paul).

McLachlan, G. and Maynard, A. (eds) (1982) *The public/private mix for health: The relevance and effects of change* (London: Nuffield Provincial Hospitals Trust).

Meade, J. (1964) *Efficiency, Equality and Ownership of Property* (London: George Allen & Unwin).

Miller, D. (1989) *Market, State and Community* (Oxford: Oxford University Press).

Minford, P. (1988) 'Outlook After the Budget', *Fiscal Studies*, 9, 30–7.

Mishan, E. J. (1969) *The Costs of Economic Growth* (Harmondsworth: Penguin).

Mueller, D. (1989) *Public Choice II* (Cambridge: Cambridge University Press).

Murray, C. (1984) *Losing Ground: American Social Policy 1950–1980* (New York: Basic Books).

MVA *et al.* (1988) *The Value of Time* (Berkshire: Policy Journals).

Nash, C. (1982) *The Economics of Public Transport* (London: Longman).

Newbery, D. M. (1990) 'Pricing and congestion: economic principles relevant to road congestion', *Oxford Review and Economic Policy*, 6, 2, 22–38.

Nolan, B. (1989) 'An examination of the new official low income statistics', *Fiscal Studies*, 10, 53–65.

O'Donnell, O. and Propper, C. (1991) 'Equity in the distribution of NHS resources', *Journal of Health Economics*, 10, 1–19.

Organisation for Economic Co-operation and Development (1987), *Financing and Delivering Health Care: A Comparative Analysis of OECD Countries* (Paris: OECD).

Organisation for Economic Co-operation and Development (1988a) *Reforming Public Pensions* (Paris: OECD).

Organisation for Economic Co-operation and Development (1988b) *The Future of Social Protection* (Paris: OECD).

Organisation for Economic Co-operation and Development (1988c) *Urban Housing Finance* (Paris: OECD).

Organisation for Economic Co-operation and Development (1990) *Health Care Systems in Transition: The Search for Efficiency* (Paris: OECD).

Oxford Review of Economic Policy (1990a) *Oxford Review of Economic Policy*, 6, 1.

Oxford Review of Economic Policy (1990b) *Oxford Review of Economic Policy*, 6, 2.

Pearce, D. and Turner, K. (1990) *The Economics of Natural Resources and the Environment* (London: Harvester Wheatsheaf).

Pearson, M. and Smith, S. (1990) 'Taxation and environmental policy: some initial evidence', *IFS Commentary*, 19 (London: Institute for Fiscal Studies).

Piachaud, D. (1988) 'Poverty in Britain 1899 to 1983', *Journal of Social Policy*, 17, 335–49.

Psacharopoulos, G. (1987) (ed.) *Economics of Education* (Oxford: Pergamon).

Rawls, J. (1972) *A Theory of Justice* (Oxford: Oxford University Press).

Seldon, A. (1981) *Whither the Welfare State* (London: Institute for Economic Affairs).

Seldon, A. (1990) *Capitalism* (Oxford: Basil Blackwell).

Sinclair, I. (1988) (ed.) *Residential Care: The Research Reviewed*, Literature Surveys commissioned by the Independent Review of Residential Care, Chaired by Gillian Wagner, National Institute of Social Work (London: HMSO).

Stiglitz, J. (1988) *The Economics of the Public Sector*, 2nd edn (New York: Norton).

Sugden, R. (1984) 'Voluntary organisations and the welfare state', Chapter 5 in Le Grand and Robinson (1984).

Titmuss, R. (1970) *The Gift Relationship* (London: George Allen & Unwin).

Townsend, P. (1979) *Poverty in the United Kingdom* (Harmondsworth: Penguin).

Verry, D. (1977) 'Some Distributional and Equity Aspects of the Student Loans Debate' in *Education, Equity and Income Distribution* (Milton Keynes: Open University Press).

Vickers, J. and Yarrow, G. (1988) *Privatisation: An Economic Analysis* (London: MIT Press).

Weiller, D. *et al.* (1984) 'A public school voucher demonstration: the first year at Alum Rock' (Santa Monica, California: Round Corporation). Also reprinted in Baxter, C., O'Leary, P.T. and Westoby, A. (1977) *Economics and Education Policy: A Reader* (London: Longman).

Williams, A. (1974) 'The cost-benefit approach', *British Medical Bulletin*, 30, 252–6.

Williams, A. (1985) 'The economics of coronary artery bypass grafting', *British Medical Journal*, 291, 326–9.

Williams, A. (1987) 'Health economics: the cheerful face of the dismal science' in A. Williams (ed.) *Health and Economics* (London: Macmillan).

Wolf, C. (1988) *Markets or Governments: Choosing between Imperfect Alternatives* (Cambridge, Mass: MIT Press).

# Index

*Note:* references to tables and figures are shown in **bold** type.

**253**